FLIGHT CAPITAL

ALSO BY **DAVID HEENAN**

DOUBLE LIVES

CO-LEADERS
WITH WARREN BENNIS

THE NEW CORPORATE FRONTIER

THE RE-UNITED STATES OF AMERICA

MULTINATIONAL ORGANIZATION DEVELOPMENT
WITH HOWARD PERLMUTTER

FLIGHT CAPITAL

THE ALARMING EXODUS OF
AMERICA'S BEST AND BRIGHTEST

DAVID HEENAN

Davies-Black Publishing

Mountain View, California

To the Pao family

with admiration and respect

Published by Davies-Black Publishing, a division of CPP, Inc., 1055 Joaquin Road, Suite 200, Mountain View, CA 94043; 800-624-1765.

Special discounts on bulk quantities of Davies-Black books are available to corporations, professional associations, and other organizations. For details, contact the Director of Marketing and Sales at Davies-Black Publishing: 650-691-9123; fax 650-623-9271.

Visit the Davies-Black Publishing Web site at www.daviesblack.com.

09 08 07 06 05   10 9 8 7 6 5 4 3 2 1
Printed in the United States of America

Library of Congress Cataloging-in-Publication Data
Heenan, David, A.
  Flight capital : the alarming exodus of America's best and brightest / David Heenan.
— 1st ed.
    p. cm.
Includes bibliographical references and index.
ISBN 0-89106-202-5 (hardcover)
1. Brain drain—United States. 2. Professional employees—United States. 3. United States—Emigration and immigration—Government policy. 4. Return migration—Economic aspects. 5. Globalization—Economic aspects. I. Title.
HD8038.A1H44 2005
331.12'791—dc22

2005019997

FIRST EDITION
First printing 2005

"Man cannot discover new oceans unless he has courage to lose sight of the shore."

—André Gide

contents

preface

For centuries, immigration was America's secret weapon, "one of the defining strengths of our country," declared President George W. Bush. Legions of newcomers from all over the world became a major force in American Exceptionalism. Undergirding the country's ascendancy was the belief that the United States was so powerful, its allure so magnetic, that it would remain the unquestioned destination of those seeking a better life. Simply put, coming to America meant staying in America. Not so today.

In the current rough-and-tumble world of international talent grabbing, immigrants of all stripes are discovering that there is no place like home. Thousands of New Americans have begun boomeranging back to their native countries. What's more, although the exodus is taking place across a wide spectrum, it is especially strong in leading-edge professions in science, technology, and business—the "high-end" sectors so much in demand in today's Innovation Economy.

The flight of any country's brightest minds is a sure sign that that country is in serious trouble. Left unchecked, it can erode a nation's competitive edge and, ultimately, its standard of living. Therefore, the reverse brain drain could send the United States "back to the Dark Ages" warns Craig Barrett, chairman of Intel, the giant semiconductor firm. To make matters worse, America's traditional source of imported capital is beginning to shrivel up exactly when its stock of homegrown brainpower is shrinking. As a result, the country faces the perfect storm: a wrenching talent gap—a situation that is unsustainable.

"To produce a mighty book, you must choose a mighty theme," wrote Herman Melville. Is there any theme mightier than safeguarding a nation's precious human capital? Clearly, the United States must hang on to its best minds, while continuing to serve as a beacon to highly skilled immigrants. But how?

To better understand the flight capital phenomenon, I crisscrossed the globe, interviewing repatriates in eight countries: Ireland, Iceland, Israel, India, China, Taiwan, Singapore, and Mexico. As you will see, the stories they told are as different as chalk and cheese. However, they all offer important insights into how other nations are rolling out the red carpet for accomplished Americans.

In my travels, I found that the exodus extends far beyond the swelling ranks of gifted emigrants. When highly sought-after professionals return home, they take their family members—particularly, their high-achieving children—with them. Obviously, that is America's loss. In addition, prospective immigrants to the United States, observing the return of their emigrant neighbors, are much more reluctant to leave the nest and venture overseas. Another missed opportunity. Finally, more and more native-born Americans are becoming geographically adventurous, heeding the call to pursue the American Dream on foreign soil.

A few notes of caution. First, I discovered that getting an accurate assessment of this emerging trend is almost impossible. Smoke-and-mirror statistics abound, as very few countries monitor the quantity and quality of their returnees. Ireland and Israel are the exceptions, using this information as marketing fodder to lure more wanderers home. The number of Americans seeking greener pastures is equally elusive. Many acquire dual citizenship or revalidate their "green cards," although their allegiance is no longer to the Red, White, and Blue. In addition, since a large number of repats drafted off a spouse or dependent passport while in the United States, they don't appear in the official rolls of the departed. Then, there is the growing pool of "virtual Americans"—those in almost perpetual transit, who prefer a truly multinational lifestyle. They, too, fly below the radar. Yet, despite the absence of reliable statistics, there is a litany of anecdotal evidence to support the growing force of out-migration.

Second, *Flight Capital* focuses on diagnosing the problem and analyzing the prospects of retaining America's best minds. By understanding more fully the present dilemma, better solutions—it is hoped—will emerge. Of course, any action agenda adopted by the United States will prompt a series of responses from other nations. These, in turn, will trigger an American counterresponse, and so on. To speculate how this sequence of parries and thrusts will evolve is beyond the scope of this book.

As a final caveat, readers will appreciate that any serious effort to stop the reverse brain drain is not a cure-all for the nation's burgeoning talent deficit. Retaining imported brainpower is only half the solution; the other half is upgrading the quantity and quality of our native-born workforce. Therefore, the United States must place equal attention on such thorny problems as reforming public education, upgrading universities, and stimulating science and technology.

America cannot afford to equivocate. History offers many examples of great countries that came to a catastrophic end because of their unwillingness to respond to change. Nothing short of stopping the

present threat will safeguard America's talent base and shape the kind
of society in which our children and their children will prosper. The
time to act is now.

David Heenan
Honolulu, Hawaii
July 2005

acknowledgments

There are many friends and colleagues I would like to thank. Brett Uprichard gave my ideas flight and elegance and brought a journalist's eye to the process. He read and critiqued the book's overall presentation. Marie MacCord assisted on selected research assignments. Jennifer Pao Heenan and Anne Pao arranged and conducted the interviews in Taiwan and Mexico, respectively, and provided invaluable feedback and advice. My conclusions in those chapters are, of course, my own.

I also benefited enormously from the contributions of various people who read portions of earlier versions of the manuscript. Their efforts in sharpening both my arguments and my prose are deeply appreciated. I especially want to thank Kevin Whelan, John FitzGerald, Brian Farren and Linda O'Shea-Farren, Sveinn Valfells,

M. P. Singh, Nags Nagarajan, T. C. Chan, Y. C. Boon, Dean Ho, Anne Stevenson-Yang, Arnon Gutfeld, and Menny Mautner.

Also providing valuable input and kind words of encouragement were Warren Bennis, Jerry Porras, Larry Pulley, Bill Hamilton, Stan Davis, Peter Brockett, Marty Stein, Richard Halloran, Michael Heihre, Phil Norris, Ralph Cossa, Ray Tsuchiyama, Tadanobu Kashiwa, Hiroshi Yasuda, Marty Jaskot, Robert Witt, David Bess, Samuel Wong, Ed Perkins, Joe Griesedieck, Warren and Carolyn Luke, Clark Hatch, Dick Tomey, Nanci Kincaid, Clint Churchill, Dick Gushman, Zap Zlatoper, Karen Ramos, and Marc and Eric Heenan. My longtime friend and colleague Bob Sutton provided special insights into repatriation "down under" and regrettably passed away before this book was completed.

There were scores of others who consented to be interviewed, or assist with interviews, some of them repeatedly. Every session was a profound learning experience that enhanced my understanding of the reverse brain drain. I am especially indebted to:

Ireland: Seamus McManus, Edel McCarville, Deidre McDonnell-Lee, Frank Barry, John Moroney, Mary Harney, Bill Harris, Kevin Whelan, Steve Coronella, John FitzGerald, David Givens, Mary Corcoran, Gerard Denneny, Sarah Maxwell, Thomas Lynch, Adrian Coyle, Kate Gunning, Anthony O'Neill, Cormac Kilty, James Burnham, Michael Ryan, Tony Glynn, Austin Cooney, Luke O'Neill, Denis Headon, Pearce Lyons, John Hegarty, Eugenie Houston, Brian Farren, Linda O'Shea-Farren, Dermot Kelleher, Dennis Kelleher, Linda Dowling Almeida, Kerby Miller, Tony Shiels, and Sally-Anne Fisher.

Iceland: Kári Stefánnson, Páll Magnusson, Larus Vilhjalmsson, Gudrun Bjarnadóttir, Ebba Thora Hvannberg, Peter Oskarsson, Bragi Árnason, Skuli Mogensen, Daddi Gudbergsson, Sveinn Valfells, Kristín Zoëga, Einar Snorri, Edda Sverrisdóttir, Ingibjörg Palmadóttir, Martin Wilhelm, Stefán Jónsson, and Jón Kaldal.

India: S. D. Shinbulal, Vivek Kulkarni, Vishal Bali, Nags Nagarajan, Bhavna Mehra, Ananda Mukerji, Kiran Mazumdar-Shaw,

M. P. Singh, Beena Pradham, Susan Kumar, Tina George, Raj Kondur, and Vijay Anand.

Israel: Avi Soifer, Rabbi Joshua Fass, Shabtai Adlersberg, Joseph Morgenstern, Yoram Yahav, Arnon and Sara Gutfeld, Oren Gross, Eli Barkat, Menny Mautner, Isaac Applbaum, Joseph Ben-Dak, Ralph Robbins, Josie Arbel and Yaacov Bartura.

China: Greg Andermann, Jill and Sandy Friedman, Randall and Norma Chang, Edward Tian, Oliver Chen, Kai-Fu Lee, Tony Horton, Diana Chen, Chris Bachran, Soucheng Zhang, Dongping Zhu, Dean and Eva Ho, Anne Stevenson-Yang, Tang Ning, Peggy Yu, and Ying Luo.

Taiwan: Cecilia and David Lee, David Zhu, Jim Morris, Morris Chang, Bobo Wang, Wen-Sen Chu, T. C. Chan, James Soong, Brian Mann, Richard Vuylsteke, Eric Lean, Charles Trappey, William and Jennie Yeh, and James Pao.

Singapore: Jack and Kay Tai, Ron Frank, Y. C. Boon, David Tan, Lan Kong-Peng, Beh Swan Gin, Lee Ying Adams, Yeo Siak Ling, Ang Boon Kheng, Ian Speirs, Edison Liu, Kong Hwai Loong, and James Tan.

Mexico: Ana Mollinedo, Alejandro Valadez, Ana Maria Salazar, Tim and Sandee Cottrell, Chad Barton, Miquel de Icaza, Jorge Zavala, Jorge Santistevan, Daniel Guzman, and Eduardo Flores.

United States: Senator Tom Tancredo; Carlos Espinosa; Dan Grossman, Colorado state senator; Gay Gilbert, Lorette Post; Theresa Cardinal Brown; Colleen Coffey; Annalisa Leandri; Ben Johnson; Chad Aleshire; Randy Johnson; Walter Ewing; Demetrios Papademetriou; Kevin O'Neill; and Lynn Shotwell.

All of these kind souls graciously accommodated my endless questions and were uncommonly generous with their time. My efforts were also influenced by a number of excellent writers who are duly cited in the notes. My heartfelt thanks go to them.

At Davies-Black, once again I had the pleasure of working with a talented team of wonderful professionals—especially my editor, Lee Langhammer Law. This book benefited tremendously from her vision, wisdom, and rigor. She saw the project from the very beginning, guiding and inspiring me every step of the way. A special salute, too, to Jill Anderson-Wilson for her careful copyediting skills and wonderful enthusiasm. Connie Kallback, Laura Ackerman-Shaw, Laura Simonds, and Patti Danos offered exceptional assistance in bringing *Flight Capital* to market.

Martha Miller's competence, diligence, and unfailing good cheer through successive versions of the manuscript contributed greatly to its completion. A consummate professional, Martha coordinated the production of each major draft of the book. She was assisted by Debbie Miyagi and Jenny Okano.

I reserve my most special thanks for my wife, Nery, who has been at my side throughout this project. She read and commented on the entire manuscript and helped shape its principal arguments. To this loving and most constructive critic goes a very special *Mahalo*.

about the author

David Heenan is a trustee of the Estate of James Campbell, one of the nation's largest landowners with assets valued at over $2 billion. Formerly, he served as chairman and CEO of Theo H. Davies & Co., the North American holding company for the Hong Kong–based multinational Jardine Matheson. Earlier, he was vice president for academic affairs at the University of Hawai'i and, before that, dean of its business school.

Educated at the College of William and Mary, Columbia University, and the University of Pennsylvania, Heenan has served on the faculties of the Wharton School, the Columbia Graduate School of Business, and the University of Hawai'i. His articles have appeared in such leading publications as the *Harvard Business Review,* the *Sloan Management Review,* the *Wall Street Journal,* the *New York Times,* and the *Christian Science Monitor*. He is author or coauthor of five other books, including *Double Lives* and *Co-Leaders*.

David Heenan lives in Honolulu, Hawai'i. He can be reached at www.flight-capital.com.

heading **home**

Give me your tired, your poor, your huddled
masses yearning to breathe free . . .

—EMMA LAZARUS

Forget terrorism and weapons of mass destruction. The next global war will be fought over human capital. For years, immigrants provided a pipeline of brainpower to the United States. From Alfred Hitchcock to Albert Einstein, a steady stream of energetic and highly skilled newcomers yearning to breathe free propelled America's ascendancy.

Today, the country continues to benefit enormously from being a magnet for inventive and ambitious people who stimulate the economy, create wealth, and improve overall living standards. Chinese and Indian immigrants run nearly a quarter of Silicon Valley's high-tech firms. Half of the Americans who shared Nobel Prizes in physics and chemistry in the past seven years were born elsewhere. Nearly 40 percent of MIT graduate students are from abroad. More than half of all Ph.D.s working here are foreign-born, as are 45 percent of physicists, computer scientists, and mathematicians. One-third of all current physics teachers and one-fourth of all women doctors immigrated to this country.

However, the United States can no longer live off its transplanted foreigners. Beginning in the 1990s, a giant sucking sound could be heard as these immigrants' native countries improved economically and politically. In a world economy that placed an increasing premium on knowledge, many of America's best and brightest began hotfooting it home in search of another promised land.

A decade ago Edward Tian said goodbye to Lubbock, Texas, his pickup truck, horseback riding, and seven years of studying an obscure poisonous weed to return to Beijing. He took with him a Texas Tech doctorate in ecology and a small Internet software company he had cofounded in Dallas. That business, NASDAQ-listed AsiaInfo, became China's premier systems-integration company, creating as much as 70 percent of China's Internet infrastructure. "I wanted to do something to change people's lives in the next five years, not the next two hundred years," says the forty-one-year-old entrepreneur. (On the heels of AsiaInfo's success, Tian went on to found telecom giant China Netcom, where he serves as chief executive.)

After centuries of importing brainpower, the United States is now a net exporter. Global mobility, once a cause for celebration, has become a nuisance. In each of the past few years, nearly 200,000 foreign-born Americans—many of them, like Tian, highly talented techies—have, on average, returned to their motherland. This reverse brain drain, or "flight capital," stimulated in part by lucrative government incentives, has spawned flourishing new scientific havens from South Asia to Scandinavia. Among these are Bangalore, India's Silicon Valley; Hsinchu, Taiwan's scientific and engineering hub; Israel's Malkha Technology Park in Jerusalem; Sweden's Kista Science Park, outside Stockholm; and Japan's Tskuba Science City.

This alarming exodus of invaluable human capital is an unintended consequence of today's more tightly knit world economy. Globalization, while generally a good servant, can be a bad master.

What is especially difficult for many Americans to accept is the growing threat posed by these emigrants, educated and trained here, who are rushing home to build their own competitive ventures. It's good news for other nations, bad news for the United States.

Given the departure of Edward Tian and many others, it was perhaps inevitable that the land of opportunity would turn its back on newcomers. In the aftermath of the September 11, 2001, terrorist attacks, more and more Americans have sought to pull up the drawbridge. U.S. Citizenship and Immigration Services has issued fewer temporary H-1B guest-worker and student visas and applied much stiffer requirements for newcomers. The number of foreigners with exceptional skills or advanced degrees allowed into the country dropped 65 percent in 2003. Fanning the fire, Patrick Buchanan, Richard Lamm, and Michelle Malkin wrote best-sellers advocating highly restrictive immigration policies. Anti-immigrant sentiment could not have come at a worse time. Survey after survey reveals that the United States faces a massive labor shortage, particularly of knowledge-oriented workers. The same is true for Germany, Japan, and the other industrial powers. But while many countries are putting out the welcome mat to gifted outsiders, the United States is doing just the opposite. On its present course, our nation of immigrants could become a nation of emigrants.

This comprehensive study of the reverse brain drain challenges the time-honored belief that the United States is the unchallenged repository of human capital. It is a fallacy that dies hard. But everything changed on 9/11. What had been a trickle of brainpower became a steady flow. Left unchecked, the outflow poses a serious threat to America's security and scientific and economic preeminence.

In researching this book, I spent several years analyzing the worldwide battle for top talent. Because personal stories are a lively and effective way to get important points across, I've chosen to examine this emerging phenomenon by telling stories of people who have left the United States to pursue their dreams elsewhere—many in countries once viewed as shiftless, impoverished, and in general disrepair. We'll travel from Ireland to India, from Iceland to Israel, looking at some extraordinary individuals who boomeranged back to their native lands. At the end of our journey, the lesson for Americans will be clear: Gear up for a contemporary replay of David and Goliath—or suffer the consequences.

Flight Capital is intended to sound a loud wake-up call to a nation often blinded by hubris. Designed to provoke and inspire, its message goes out to every American concerned about the country's future. To understand the present dilemma and the reasons for its emergence, readers can delve into the tales told here. The best minds going elsewhere could spell the beginning of the end of American Exceptionalism. However, this is not a forecast of certain doom: reverse migration is reversible. Simply put, it's America's game to lose.

Which corrective actions might be taken to halt or at least slow the exodus of human capital depends on one's analysis of the reasons for America's diminished allure. The answers, as my research suggests, are not to be found in any dramatic turn from our present course. In many cases, they call for the kinds of innovative reforms— from overhauling public education to revamping immigration policies—now being applied in countries once considered unlikely magnets for gifted professionals. As you can see, I've identified a dozen actions to recoup our talent losses—actions we will explore in the next eight chapters and amplify in chapter 10.

Credit Taiwan with inciting the exodus. With the creation of its Hsinchu Science-Based Industrial Park in the 1980s, the Republic of China began cashing in on the knowledge-economy sweepstakes, recruiting hundreds of Taiwan-born engineers and scientists from the United States with valuable skills, experience, and contacts. Located near top universities and government research institutes and offering low-cost land, green vistas, and a minimum of bureaucracy, the Silicon Valley–style technology park helped spur a high-tech gold rush, building a critical mass of repatriated "brainiacs." Roughly one-third of its companies were founded by returnees from America. One of the first recruits was Stanford-educated Miin Wu, who, in turn,

A **Call to Action**

1 • Know thy competition

2 • Adapt—or die

3 • Spur immigration reform

4 • Dust off the welcome mat

5 • Target the best minds

6 • Encourage dual loyalties

7 • Reform—really reform—public education

8 • Nourish the halls of ivy

9 • Celebrate science and technology

10 • Expand the workforce

11 • Reconsider national service

12 • Act now

enticed a group of twenty-eight Taiwanese homeboys to launch Macronix International Co., Ltd., in Hsinchu. "When I was at Intel, I dreamed of starting my own company," recalls Wu. "Here we mix a U.S. technology base with Taiwanese manufacturing technology." Today, the manufacturer of high-end computer chips boasts a stock market capitalization of $2 billion.

Singapore is also rolling out the red carpet for foreign scientists and entrepreneurs. One highly prized globetrotter is Hong Kong–born Edison Liu, former director of clinical sciences at the U.S. National Cancer Institute, who was wooed to head the impressive Singapore Genome Institute. "It's a little like surfing—you see a great wave and you paddle like crazy to catch it," says Liu of his new employer. "What they have done in coordinating investment, immigration, education, infrastructure, and medical systems has been masterful. It's the most astounding social engineering I've seen in my life."

For other Western scientists, the chance to conduct leading-edge research in this pleasant city-state is a big draw. Poaching top talent comes easily: about 70 percent of the Genome Institute's team of 170 scientists comes from abroad. Singapore's embrace of foreign expertise makes good sense to the mobile Liu. "If you were to say that you could only build Harvard with second-generation Bostonians, you'd see what would happen to Harvard," he says. "The idea that any country can have hegemony over biology by virtue of just training its own people is not rational."

China's great leap forward began in the late 1980s with its commitment to becoming an economic colossus. To help realize its high-tech and scientific dreams, the Middle Kingdom tapped more than 400,000 of its students who had been trained in foreign universities, mostly in North America and Europe. Despite some stops and starts, these sharp-witted émigrés are helping boost China's modernization drive to warp speed.

From Beijing to Guangzhou, local governments are enticing overseas Chinese with everything from cheap rent and lower taxes to dual citizenships. After working for eleven years in the United States, James Gao went to Shanghai three years ago to set up his integrated-circuit design company. In return, the Nanjing native received modest public funding. "Everything comes to Shanghai in the semiconductor business," says Gao, noting that government incentives are a "sign of support that the government gives returnees."

But there is more to the equation than just money. The tug of family and the chance to reconnect with their roots while contributing to nation building are powerful magnets for many returnees. For Gao Weining, the American Dream faded with the burst of the Internet bubble. In 2002, the thirty-eight-year-old electrical engineer emigrated to Shanghai, where he serves as senior vice president for sales and marketing for Intrinsic Technology, Ltd., a China-based software developer. "I'm trying to enjoy my apple instead of thinking about the orange I gave up," says Gao, a native of Jiangxi Province in central China, who graduated from Vanderbilt University and lived in America for twelve years. "It's more challenging to work in a maturing market like China than in a saturated one like the United States because there's more room for growth."

Since the liberalization of its state-run economy, India has been emulating China's program of tapping émigrés to boost its economy. "We want the richness of your experience," proclaimed former prime minister Atal Bihari Vajpayre at the January 2003 Overseas Indian Day, a lavish three-day conference in New Delhi designed to attract and retrieve the Indian diaspora. His successor, Manmohan Singh, sees the 20 million Indians working overseas as a gold mine of scientific and management know-how. The government's message is loud and clear: Come home, we need you!

Among those heading home is Rama Velpuri, an Indian-born engineer and U.S. citizen with a degree from Louisiana State, who had spent the 1990s working for Oracle. But when he started his own firm, Oramasters, he decamped for one of India's emerging high-tech hubs, Hyderabad. There, he runs his company for only $30,000 a month (including payroll for his twenty-five employees) and pays

$1,000 a month for a five-bedroom house in Hyderabad's tony Jubilee Hills, complete with three maids, a chauffeur, and a gardener. Given these perks and the obvious advantages entrepreneurs such as Velpuri enjoy, it is hardly surprising that the flight capital movement is taking hold. "India is slowly becoming a land of opportunity," says Kalash Joshi, president of IndUS Entrepreneurs in Silicon Valley, where Indians founded or are top executives at close to a thousand companies.

Even Vietnam is trying to bring home its transplanted talent. For years, its nearly 2.7 million emigrants—a community half the size of Ho Chi Minh City—were called *Viet Kieu*, or "overseas Vietnamese." More than half—1.5 million—live in the United States. In the early 1990s, they started to trickle back to check out the new, more liberalized Vietnam. Now, the trickle has become a flood, with up to 300,000 returning each year, many permanently.

One prodigal son is David Thai, a thirtyish Californian who left his homeland in 1972. After graduating from the University of Washington, he returned to Vietnam with $700 to look for an opportunity. Today, Thai runs a successful string of coffee shops in Hanoi and has investments in a coffee plantation and a coffee-export business. With its darker years behind it, the Communist-controlled government is pulling out all stops to make other *Viet Kieu* feel welcome, including posting jobs on VietnamExpress and VietnamWorks, Web sites directed at overseas Vietnamese. Vietnam is even making a major push to turn itself into an outsourcing powerhouse. One wonders, What would Ho Chi Minh think?

South of the U.S. border, Brazil, Mexico, Chile, and Costa Rica are among the Latin pacesetters trying to tap the rich vein of overseas engineers, scientists, and entrepreneurs. In the early 1980s, Brazilian professor Fernando Macondes de Mattos introduced the idea of creating a Silicon Valley South. He convinced local government officials to lure overseas companies and Brazilian-born talent to Tecnópolis in seaside Florianópolis, a city of 330,000 inhabitants and forty-two balmy beaches. In 1985, Paulo Guimarães, a U.S.-trained computer scientist, beat a retreat to this picturesque locale to launch Compusoft, a software company that has won prizes for its groundbreaking inventions, including an infrared wireless communications system. Today, Guimarães is a national star—"our Bill Gates," says one Tecnópolis colleague. Like Compusoft, other Brazilian companies are slowly making serious inroads into markets once dominated by the United States.

Ironically, I've found that almost all returnees speak highly of their U.S. experience. Many serve proudly as America's informal ambassadors, with amazing fondness and close ties to their former institutions. Some can even cite the name of Stanford's third-string quarterback or the status of Boston's "Big Dig." But make no mistake: their primary loyalty rests with their motherland.

Many of these well-trained repatriates are more turned off by America's eroding values than by its vexing, heavy-handed immigration policies. Single-parent families, bare midriffs, drug abuse, and public vulgarity—the coarsening of America—are especially troublesome. Second-rate schools focus more on metal detectors than mathematics The nation is obsessed with power and money. "A culture with no culture," is how one disenchanted scientist puts it. Three years ago, Kwume Botsu, vice president of Rising Data Solutions, an Internet call company based in Gaithersburg, Maryland, returned to Ghana to set up a hundred-employee operation. The twenty-year IBM veteran traded in his white button-down for a dashiki, the colorful shirt of his homeland, largely to reconnect with his core values.

The cultural rebirth and immigrant-led boom has even extended to isolated Iceland. For a thousand years, generations of descendants of the Vikings set out for the New World. More recently, Iceland's sons and daughters have been busily transforming this once-remote fishing center into a high-tech haven. The subarctic island of 290,000 now ranks among the world's five richest countries per capita. Shucking a Harvard professorship in 1996, Kárí Stefánsson came home to Reykjavík, the capital, to found deCode Genetics, Inc., a gene-sequencing company whose goal is to identify specific genes that may cause cancer and other diseases. Stefánsson is proud of the work he and other Icelanders are doing to create a hotbed of new biotech businesses. "People thought I was crazy," he recalls of his departure from Cambridge. "They said, 'Nobody leaves tenure at Harvard to found a biotech company in Iceland.' But this is my country."

For similar reasons, Daddi Gudbergsson continues to turn down stateside jobs. The cofounder of Web site developer GM.com had lucrative jobs in New York and San Francisco. But what makes Iceland attractive is the mentality of its people. Folks in this tight-knit, largely homogeneous population tend to work ten-hour-plus days, and they are consummate pragmatists. "You can make things happen faster in Iceland [than in the U.S.]," says Gudbergsson. "You go out on a Saturday night and, next thing you know, you've made a deal. There are no formal proposals. People know you and you get along."

The Irish, too, are finding they *can* go home again. Like millions of men and women before them, Brian Farren and his wife, Linda O'Shea-Farren, left the Emerald Isle hoping to find a better life in America. Their dreams materialized. The two practicing attorneys gained valuable courtroom experience and fat salaries years sooner than they would have back home. But after five years, they did something earlier generations of Irish immigrants would never have imagined: they moved home.

In the 1990s, Ireland became the "Celtic Tiger," thanks largely to American and other foreign investments, as well as its membership in the European Union. Then this once-blighted island began reversing one of the largest and longest migrations in history: its native sons and daughters started heading home. Net immigration, the number of those moving to Ireland minus those who leave, has been positive for several years. Besides the improved economy, Irish immigration counselors report that the current anti-immigration climate in the United States is contributing to the exodus. In the post–9/11 world, many newcomers feel like second-class citizens, with their sense of belonging tested. Capitalizing on this, the Irish government has been actively courting them, establishing a special fund to help Irish entrepreneurs repatriate, particularly those interested in launching high-tech and scientific companies.

The rejuvenated nation has lots to offer. "Now, in Dublin, we can get everything we could in the States, which we couldn't have before," says Farren, forty-three. "What I miss about the U.S. can be satisfied with a trip every year or so."

The ripple effect of out-migration reaches beyond skilled foreign-born professionals like the Farrens to include their high-achieving children. In a typical year, almost two-thirds of *USA Today*'s All-USA High School Academic Team is represented by the gifted offspring of New Americans. According to a recent study by Stuart Anderson of the nonprofit National Foundation for American Policy, in Arlington, Virginia, they account for 65 percent of the 2004 U.S. Math Olympiad's top scorers and 46 percent of the U.S. Physics Team. In Intel Corp.'s Science and Talent Search (the "Junior Nobel Prize"), 60 percent of the forty finalists were prodigy of foreign-born residents, a large number of them here on H-1B visas.

The legacy of learning imparted by immigrant parents is well known. America's newcomers are passionate about education and plant the seeds that often produce the next generation of whiz kids. Take Harvard-bound Arjun Suri, a member of the 2004 *USA Today* team. His Indian-born parents, both physicians, came to the United States with $500 between them. Through hard work, they provided educational opportunities and support, as well as a perspective broadened by family travel to five of the six continents. "Their example speaks for itself," says their grateful son.

When America's imports return home, their children go with them. It's a tremendous loss. Indeed, the Anderson report concluded that if anti-immigrant policy had existed over the past twenty years, "we would have wiped out two-thirds of the top future scientists and mathematicians in the United States because we would have barred their parents from ever entering America."

But there's more collateral damage: the loss of potential overseas recruits, who see little or no value in coming to America. Comeback kids such as Edward Tian and Kári Stefánsson are given celebrity status in their motherland. They are the role models for future generations. That these superstars have abandoned the United States—a land once considered the zenith of the postindustrial world—for life in their home countries is a powerful incentive for others to stay put. As their economies improve and educational institutions grow in stature, many bright young Indians, Chinese, Israelis, and others are perfectly content to build their careers on home soil.

And what of the estimated 4 million Americans living abroad? International life has given them new skills and a cosmopolitan perspective they do not want to see compromised if and when they return to the United States. According to a survey conducted by health insurer Cigna International Expatriate Benefits and WorldatWork, a nonprofit research organization, 77 percent of American expatriates said they would rather accept another job abroad with a new employer than be repatriated by their current organization.

Even Yanks unfamiliar with overseas living are succumbing to global hiring. Declining corporate loyalty and the rise of the free-agent workforce has made Americans much more geographically adventurous. The Association of Executive Search Consultants reports that its member firms are flooded with requests from U.S. executives willing to pack their bags. Fully half of respondents surveyed say they would go to China; 34 percent would take a job in either India or Russia.

Sensing these attitudinal shifts, many countries are intensifying their courtship of homegrown Americans. In the global economy, turnabout is fair play. One Yankee joining in the wanderlust is Norman Prouty. The sixtyish executive arrived in Bangalore in 1992 to provide venture capital to high-tech entrepreneurs in India's "Silicon Plateau." The Yale graduate worked for thirty-five years in senior financial jobs at Citibank and Lazard Frères. Rather than retire, he brought a lifetime of powerful contacts and business acumen to the capital-starved country. Why India? It houses the world's largest English-speaking population outside the United States. Since most software engineering is done in English, this is a major advantage. In addition, the world's second-most populous nation has 4 million scientific and technical professionals, including thousands who hold American doctorates.

Already, Prouty's company, ICF Ventures, has done dozens of deals to fund Indian start-ups. "ICF funds come from some of the United States' most successful investment bankers, venture capitalists, and institutions," says Prouty. "These people have ridden some very fast horses in the U.S., and in India they see the opportunity to ride even faster ones."

For Sandra "Sam" Gershenfield, a slower, not faster, pace was the watchword. When terrorists flew two airplanes into the World Trade Center, where she worked as a top business consultant, she headed straight for the safest spot she could think of: New Zealand. "The U.S. had just become so unsafe and scary," she says from her new digs north of Auckland. "I'm so incredibly grateful to be here. If I had to describe this experience in one sentence, it's this: I found peace."

Besides peace and quiet, a first-rate lifestyle has attracted a growing number of Americans to France's "technopoles," specialized industrial zones that cross-fertilize universities, research institutions, and business. The most prominent is Sophia Antipolis, halfway between Cannes and Nice on the French Riviera—a setting F. Scott Fitzgerald called "the most beautiful place in the world."

Founded in the 1960s, Sophia Antipolis (its name combines the Greek word for wisdom and the nearby city of Antibes) has attracted thousands of high-tech and scientific companies and many talented expatriates. Besides being a serious center where creativity flourishes, the mild climate and beauty make it an easy sell. "It's like California with baguettes," beams Stephanie Longo Denman, marketing manager at Theseus International Management Institute.

Another adventurous American, Keith Ross, the founder of start-up Wimba.com and professor at the Institute Eurécom graduate school in France's Silicon Valley, agrees: "We scientific types like this environment. It's just like California." Fragrant olive groves and nearby beaches give the imported techies a place to reflect. After teaching computer science and engineering at the University of Pennsylvania for thirteen years, Ross moved to the Côte d'Azur with his wife to take up his post at Eurécom. "We wanted to be in a great place where the weather's nice," he says of his new home, where it's *"Bienvenue, les Américans!"*

Mark Davies, a Welsh-born American and a dot-com millionaire, moved to Ghana for business reasons: to provide Internet access to a technology-starved people. His company, BusyInternet, headquartered in Accra, offers services for Internet entrepreneurs needing space, infrastructure, and moral support. Despite many obstacles, the firm now employs fifty people and boasts a client base of 1,500 customers. Frontiersman Davies, forty-one, plans to open branches in other African cities.

Equally adventurous are the rising ranks of Americans making their home in Eastern Europe. In 1999, Fernando Zacca and his wife, Magdalena Wullert-Zacca, abandoned the United States for Poland. The husband-and-wife team moved their Southeast Asian furniture business from Thousand Oaks, California, to Poznan, a cosmopolitan city of 750,000, midway between Berlin and Warsaw. Within months, the company was operating in the black, thanks to significantly lower rents and labor costs—and a fresh product line. "In Poland, people are always looking for new things," Zacca explains. "They're anxious for something new."

Even U.S. farmers are putting down roots in foreign soil. More than a century after his ancestors began toiling in the midwestern United States, Dan Carroll bought a soybean farm in the western part of Bahia State in Brazil. He joined more than a dozen other Yanks who had recently begun farming there. Most are lured by the relatively cheap land. "It's prohibitively expensive to buy land in the States right now," says the forty-nine-year-old Carroll. "I have no doubt that Brazil is the future of global agriculture." The local mayor is cozying up to all comers: "I don't care if they are Americans, Chinese, Africans, Argentineans," he says. "Anyone who wants to come here is welcome."

For many years, the United States benefited from minimal competition in stockpiling talent. But in the ebb and flow of globalization, attractive alternatives became available elsewhere. "We are losing our lead every day," warns Andrew S. Grove, the Hungarian émigré who cofounded Intel and made Silicon Valley all but synonymous with the entrepreneurial spirit that drives the Innovation Economy. "The distance between us and the rest of the world is eroding every day because knowledge doesn't stay confined and people don't stay confined."

The Global Village that Marshall McLuhan foresaw in the 1960s is a reality today. Technology and globalization, the two most powerful forces of our age, are recharting the landscape. New Age technology is obliterating geography. By redistributing power around the world, it is creating a more footloose economy that permits modern-day adventurers to explore a variety of venues. It really is a small world after all. In the tiniest burg, one can be physically absent but professionally present—thanks to fiber optics, wireless networks, PCs, videoconferencing, and the like. Professionals around the globe can study virtually at the same schools, read and publish in the same journals, and communicate across time zones using similar technological gizmos.

Any nation can play the global business game provided it is prepared to invest in science and technology. The end game is to cash out of lower-value industries and move upstream to more profitable ones. Consequently, we are witnessing the rise of new arenas of industry and knowledge in what were once thought to be the most unlikely locations. As we will see, the new kids on the block possess an unbeatable combination: advanced technology, strong government support, and an industrious, well-educated workforce—composed increasingly of repatriated and imported talent. "We are in a new world, and it is increasingly going to be dominated by countries other than the United

States," says Denis Simon, dean of management and technology at Rensselaer Polytechnic Institute.

Interestingly, the global hiring hall embraces brawnpower as well as brainpower. Take sports, where renowned stars such as China's Yao Ming, Sweden's Annika Sorenstam, and America's Lance Armstrong transcend national borders. Like everything else about athletics these days, going global is driven by commerce; almost every professional franchise is banking on big help from abroad to generate growth and fan interest. Winning over foreign cultures and colonizing overseas markets are critical to financial success. For example, some 30 percent of players in Major League Baseball are foreign-born.

What we are seeing is the transformation of national pastimes into international pastimes, as the world's best athletes flash their talents around the planet. "Have ball, will travel," is the current mantra in international hoops. Former National Basketball Association (NBA) coach Del Harris, who was hired to lead China's Olympic team, points out, "Pick-and-roll is really pick-and-roll in any language." Stateside, non-Americans have given the sport added flair. "They play really hard and they don't have a posse," says Charles Barkley, the former pro star turned TV analyst, on why he likes the swelling corps of foreign players. "They come here and they aren't spoiled. America is the greatest country in the world, but we have some spoiled __ ."

NBA Commissioner David Stern gets the credit for pioneering the sport's globalization. Today, the league's telecasts are available in 205 countries and forty-three languages. Fifty percent of the visitors to its Web site, NBA.com, come from outside the United States. "Capitalism is a wonderful thing," says Stern. "It's all about competition, about skills—regardless of ethnicity, race, or national origin."

If anyone doubted the ubiquity of elite athletes, the events of October 2, 2004, laid those doubts to rest. Ever since Commodore Matthew Perry and his Black Ships opened Japan at gunpoint in 1853, Japan has kept *gaijin,* foreigners, at arm's length. Yet, on this special day, before a crowd of about 10,000 in Tokyo's Ryogoku Kokugikan ring, the career of Hawai'i-born Musashimaru officially came to an end. In a tearful ceremony, the thirty-three-year-old, 500-pound *yokuzuna,* grand champion, had the traditional topknot of hair cut off in a ritual that concluded his illustrious career, spanning fourteen record-setting years.

The final snip of the scissors before a nationwide television audience marked the end of forty years of competitive Hawaiian *sumitori.* More and more, organizers today are looking to Asia, notably Mongolia, and Europe to spice up the competition and boost ancient wrestling's appeal.

On the same day, Japan was also watching its favorite son, Seattle Mariners outfielder Ichiro Suzuki, break one of American baseball's most durable records—George Sisler's 257 hits in a season, set in 1920. This incredible accomplishment had taken eighty-four years, and it took a Japanese *besuboru* migrant with superior speed and bat control to change the course of history. Suzuki's feat, and the hearty celebrations that followed on both sides of the Pacific, prompted one Japanese ballplayer to remark: "America is not just a country for America. It always welcomes people from outside—so maybe more foreign-born players will be the American way."

Yet grappling with globalization in an environment where brains, more than brawn, are paramount has not been easy for most Americans. In the minds of many, the outsourcing of jobs has become the bogeyman of the times. The truth is far more complex. Most research has shown that exportation of work, if anything, is mildly positive to U.S. economic well-being. The McKinsey Global Institute, for instance, has found that for every dollar of corporate spending shifted offshore by an American firm, $1.13 in new wealth is generated back home. Besides, it's here to stay. "You couldn't stop it if you wanted to," says economist Lester Thurow, the former business school dean at MIT. "If you add the pluses and the minuses, the pluses exceed the minuses."

Truth be told, flight capital is a story of good news and bad news. Whether it is viewed as a threat or an opportunity, there almost certainly will be long-term benefits to the global economy. For one thing, a rising tide lifts all ships. Therefore, a more equal distribution of brainpower should lessen hostilities around the world as well as restore the geopolitical balance. For another thing, it should enable political leaders to distinguish more clearly between the myth and reality of contemporary capitalism. "I think it's a good thing that more and more countries are getting to participate in the capitalist economy," Microsoft chairman Bill Gates said recently in a speech on outsourcing at the University of California at Berkeley. "It's not like we have one winner and one loser in this system."

Leaking talent, though, is much more insidious than simply losing jobs or outsourcing. Americans should be far less worried about off-shore jobs and far more concerned about flight capital. Intel's Grove calls the outflow of skilled professionals "mutually assured destruction. You can't hurt the other party without hurting yourself."

Think about it. When our nation's best brains walk, they take with them their intellectual capital, as well as invaluable contacts and connections fostered over a period of years. In the best case scenario, they may continue to be employed by U.S. multinationals—providing creativity and innovation, albeit from afar. But, as our stories will show, those ties often quickly fray. Many returnees either start their own ventures or join local employers. As allegiances shift to the homeland, yesterday's colleagues become today's competitors. This trend, if left unchecked, will lead to a day of reckoning. Eventually, America's share of the global economy will be diminished. It's that simple.

As the winds of technological change sweep the planet, every far-sighted country is tapping the global hiring hall for the same reservoir of human capital. Nations that once strove to keep people out— Germany, Japan, the United Kingdom, Spain, and Australia—are encouraging them to enter. "Brain circulation," a term coined by Berkeley professor AnnaLee Saxenian, is here to stay. Historically, the United States was the world's biggest skills magnet and the least likely country to lose gifted, well-educated people. In the Innovation

Economy, however, the flow of brainpower is no longer one-way. With the rising appeal of overseas opportunities and growing hostility toward skilled legal immigrants, many of the best minds in America are seeking new horizons. If this continues, U.S. technological and scientific prowess—along with the nation's standard of living and national security—will be endangered. Need proof?

For the first time on record, the United States ran a high-tech trade deficit in 2003, a trend that continues today. In essence, the country began importing more "advanced technology" products—representing ninety industries, from life sciences to nuclear technology—than it exported. Many link this reversal to the exodus of America's top talent. "People are going to be surprised to see how rapidly this develops," Washington economist Charles McMillion predicted in an interview with the *Christian Science Monitor*.

Flight capital could not have come at a worse time. America's Achilles' heel is its growing shortage of highly trained labor. In the 1990s, after three decades of plenty, the United States began to experience a serious manpower and skills shortage. With falling birthrates and longer life spans, labor-force growth continues to flatten. Some economists predict that the college-educated component could be short by as many as 10 million by 2010, and remain at a crawl for decades to come. These numbers assume immigration remains at a record high, approximately 600,000 legal immigrants a year—a highly unlikely scenario.

Putting quantity aside, there is the related concern about the quality of the U.S. workforce. Many Americans are unprepared for Space Age work. The 2004 American Diploma Project found that 60 percent of employers rated high school graduates' proficiencies as only "fair" or "poor." "We are losing the skills war," laments Louis V. Gertsner Jr., a founder of the Carlyle Group and former chairman of IBM. While other nations are placing enormous emphasis on revving their educational engines, reformist movements here continue to sputter. U.S. high school students are no better prepared for college than they were ten years ago, according to a recent study by ACT, one of the two leading organizations that offer college entrance exams. The United States remains a nation at risk.

Especially worrisome, the math and science scores of America's schools don't add up, putting the country close to the bottom internationally. A recent survey, Trends in International Math and Science Study, found that the best-performing graduates were from, in order, Singapore, South Korea, Taiwan, Hong Kong, and Japan. The United States ranked nineteenth, just after Latvia (India and China were not surveyed). Similarly, a December 2004 study of forty countries by the Organization for Economic Cooperation and Development (OECD) ranked American teenagers twenty-eighth in math, twenty-second in science, and twenty-ninth in problem solving. In addition, fewer engineering and science students are earning degrees at U.S. colleges and universities. Concerned about being labeled geeks and shunning the rigors of math, science, and engineering, students are opting for softer disciplines, from art history to recreational administration.

"We have a serious scientific and engineering manpower problem, and it's been developing since the 1970s," warns Cornell physicist and Nobel Prize winner Robert C. Richardson. "We used to be third in the world, behind Japan and Finland, in the percentage of our students who became scientists and engineers. Now we're twenty-third. Half of our graduate students are foreign-born, and they're looking for opportunities in Australia and Europe." Without change, "we're going to be left behind in a cloud of dust."

"People have come from around the world to be educated in the United States, and they have stayed," adds Susan Hockfield, president of MIT and a renowned neuroscience researcher. "They have become part of America's economic engine. And it's not the case that we have plenty of native-born Americans to fill those roles. If we cut off the opportunities, these people will go somewhere else. Ultimately, we could lose our position as a world leader in science and technology."

The United States has two options: develop more homegrown talent or import more talented workers from abroad. The first option is unlikely to produce results, at least in the short term. Therefore, the nation will have to attract and retain more immigrants while also retaining its existing pool of native- and foreign-born workers.

Let me emphasize that heading home is not entirely new. Between 1880 and 1930, roughly 30 percent of European immigrants returned home. For the most part, they were sojourners, with no intention of residing in the United States permanently. When economic opportunities dried up, they just left. Typically, they were blue-collar workers, which were in oversupply in industrial America. Today's departing immigrants represent the creative class: gold-collar workers who could contribute to America's global prowess.

The current wave of flight capital, to be sure, is still a young phenomenon. Since its discovery, the New World has beckoned millions oppressed by religious, social, or political persecution who sought a better life. "America is God's crucible, the great melting pot," British writer Israel Zangwill once observed. That reputation, by and large, remains intact: the United States' tremendous strength, dynamism, and resiliency continue to attract gifted people from around the world.

"The true genius of America is its openness to foreigners," says Menachem Mautner, a professor and former law school dean at Tel Aviv University, who has taught at Harvard, Yale, and Michigan. "It's the best place on Earth to be a foreigner. No other country even comes close." Take Fortress Europe, which is faced with the same aging population and the same need to replenish its skilled labor pool. In stark contrast to America, Europe exhibits an ingrained wariness of newcomers—a standoffishness that inhibits its ability to attract, let alone retain, top talent. Some 100,000 European-born researchers work in the United States, and, according to a European Commission survey, more than 70 percent of EU-born recipients of U.S. doctorates between 1991 and 2000 plan to stay here. By 2010, Europe will have a human capital deficit of 700,000 scientists and engineers.

Therefore, no one is suggesting that the United States should despair. The country remains a steamroller of modernity. It is capitalism on steroids. Our economy is more than seven times bigger than

China's and represents close to one-third of the global GDP. U.S. multinational corporations dominate the Fortune Global 500 list, with 189 firms making up 39 percent of "500" revenues. American stock markets account for roughly one-half of the world's market capitalization. A rich ecosystem of risk-taking entrepreneurs, flexible companies, first-rate universities, and Silicon Valley clusters enriches national creativity. The United States outspends everyone on research and development—three times more than second-place Japan. And the gap is widening. As a result, the United States ranks highest in the world knowledge economies' index, compiled by Robert Huggins Associates, a British-based economics consultancy. Another recent poll ranks the United States second (to Sweden) in creativity.

America's universities, particularly at the graduate level, are the best in the world: "the epicenter of academic achievement," the *Financial Times* calls them. The United States has won roughly 60 percent of all Nobel Prizes awarded since World War II, and seven hundred of the world's most highly cited researchers work here. In 2004, academics at Shanghai Jiao Tong University constructed a league of the world's best universities, using a composite index of Nobel Prizes, citations, and scholarly articles. Of the top twenty, all but three—Cambridge, Oxford, and Tokyo—were American.

On many fronts, the United States appears to be winning the race for human capital. Nonetheless, the nation cannot afford to rest on its laurels. "It is far more difficult to hold and maintain leadership than it is to attain it," Samuel Jones Tilden reminded us more than a century ago. America's major rivals—China, Japan, Taiwan, South Korea, and other tiger economies—are well prepared to knock us off our perch.

The right attitude toward challenge is neither dark pessimism nor wild optimism—but rather sober realism. "No one disputes the fact that, when it comes to economic dynamism, the United States still ranks at the top," writes Alan Webber, founding editor of business magazine *Fast Company*. "But the combination of 'reverse brain drain' policies presents a clear danger to America's future competitiveness." In a world where creativity and innovation are central to growth and prosperity, keeping the best brains in the country, or encouraging them to come back, will be critical if the United States wants to stay on top.

This is a defining moment. The time to act is now if the United States is to avoid becoming a technological colony of other countries. In today's world, no one nation has a lock on creativity and innovation. History tells us that, inevitably, one country's competitive dominance passes to another. Today, the Americans, tomorrow the Chinese, Indians, Brazilians, and others.

"The history of man," wrote psychologist and thinker Erich Fromm, "is a graveyard of great cultures that came to catastrophic ends because of their incompatibility for planned, rational, and voluntary reaction to challenge." Historically, the United States has shown the ability to respond successfully to challenges. A pragmatic resiliency is deeply ingrained in the American psyche. It has served us well in the past. If we so choose, it will serve us well in the future.

Irish **uprising**

They say there's bread and work for all,
And the sun shines always there.
But I'll not forget old Ireland,
Were it fifty times as fair.

—LADY DUFFERIN

"Lament of the Irish Emigrant"

For centuries, the Irish viewed the United States as the Promised Land. Millions of men and women eagerly traded in the Old World for the New in their search for a better life. Clearly, that was the sentiment of Gerard Denneny in 1995 when he snared a visa to work in America. "It was like winning the Lotto," he recalls. "My sister was living and working in New York, and I had every intention of staying abroad for an indefinite time, even permanently." The twenty-nine-year-old hotelier quickly settled into the Big Apple as part of the management team tasked with opening the prestigious Four Seasons Hotel, smack in the heart of Manhattan's business and shopping epicenter.

Two years later, however, in a dramatic break with previous decades of Irish emigration to the United States—one of the oldest, largest, and most sustained migrating flows in history—Denneny did the unthinkable: he headed back home. In doing so, he joined the ranks of thousands of other "homing pigeons," a term coined by Irish economist John FitzGerald, who represent the burgeoning flock of people returning to the land of their birth.

Since 1996, the Irish, who once saw little choice but to move to America, have been reversing their tracks. Last year, Ireland took in nearly 29,000 more people than it sent abroad, many of them—like Denneny—homing pigeons, or returning emigrants. That's a remarkable turnabout for a nation that for most of three centuries hemorrhaged its population.

Traditionally, the exodus of Ireland's best and brightest was regarded as a death in the family. Any departure was viewed as a mortal wound, not only to the family structure but to the national psyche. Prelaunch "American wakes" took place in homes across the country as relatives and friends mourned their coming loss. The island's peak population of 8.2 million in 1845 shrank to the current population of 5.2 million, largely the by-product of out-migration.

Recently, however, thanks to a dramatic turnaround in the 1990s that doubled the size of Ireland's economy and altered the nation's economic image from waif to whiz kid, thousands of skilled professionals have been returning to share in the good times. "It's a historical change" says Mary P. Corcoran, a sociologist at the National University of Ireland in Maynooth who has studied the reverse migration. "We've always seen ourselves as an emigrant country," she says, while noting that "the story of the nineties is people coming home." Returning business-savvy expatriates have helped transform Ireland into the high-flying "Celtic Tiger."

Reflecting on his own U-turn, Denneny, now thirty-nine, cites the country's economic rebirth as a factor in his decision to journey homeward. "I kept hearing while I was away about how good the Irish economy was doing, that things had really changed." Following a brief stint at the four-star Morrison Hotel, he currently serves as resident manager of the Four Seasons Hotel in Dublin's tony Ballsbridge district. Denneny's return home also reflects a desire to reconnect with his roots. "Virtually every Irish man and woman I know in the States wants to come home," he says. "Their comfort level is simply higher here."

"The Irish have always had an enormous affection for their homeland," explains historian and author Tim Pat Coogan. "The moment any shoots of prosperity come up, they come back home." With their help, Ireland's government—in partnership with business, labor, and academia—has crafted a comprehensive industrial policy to transform the country into a model of success. At the end of 2004, the Irish Republic (representing five-sixths of the island) looked backed on fourteen years of uninterrupted prosperity. With economic growth exceeding 50 percent during the past decade, Ireland enjoys greater prosperity than does England, its former landlord. The Celtic Tiger has roared in the face of its global competitors by mixing low corporate tax rates, funds from the European Union (EU), fiscal reform, and a bright, baby-boomer workforce lured from abroad, along with locals who trained in blue-chip multinational corporations such as Intel, IBM, and Microsoft.

> **Adapt—or Die**
>
> At the start of the twenty-first century, Ireland's leaders recognized the country would have to rely on brains, not brawn.

However, the technology downturn appears to have ended the days of double-digit growth. Ireland's central bank forecasts almost 5 percent for 2005. No longer a low-wage country, Ireland also has outsourced a growing number of jobs—particularly in telecommunications and financial services—to cheaper locations in the expanded EU, Latin America, and Asia. Yet, optimism remains high. Ireland is aggressively seeking a fresh angle on the economy, especially in a variety of technology- and innovation-intensive industries. Here, too, a key component of the national game plan is to snare the latest flock of homing pigeons: the highly skilled scientists, researchers, and entrepreneurs needed to spur the next growth cycle.

The Irish uprising is the ideal prism through which to view the power and potential of reverse migration. In many respects, it offers important lessons for other countries eager to join the economic big leagues. It underscores one of the axioms of flight capital: global mobility can work to the advantage or disadvantage of any nation.

Although significant emigration occurred from the late eighteenth century, the Great Famine of the 1840s is the defining landmark in Irish departures. Sir Walter Raleigh introduced the potato to Ireland, from America, in 1586. A century later, it had become the primary food of the peasants. In southern Ireland, it was the only food eaten by one-third of the population. In a cruel twist of fate, the catastrophic blight that devastated the potato crop also came from America— onboard the notorious "coffin ships" that later carried so many Irish, hungry and jobless, to America. These ships bore both diseased potatoes and bird droppings, imported as fertilizer, that transmitted the fungus.

The blight first appeared in September 1845 and continued for three years, leaving the potatoes rotting in the ground. Once-fertile fields were transformed into barren land. Many peasants became too weak to work their farms. Landlords had the thatched huts of tenants unable to meet their rents torched and drove thousands of starving peasants off the land. Meanwhile, unaffected crops such as corn sat in warehouses waiting to be shipped to England.

In *Star of the Sea*, a chilling indictment of the period, Irish novelist Joseph O'Connor describes the misery through the eyes of his narrator, an American journalist: "Nothing had prepared him for it: the fact of famine . . . the hillocks of corpses. . . . The man arrested on the outskirts of Clifden accused of devouring the body of his child. The blankness on his face as he was carried into the courtroom, not being able to walk with hunger. The blankness when he was found guilty and carried away." In 1854, writer and historian John Mitchell offered a similar report: "Families, when all was eaten and no hope left, took their last look at the sun, locked their cottage doors that none might see them die nor hear their groans, and were found weeks afterwards, skeletons on their own hearth."

The Great Famine remains deeply etched in Ireland's psyche. Former president Mary Robinson calls it "the event which more than any other shaped us as a people. It defined our will to survive. It defined our sense of human vulnerability." Even today, it is visible in the landscape, where once-thriving settlements are little more than heaps of lichen-covered stones; where stone walls still mark fields long since taken over by bracken and heather. Famine graveyards hold the remains of 1.5 million fathers, mothers, and children buried anonymously in huge communal pits. The harrowing tales of families dying in their homesteads are matched only by the poignant accounts of those fleeing on the disease-ridden coffin ships to seek a new life in America. Many emigrants were evicted tenants, helped on their way by landlords eager to expel them. Others borrowed passage money (the equivalent of $10 in U.S. currency) from relatives left at home, promising to repay them as soon as possible.

> **Dust Off the Welcome Mat**
>
> Early immigrants to America from the Emerald Isle were greeted with signs such as "No Irish Need Apply."

Conditions onboard were miserable. In steerage, hundreds of men, women, and children were crowded together for a month or more. On daily rations consisting of half a pound of hardtack and a quart of water, they fought hunger and seasickness. If the weather was bad, they were not allowed on deck for fresh air. Nearly half of them died during the voyage, their corpses unceremoniously tossed overboard.

These ships were still seen by many as cradles of opportunity rather than coffins, says historian Kevin Whelan, who directs Notre Dame University's Keough Center in Dublin. For them, the choice was simple: emigrate or die. However tinged with sadness, more than a million Irish carried their hopes, their enterprise and ambition to America. Those who survived the wretched journey often were quarantined in disease-ridden camps. Then, thousands of "Shanty Irish" were crammed into shanty towns or filthy tenements. By 1850, one-fourth of New York City's population of 696,000 was Irish-born; by 1855, 1.5 million people of Irish descent were living in the United States.

The early arrivals experienced widespread ridicule and discrimination. Job-seekers were greeted with notices proclaiming, "No Irish Need Apply." Those fortunate enough to find work held menial jobs. Generally unskilled, unfamiliar with urban living, and often speaking only Gaelic, the Irish established protective associations under the umbrella of the United Irish Counties, providing a lifeline of contacts, tips, and support. Eventually, they fanned out across the country to Boston, Philadelphia, and Chicago, as well as more remote locales: Butte, Charleston, Spokane, and San Antonio.

Once having left Ireland's shores, an emigrant never dreamed of returning or even visits back home. There were new lives to be built and families to rear. "The Irish emigrant was expected to make good in his new country, but never forget the old one," writes Geraldine O'Connell in *The Children of the Far-Flung*. "He had a duty to remember the folks at home. But he was not meant to go home."

Consequently, Irish settlers traveled as families with no objective other than survival and assimilation into their new country. Almost from the beginning of their history in America, they professed their allegiance by answering the call to arms. They were, and remain, disproportionately represented in every major military conflict. For instance, 80,000 native Irishmen fought for the Union in the Civil War; 20,000 for the Confederacy.

By the 1870s, the emigrant profile had changed. "Healthy single young men and women left Ireland with a goal to create a new life for themselves," writes professor Linda Dowling Almeida of New York University. "They were ambitious workers, who were welcomed into Irish neighborhoods, many of which were built by the survivors and descendants of the Famine refugees."

By the turn of the twentieth century, more than 4 million Irish had crossed the Atlantic. In fact, as many Irish lived outside the country as in it. What had been one of Europe's most densely populated countries became quite the opposite. In turn, the exodus helped populate the United States, where today an estimated 44 million Americans claim Irish ancestry.

With the passage of time, the Irish overcame much of the discrimination and poverty that characterized their earlier history. As waves of immigrants from Europe arrived, the Irish slowly advanced from largely unskilled labor to skilled and managerial positions. They began to make their mark in a variety of professions.

In politics, the Irish began their ascent to America's highest offices. New Yorker Al Smith was the first Irish Catholic to run for president. Later, Presidents John Kennedy, Richard Nixon, and Bill Clinton would proudly proclaim their Irish roots. Irish Americans were also successful in big cities. Boston mayor and Massachusetts governor James Michael Curley and Chicago mayor Richard J. Daley were beneficiaries of urban political machines run by the Irish.

The descendants of Irish immigrants achieved distinction in other fields as well. Automobile manufacturer Henry Ford, the son of immigrants from Cork, revolutionized how the world traveled. Maine-born John Ford, whose parents came from Connemara, directed some of his era's most memorable films, many with Irish subjects. Famous Americans of Irish descent include filmmaker Walt Disney, singer Bing Crosby, artist Georgia O'Keeffe, Nobel Prize–winning playwright Eugene O'Neill, and novelists F. Scott Fitzgerald and John O'Hara.

After the Great Depression, the pattern of massive emigration changed. In the 1930s, much tighter U.S. immigration laws ended the era of open access and deflected the Irish away from America. Between 1946 and 1961, 531,000 men and women left Ireland in search of jobs and a better future. Almost 90,000 of these "vanishing Irish" (a term introduced by Notre Dame's Rev. John O'Brien) made their way to the United States. The outflow continued into the 1960s, although at a somewhat slower rate. Between 1846 and 1969, an estimated 6 million Irish had emigrated.

In the 1960s, the Irish Republic for the first time experienced net immigration as the economy briefly improved, but when it soured, outflow increased again. The country lost close to 170,000 people in the 1980s and early 1990s, but the tide turned once again in 1996, when a net 5,700 people returned home. Subsequent years have seen a steady rise in homing pigeons, who make up almost 40 percent of the inflow.

Traditionally, those who left Ireland were predominantly unskilled and poorly educated, many of them straight off the farms. Even in the late 1960s, only one-third of those emigrating had a high school diploma; but by the late 1980s, 80 percent had completed high school. During the past two decades, many émigrés have been highly qualified men and women whose movement abroad was prompted primarily by career considerations. These "global cosmopolites," a phrase used by professor Mary Corcoran, represent the "transnationally mobile, educated elite" drawn to life in global cities who have "amassed considerable cultural and capital experience during their sojourns abroad." They bring with them "experience of business and culture outside Ireland along with new ideas, new contacts, and even additional capital," says John FitzGerald of the Dublin-based Economic and Social Research Institute. "Across wide areas of Irish society, such as business and academic life, many of those in positions of authority are these special pigeons. They've added directly to the skills of the economy and helped create a much more cosmopolitan and innovative society. They're part of the human capital accumulation process."

Target the Best Minds

Recently, the country has been focusing on "global cosmopolites," who bring with them considerable skills acquired from living and working abroad.

The local marketplace recognizes the global cosmopolites' talents, and companies are eager to pay for their experience. Recently, two Irish professors, Alan Barrett and Philip O'Connell, quantified the "wage premium" for professionals who ventured abroad compared to their counterparts who remained home. On average, they earn 10 percent more when they return as a result of their foreign experiences. (Business executives I spoke to contend that this statistic is woefully understated and may be as high as 35 percent.)

For some time now, Ireland has aggressively targeted this sub-species of homing pigeon for nation building. Government and private agencies are engaged in various campaigns to lure them home. Using everything from job fairs to advertisements in overseas media, businesses and government are attempting to retrieve Irish brainpower. In the United States, Irish Development Authority ads claim, "People are to Ireland as oil is to Texas." FAS, the republic's state-run training and recruiting arm, is scouring the country for skilled personnel, probing Irish cultural centers and community associations. Private headhunters such as TransSearch International and the Marlborough Group are also keen to tap overseas talent. "There's a massive pool of people we want to bring home," says Marlborough's Jason Kennedy, who has placed returning expats with local affiliates of Microsoft, Dell, Citigroup, and General Electric.

Emigration today is driven by a different purpose. Professor Edward Walsh, who spent several years in America before serving as president of the University of Limerick, argues that going abroad enables graduates to gain scientific and high-technology experience that they couldn't acquire in Ireland. When they return home, their contributions are often invaluable. Another proponent of overseas living, English historian John Ardagh, predicts emigration is likely to remain a feature of Irish life for many years. "There will always be plenty of young Irish seeking to explore this wider world, outside their tight little island," he writes. "This is healthy and positive in so many ways—so long as they can go willingly, without economic coercion, and can return to jobs in Ireland if and when they wish." These present-day advocates of emigration stand in stark contrast to earlier generations.

Prior to the 1960s, the Irish Republic, which secured its independence from Britain in 1922, was turned inward. The long-standing reign of American-born prime minister Éamon De Valera held fast to a vision of Ireland as pure, uncontaminated by other cultures or countries. The Taoiseach ("Chief" in Gaelic, pronounced *tea-shook*) and his Fianna Fail ("Soldiers of Destiny") Party emphasized the reclamation of Irish heritage and restoration of the Irish language. Not unlike

early American patriots, De Valera argued that limiting British economic influence would allow both national culture and domestic
industry to flourish. But his policies of stiff protectionism, tight controls of foreign capital, and heavy reliance on state-owned enterprises
produced economic stagnation.

In 1959, Séan Lemass, who advocated modernizing the economy,
became Taoiseach. In a sharp break with his predecessor, the reformist
prime minister turned outward and emphasized massive investments
in Ireland's youth. The now-legendary "Lemass era" led to important
changes on several fronts.

First, the country traded in its philosophy of economic independence for interdependence. Tariff barriers were slashed, foreign
capital welcomed, and generous tax concessions offered to multinational companies. Ireland joined the World Bank and International
Monetary Fund. In 1961, it applied
for and later joined the European
Economic Community, forerunner
of the European Union. With EU
membership came access to infrastructure funds," which did much
to boost the nation's recovery efforts. Initially, these funds brought
aid to large farmers, but later they became more widespread, leading
to major airport, highway, and education improvements.

Reform Public Education

In the 1960s, Ireland began a
massive program to upgrade its
public schools.

Second, the government overhauled its archaic education system.
On the heels of several national and international reports highly critical of Irish schools, a massive reform movement took place in the late
1960s. Free education became compulsory from ages six to fifteen.
Curricula were stiffened: much greater emphasis was placed on science and math, as well as on proficiency in foreign languages. The
number of students receiving leaving certificates (the equivalent of
high school diplomas) skyrocketed. At the urging of industry, a new
tier of Regional Technical Colleges, as well as two new universities,

were established. Thirty years ago, only 15 percent of Ireland's young people attended a college or university; now almost 60 percent do.

Today, the quality of Irish education is exceptionally high. The republic stands second only to Finland among advanced countries in reading, math, and scientific literacy, and second only to Japan in number of science graduates on a per-capita basis. The *Financial Times* ranks Ireland as fourth (behind Switzerland, Sweden, and the United States) in its latest survey of countries most likely to succeed in knowledge industries.

Third, Ireland worked hard to secure labor harmony. Although 43 percent of its workforce is unionized (roughly the average for Europe), the country's labor climate has tilted more toward collaboration than confrontation. In 1987, the government joined business and labor in a landmark social partnership that rewarded wage restraints with income tax breaks. It also allowed most multinational companies to operate in a flexible union-free environment. One benefit: Ireland's labor productivity has grown by 5 percent a year since 1995—double the rate of the United States and most major European economies.

As part of the national move to restore competitiveness, government officials were encouraged to bring deficits under control. As important, once-ham-fisted bureaucrats came to appreciate that the country's economic revival depended in no small way on their ability to accommodate, not handcuff, business. Civil servants now stand ready to assist any company eager to participate in the nation's economic rebuilding. A few years ago, for example, Wyeth BioPharma, a division of U.S.-based American Home Products Corp., was contemplating investing $1.7 billion in what would be the world's largest integrated biopharmaceutical facility, at the Grange Castle, in the south Dublin suburbs. Although familiar with the Irish political climate (Wyeth first invested there in 1974), company executives feared possible delays in the planning process. However, government officials, noting that the facility would employ 1,300 highly skilled people and undertake leading-edge drug development and design, pushed through the plans for the mammoth 1.2-million-square-foot project in a record six weeks.

Taken together, these initiatives began to transform Ireland into Europe's darling. Success didn't happen overnight. It took nearly three decades for these strategies to take hold. There were numerous stops and starts along the way, including the oil shocks of the 1970s and the dark days of the 1980s when Ireland's unemployment rate reached 18 percent and a thousand people a week were emigrating. But by the 1990s, the country's well-educated, hardworking workforce began to generate results, and Ireland became the export base of Europe.

Over the past three decades, more than 1,200 foreign companies—in areas ranging from electronics to financial services—have joined the strong corps of firms trading successfully from Ireland. Employing more than 138,000 people, U.S. multinationals include Microsoft, Intel, Hewlett-Packard, Hertz, and Citigroup. Ireland's stable, pro-business environment also explains why close to one-fourth of U.S. foreign direct investment in Europe resides there, although Ireland accounts for just 1 percent of Europe's population. As for the bottom line, U.S. manufacturing companies report after-tax returns of 24 percent a year, on average, on Irish investments.

Celebrate Science and Technology

"Technology is clearly the driving force for us," says Prime Minister Ahern. "It has given a whole new generation of Irish people confidence."

Especially satisfying to the Irish is their country's status as a major player in knowledge-oriented industries, from computer software to biotechnology. "Technology is clearly the driving force for us," says Prime Minister Bertie Ahern. "It has given a whole new generation of Irish people confidence. It has helped create employment and stem the huge tide of emigration by giving our people a future."

That future appears promising. Take the highly competitive software industry, where Irish-designed products easily exceed $1 billion in average annual sales. Microsoft, which has its European headquarters in Dublin, accounts for almost 3 percent of the country's gross domestic product and 4 percent of its exports. Ireland is now the world's largest exporter of software and accounts for roughly one-third of the packaged software sold in Europe.

With seven of the top ten foreign software companies operating in Ireland, the government has been nurturing homegrown companies in recent years. With help from Enterprise Ireland, the state agency that encourages local businesses, there are now some six hundred indigenous software firms. Many of them are run by homing pigeons who made their money in America and returned home to start their own companies. Aldiscon, Baltimore Technologies, Office Integration Solutions Ltd., and CSI are just a few of the firms founded by American-trained returnees—who are treated royally. "Ten years ago, we looked down on a guy who was a businessman," says Eoin O'Neill, director of Trinity College's Innovation Services, the school's technology incubator. "Today, Ireland's technology entrepreneurs are national heroes."

Indeed, a number of Irish companies have global ambitions. For many, the U.S. market is key to their success. "The message was very clear to us. If we were to grow as a company, we needed to establish a U.S. presence," says Ed Ryan, vice president of marketing for Clockworks International, a company that produces international versions of software for Lotus, Symantec, Disney Interactive, and others. Other multinationals include software vendor Iona Technologies, smartcard seller Card Services International, Internet security firm Teinteck, and software encryption and security company Baltimore Technologies. Some Irish companies, such as Iona and Computer Basic Training Systems, list their stock on the NASDAQ like their Silicon Valley counterparts.

Ireland, of course, didn't create a bevy of homegrown tech shops overnight. At Dublin City University (one of the Regional Technology Colleges mentioned earlier), professor Michael Ryan reminded me of the lean years in the late 1980s when graduation from the School of

Computer Applications meant a one-way ticket overseas. "There were simply too few jobs here," he says, recounting the time when Philips, the Dutch electronics giant, chartered a jet to recruit his techies to the Netherlands. "Virtually every one of them got a job offer." Over the past decade, though, the tide has changed: "We can't generate enough supply for the local market," Ryan explains. "Ireland is the only place in Europe where kids think computers are cool."

The economic transformation to a paragon of high technology was born of desperation. Leapfrogging from a largely agrarian society to a postindustrial world took special grit. But that had its advantages. "We skipped heavy industry for New Age jobs like software, electronics, and healthcare," says Deputy Prime Minister Mary Harney, who, until October 2004, also served as the nation's loudest economic cheerleader as minister for enterprise, trade, and employment. As a result, Ireland sidestepped many of the lingering problems of the Industrial Revolution. There are no Rust Belts—hence, none of the thorny labor dislocations that confronted cities such as Glasgow, Cologne, and Cleveland.

Ireland's big bet on technology sent money flowing into several key sectors. With the help of the Industrial Development Authority (IDA) and a $5 billion budget, the country overhauled what was perhaps the worst telecommunications system in Western Europe. The overstaffed, antiquated operation became a highly efficient, self-financing state enterprise and later was privatized. Today, Ireland is Europe's recognized telecom leader. "It's the end of the first industrial revolution in Ireland," said IDA spokesman Colm Donlon, "and the beginning of the second."

These improvements convinced hundreds of IT companies to add e-business hubs to their Irish operations. Taking advantage of the massive available bandwidth, Dell, IBM, UPS, Radisson Hotels, and Google are among the sixty global firms that set up call or data-hosting centers in Ireland. The country's English-speaking workforce and its commitment to foreign languages (including Polish and Czech) have made it the region's telemarketing champion.

The government has also been attempting to make Dublin a regional finance center, a kind of mini-Frankfurt. In 1987, it created the International Financial Services Center in the former wasteland of Dublin's abandoned docks. Modeled on Canary Wharf in London, the forty-acre business park has managed to attract over half of the world's top fifty banks, including Citigroup, Bank of America, and JP Morgan Chase. Imposing office towers on both banks of the River Liffey contain 16,000 workers, primarily in back-office operations. In addition, the New York Futures Exchange maintains its European currency tracking floor there. Relying on tax incentives and direct subsidies, the government also plans to develop the Digital Media District, a proposed village of start-up companies and research labs, on an eight-acre parcel, once home to Guinness warehouses and breweries, on Thomas Street in Dublin. The District will take about seven years to complete and will eventually encompass thirty to forty acres. If all goes well, it will include firms in a variety of high-tech fields, ranging from special effects to digital TV, while attracting hundreds of entrepreneurs eager to start businesses.

The Irish government, in partnership with business and academia, played a visible hand in all these bold initiatives. "The state had a major role to play in economic development," writes economist James B. Burnham of Duquesne University in Pittsburgh. "While doctrinaire socialism has never been a prominent feature in Irish economic policy (as it was in England for a time), neither has there been a Reaganesque—or Thatcherite—commitment to the 'magic of the marketplace' by political leaders or their economic policymakers." "Ireland Inc." stands somewhere between the seemingly slapdash, adversarial model of the United States and the more unified approaches of Western Europe.

What triggered Ireland's breathtaking turnaround—laissez-faire economics or creative statecraft? "Clearly, economic opening, foreign capital, and tax breaks helped," writes economist Robert Kuttner in *Business Week*. "Score one for laissez-faire. But so did massive investment in education and public infrastructure. Score one for social outlay." Kuttner's conclusion: "The marketplace didn't do it alone."

Today, the Irish model is tilting decidedly in the U.S. direction. "Ireland has more in common with Boston than Berlin," says Deputy Prime Minister Harney, who claims that, because its success was rooted in lower taxes and other free-market policies, Ireland—though geographically closer to Berlin—is spiritually closer to Boston. It is an appealing thesis. "In the end, we didn't go for the European model," adds Eamon Delaney. "Despite all the dosh they gave us to kick-start our boom and despite all our protestations about being good Europeans, Harney is right, we are closer to Boston than Berlin."

Encourage Dual Loyalties

"Ireland has more in common with Boston than Berlin," says Deputy Prime Minister Harney. Many Irish professionals also keep a foot in the United States.

More than at any time in recent history, the government is now forced to reassert itself. But don't look for political leaders to make a dramatic turn from their present course. Rather, they must look toward shifting from a low-cost economy to one focusing on strategic research and development. Ireland is pursuing this course through a massive development plan, worth $2.3 billion, aimed at bringing its brainpower back home.

• • •

It's a bright, clear Thursday morning in October 2003. Two hundred Irish and Irish descendants have been summoned to Bayard's on Hanover Square in Manhattan, not far from the Statue of Liberty, which beckoned millions of their ancestors. Enterprise Ireland, the Irish business development agency, has organized a two-day conference called "BioLink USA-Ireland." Its purpose: to attract expatriates and Americans of Irish descent to Ireland. Not every Dermot or Colleen, mind you. Invitees are biotech's best and brightest, highly trained life scientists. "We've identified about 375 Irish experts, scientists, and researchers," says Edel McCarville of Enterprise Ireland's

New York office. "Of them, 75 percent claim they want to return to Ireland within five years."

Targeting biotechnology makes good sense. The industry finds ways to use living organisms in manufacturing food, drugs, and other products. In healthcare, it leads to diagnosing and treating illnesses such as cancer with new drugs, software, and medical instruments; in agriculture, genetic engineering of plants and animals makes them more resistant to pests. Hence, Ireland and many other countries are betting millions of dollars that biotech can be their next job engine.

> **Know Thy Competition**
>
> "We can't compete with low-wage countries," says Harney. "I've been to India, and I've seen what they can do."

"Bio has become everybody's best friend," says Rich Weddle, head of the International Economic Development Council. In the next several years, life sciences are expected to be one of the fastest-growing job sectors in the world. Also, biotech jobs pay $50,000 or more a year—one-third higher than the Irish median.

Although the United States dominates the biotech industry, Ireland has many of the building blocks needed to develop the sector. It houses the operations of nine of the world's top ten pharmaceutical companies and ten of the fifteen largest medical products companies. One of the strongest underpinnings of the Irish economy, the "pharmas" (as those in the drug and medical device industry are often called) are keenly interested in expanding their biotech capabilities in Ireland. But they need highly skilled people—such as those at the BioLink conference.

Deputy Prime Minister Harney explains to the conference attendees how Ireland has fundamentally changed over the past twenty years, while admitting that the country is still in transition. "We can't compete any longer with low-wage countries," she says. "I've been to India, and I've seen what they can do. Our future is with brainpower, with people like you." With the verve of a military recruiter, Harney barks, "We want you! We want you home! I don't expect all of you to come home. But the door is always open."

The deputy PM spends much of her time overseas at recruiting shows explaining to the attendees—many of whom have been away from Ireland for more than twenty years—how she and her colleagues have been changing the science culture in Ireland, what funds and other resources would be available to them, and what their return would mean to the country. "Above all, I appreciate and admire the 'can-do' attitude it takes to make a success of it in the States," she says. "We want you to bring that same attitude and spirit back home."

A series of speakers echoed Harney's patriotic plea. Ena Prosser, director of BioResearch Ireland, the arm of Enterprise Ireland that facilitates the commercialization of biotech opportunities, tells the attendees how indigenous companies are feeding off established multinationals such as Pfizer, Roche, Glaxo, Genzyne, and Merck—all sources of high-paying work. Her goal: 5,000 biotech jobs by the end of the decade—up from just 350 in 2000. Equally important is "moving into the R&D space," Prosser says. No longer content to simply manufacture drugs and medical equipment, Ireland aspires to conduct leading-edge research. "We have been excellent musicians of others' music. Now we want to be excellent composers of our own music."

One such composer is professor Luke O'Neill, director of the Biotechnology Institute at Trinity College Dublin, founded by Queen Elizabeth in 1591. One of the nation's preeminent scientists, O'Neill has attracted worldwide attention and support for his work in bio-chemistry and immunology. "There's plenty of money out there," he tells the audience, noting that he's received close to $10 million in various research grants over the past ten years. "In many respects, the funding climate is better, more consistent than in the U.S." Then, in a brazen pitch for the home team, O'Neill lets the conference attendees know that he took the road less traveled, turning down a job with Seattle-based Immunex Corp. to participate in Ireland's rebirth. "Please join me in delivering leading-edge scientific research to the next generation," he urges.

Mindful of the Irish propensity for blarney, several outsiders try to inject reality into the sessions. Michael Kamarck, senior vice president of Wyeth BioPharma, based in New Jersey, tells the group that first-rate biotech clusters today exist only in Boston, San Francisco, Seattle, and San Diego. "But maybe, just maybe, Dublin could join a short list of perhaps six or seven finalists by 2010," he says. Next, Robert Ulrich of Vanguard Venture, a firm specializing in funding high-tech start-ups in Silicon Valley, warns the attendees to "get real." He argues that any biotech company that proves itself able to move a drug through the development process with the help of private investors must provide a feasible product. Promising early-stage drugs don't automatically make it through the approval process; and one-half of late-stage products fail. Finally, Irish expat and former Citibanker John Moroney of Landmark Financial Corp. reminds the group how difficult biotech start-ups are to create, largely because they depend so much on being close to premier research universities.

"You're right," says Pierre Meulien, who tells how a consortium of Irish universities has banded together to become a powerful force in applied genetics. Given the country's small size and homogenous population, Ireland is among the best locations in the world to undertake large-scale investigations in cardiovascular disease, cancer, and other genetically based disorders that disproportionately affect the population. Meulien's Dublin Molecular Medical Center, established in 2002, attempts to address the major causes of death through leading-edge genetic research.

> **Nourish the Halls of Ivy**
>
> At the heart of the country's scientific resurgence has been a longstanding pledge to upgrade a consortium of top-tier universities.

The center is an interdisciplinary unit directed by three homing pigeons from America. Dermot Kelleher, now at Dublin's Trinity College, spent considerable time investigating human genomics at Scripps Medical Center and the University of California, San Diego.

His colleague, Desmond FitzGerald, a professor of clinical pharmacology at the Royal College of Surgeons, held important posts at Vanderbilt and the University of Pennsylvania. Hugh Redmond Brady, president of the University College Dublin, spent ten years at Harvard Medical School and Boston's Brigham and Women's Hospital. Thanks to these returnees, the Dublin Molecular Medical Center has attracted close to $140 million from Ireland's Higher Education Authority. But moving to the next level, CEO Meulien says, "will require attracting even more new blood to Ireland."

Changes at the top of Ireland's leading universities also reflect the country's affection for scientific experience gained in America. Medical researcher Brady was recently appointed to head up University College Dublin. In 2001, at crosstown rival Trinity College, the faculty chose laser physicist John Hegarty as their leader. Hegarty had spent almost ten years in America, initially as a postdoctoral fellow at the University of Wisconsin and later at the prestigious Bell Laboratories in New Jersey, where he worked with several eminent researchers, including a number of Nobel Prize winners. These presidential appointments signal the skill set Irish universities are seeking in their leaders.

Besides hearing about the growing premium on science, BioLink participants wanted to be convinced that there would be substantial, long-term funding for state-of-the-art research. So when William Harris, director general of Science Foundation Ireland (SFI), took the microphone, all eyes were on him. Harris needed no introduction. Before moving to Dublin in September 2001, the distinguished American chemist had worked for the National Science Foundation in the United States and had held top administrative positions at Columbia and several other universities.

Harris claims this is "Sputnik time" for the republic. "Ireland today is where the U.S. was in the 1950s when the former Soviet Union launched the first spacecraft," he says. "My country had to reevaluate its priorities for research and postgraduate training if it were not to fall behind Russia in the space race. Ireland's in a similar race. It must develop a science-friendly environment with limited bureaucracies. Above all," he adds, "Ireland must develop the minds of its own people."

Created in 2000 by the Irish government, SFI administers more than $700 million, with roughly half earmarked for biotechnology. "So far, we've distributed over $150 million on a variety of projects in fields such as genomics, drug delivery, and bioremediation," says Harris. At the core of SFI's mission is attracting leading researchers from around the world to Ireland. "We've set a goal of recruiting at least fifty researchers or research teams whose accomplishments place them in the top tier of their disciplines," he says. Of course, Harris knows that not every scientist wants to settle in Ireland permanently. To accommodate those who don't, SFI's generous "visitor awards" bring in international researchers for periods ranging up to one year.

From all reports, the work Harris and his colleagues are doing at SFI is catapulting Ireland into the biotech race. "It has made all the difference," says Trinity College's O'Neill, the recipient of more than $4 million in funding. "Bill Harris really understands the benefits of university-based research, and we're seeing a dramatic upswing in applied biotechnology."

In wrapping up the conference, Denis Headon, president of BioNetwork USA-Ireland, reminds attendees that the objective is to attract U.S.-based scientists and managers to create a self-sustaining biotechnology sector in Ireland. "This initiative follows attempts in the past few years to bring Irish expatriates back to their country through U.S. road shows and the creation of a human database, dubbed the 'Ex-Pat Project,'" he says. "Our next BioLink event will be on the West Coast in March. For it to succeed, we'll be relying on our 'regional champions.'" Those champions include ten distinguished Irish scientists, including Karine Egan at the University of Pennsylvania and David Oliver at Biopharmaceutical Solutions in San Francisco.

What are Ireland's chances of success? "This initiative is excellent because it relies on the Irish community to create a strong scientific network," says professor Austin Cooney of the Houston-based Baylor

College of Medicine. "Unfortunately, though, I'm not that mobile. You see, I married a Texas girl. So I'm pretty much confined to Texas." However, the great majority of scientists and researchers I spoke to were swayed to return home in the next few years. For instance, Baltimore-based Osiris Therapeutics's director of arthritis research, Frank Barry, in his late thirties with two children, plans to go back within the next six to twelve months. "I'm very impressed with what's happening back home," he says, "particularly the prospects for research awards and concrete job opportunities."

But Ireland cannot rely solely on its homing pigeons to build its biotech base. "Bringing in expatriates is not enough to build an industry," says Evelyn Combat, head of Forum USA 2004, roughly the European equivalent to Enterprise Ireland. "You also need people in the country who know companies and national networks to develop the industry."

A week after the conference, I'm in Dublin to search out the Ireland-based scientists Combat spoke of. My first meeting is with Cormac Kilty, chief executive of Biotrin International, one of Ireland's leading healthcare diagnostics companies. From his corporate headquarters on The Rise in the Mount Merrion suburbs, near Dublin Bay, the fifty-year-old scientist turned business executive tells me of his odyssey.

After finishing his doctorate at University College Dublin, Kilty went to the University of Texas at Austin in 1979 for postdoctoral work in genetics. Three years later, it was back home. The Irish economy was in the tank. "I was on the dole, broke and out of work for five months," he recalls. "Fortunately, my wife was teaching biology at the time and easily found work." After surviving on a research fellowship, Kilty's fortunes turned. A headhunter offered him a position in Switzerland with Baxter Diagnostics, a division of U.S. drugmaker Baxter International. A few years later, Kilty became the company's director of research and development. That, in turn, led to greater responsibilities for business development across Europe. "Previously, I knew a lot about science and technology, but very little about commercialization," he says. "But in my new role, I discovered two important things: first, the critical need for patent protection in the biotech business and, second, the economic advantages of developing diagnostics as opposed to drugs, which take so long to certify."

In the early 1990s, Kilty decided to break out on his own. But where? He looked carefully at France, Scotland, and Ireland, eventually choosing his homeland. Why? "I really believed—and still do—that Ireland is an excellent place to start a business," he answers. "Our corporate tax rates [now 12.5 percent, formerly 10 percent] are a major draw. And if the bulk of a company's research is done in Ireland, the worldwide royalties on those products or ideas are tax-free. That's a major incentive for any knowledge-oriented company." But there was more to Kilty's return home than sheer economics.

> **Celebrate Science and Technology**
>
> "The continuing commitment to investment in science will make Ireland attractive for biotech," says Biotrin CEO Kilty.

"Most important to every Irishman is what we call *grá*," he explains. "Loosely defined, it means a 'love of' something—in my case, a spiritual attachment to this country."

In 1992, Kilty returned home, founding Biotrin International with the specific aim of delivering novel diagnostic technologies for niches often missed by larger companies. "In the early nineties, European technology was not being commercialized because of the lack of appropriate commercial and funding vehicles," he recalls. "My idea for Biotrin was to commercialize these orphan technologies and explore their clinical usefulness."

Over the past decade, Biotrin has developed a variety of proprietary tests, which it distributes in the United States through its subsidiaries in Germany and France and through a network of forty distributors worldwide. Today, the sixty-seven-person company is the world leader in Parvovirus B19, testing for viral infections that can cause pregnancy miscarriages. Among its other products are unique measures to detect levels of DNA and liver damage.

Kilty credits the Irish government with his company's—as well as the industry's—success. Biotrin was one of the first recipients of an e-business grant from Enterprise Ireland. Its Web site provides information on a wide range of company products. "The continuing commitment to investment in science will make Ireland more attractive for biotech-based industry," he says.

Since most of Biotrin's key customers are large multinationals, access to them is critical. Kilty cites the Irish-American Business Summit, organized by Tommy Thompson, then-U.S. secretary of health and human services, which put him and other captains of Irish industry in touch with their U.S. counterparts in the life sciences. "These contacts have made a world of difference," says Kilty.

In return, Kilty has offered up a good deal of his time to his country as chairman of the Irish BioIndustry Association. "Our greatest need isn't scientists. It's entrepreneurs and experienced managers," he contends. "It's the major constraint on Ireland's future growth." To that end, he applauds Enterprise Ireland for developing a mentor network of experienced Irish CEOs who volunteer to become trusted advisers to up-and-coming executives. Mentors such as Kilty confidentially provide strategic guidance and practical advice, drawing on their extensive background in industry.

For some time now, Ireland Inc. has been pulling out all the stops to lure back its entrepreneurial pigeons. Five years ago, Enterprise Ireland, together with L. M. Ericsson, the Bank of Ireland, Neil McCann, and the European Union, established the Millennium Entrepreneur Fund. With a modest $1.8 million, the fund is intended to provide a limited amount of cash with some hands-on help to motivated émigrés. Over a pint of Guinness, the fund's director, Tony Shiels, recalls, "We went after Irish nationals in the U.S., the U.K., Australia, and Europe—making contacts through ads, trade fairs, and road shows. We focused on software, information technology, and life sciences. The only qualification was that an Irish national had to be part of the venture."

Shiels, with more than twenty years of working with start-ups and thirteen years of overseas experience, brought some impressive credentials to the fund. In the end, he and his colleagues evaluated four hundred possible investments, settling on just eight. "If just three eventually make it, we'll be happy," he says, noting that the award is a one-time grant and averages $150,000. "This is really postfeasibility study money, which is often the most difficult for any entrepreneur to secure. As important, these funds are relatively long-term, lasting five to seven years. In 2006, we'll reevaluate the fund's portfolio and make any necessary changes."

Of course, not every returnee is an entrepreneur or techie. Recall lawyers Linda O'Shea-Farren and her husband, Brian Farren, from chapter 1. Now forty-five and forty-four, respectively, Linda and Brian told me about their migration over dinner one evening.

"We had both received our degrees in law and, just by coincidence, since we each had one parent who was born in the U.S., we had green cards," says Brian. "So we figured to try our luck in New York where we could get better experience and the salaries that go with it. But, in fairness, we didn't have a clue on how it would go."

In short order, both would make their mark in New York legal circles. After five years in New York, in 1989, Linda was asked to move back to Europe to open Debevoise Plimpton's London office. She remembers vividly how her American colleagues told her not to accept the assignment. "Listen, think very clearly about this," warned one attorney. "You're going to be out-of-sight, out-of-mind. You'll never make partner over there." Undeterred, Linda and Brian relocated to London, where Brian continued to work for LeBoeuf, Lamb, Greene & MacRae, representing the insurance industry. Living the good life on U.S. expatriate salaries, the couple came to appreciate the slower pace of European living and bought a fixer-upper in the historic center of Dublin.

Two-and-a-half years after moving to London, they returned to the Big Apple, which, at the time, "didn't look as good." With one child in tow and others contemplated, Brian and Linda asked themselves the crucial question: Where do we want to raise the children? "We'd seen what happens to law partners in New York, what happens to their children," says Linda. "They work so hard, but their lives never seem to get any better."

Ten years away from Ireland was enough. In 1993, the Farrens decided to leap off the legal fast track and head home. "It was incredibly risky, maybe even insane," says Brian. "We had no jobs and a very expensive house to rebuild." The transition was not easy. Shifting from the high-paying world of corporate law, Brian had a particularly difficult time. "As an attorney who'd been out of the country for a decade, I had to build a client base. That first year, I made less than $200." Fortunately, Linda's reentry was smoother as she shifted between positions in government and the law.

"It was absolutely the right decision," says Brian. Since then, the quaint, bucolic Ireland of whitewashed cottages and donkey-drawn carts has changed. "The country's not as genteel as before," he admits. Nonetheless, the benefits to their three children have been exceptional. Each youngster is gifted and has received outstanding educational and musical instruction. "Could they have received an equal level of attention in New York City?" Linda wonders. "I don't know, but I really doubt it."

The Farrens, who definitely qualify as members of professor Corcoran's global cosmopolites, are also convinced that Ireland's capital city is an important magnet. It provides the kind of world-class amenities that up-and-coming professionals expect in their living environs. "Now, in Dublin one can get everything we got in the States, which we couldn't have before," says Brian.

• • •

Since it was founded by the Vikings in the ninth century, Dublin (*Dyfflin,* or "black pool," in Old Irish) has served as the center of Irish trade and industry. In 1171, it was taken over by the Normans and made their capital. Dublin has grown ever since. Today, this city of about 1 million has more than 25 percent of the Irish Republic's total population and more than 30 percent of the country's workforce.

During the 1990s, Dublin emerged as one of Europe's hot spots, along with Barcelona and Prague. Its Georgian townhouses, cobblestone streets, fashionable Temple Bar area, high-end restaurants, and cozy pubs make it one of the world's most livable cities. Whether it's discovering the cheery babble on trendy Grafton Street (the world's fifth-most-expensive retailing street) or watching the deer lope through Phoenix Park, the largest city park in Europe, returnees and visitors quickly sense Dublin's diverse pleasures. Smart, stylish hotels such as the Four Seasons, Morrison, and Shelbourne; boisterous bars that pour cosmopolitans as well as foamy pints of Guinness; and high-energy dance clubs attract more and more people to the nation's urban center.

> **Dust Off the Welcome Mat**
>
> Dublin, Ireland's capital city, provides the kind of amenities talented professionals expect from a world-class metropolis.

"A good puzzle would be to cross Dublin without passing a pub," James Joyce once wrote. With one pub for every 450 Dubliners, it's next to impossible to avoid the city's many watering holes. You can relax with a pint of Guinness or Bulmer's sublime hard cider at The Brazen Head Inn, Ireland's oldest pub, or Kehoe's, where famous Irish writers once tippled.

Dublin's easygoing hospitality and many charms spill over into a bevy of sleek restaurants and hip cafes. For years, Irish cuisine was an oxymoron. Notre Dame's Kevin Whelan remembers his childhood days when he fed the fresh salmon and trout he had caught in the River Derry to the family cat because no one would eat it. Today's sophisticated palettes demand much more than corned beef and boiled cabbage. In Dublin, you can dine on smoked haddock risotto at Michelin-starred La Stampa, sample black sole with beurre noisette at Les Frères Jacques, or enjoy Nasi Goreng at Lemongrass. Even Irish pubs are making it possible to swill stout with tuna tartare, curry, and foie gras.

When you've finished eating and drinking, a stroll through twenty-two acres of gardens at St. Stephen's Green, which connects Trinity College with Grafton Street, offers stunning scenery. A short distance away are the Hugh Lane Gallery and the recently remodeled National Gallery; each features outstanding collections of Irish and French impressionists. For theater-goers, there's the nearby Abbey, the century-old cradle of Ireland's greatest playwrights and actors and home to a cross section of contemporary performers.

A decade of prosperity has reenergized the capital city, where the traditional idea of the *craic,* or "good time," is alive and well. "Young people dominated Dublin life in the 1990s," says economist John FitzGerald. "They developed a whole popular culture and made the city buzz with music and nightlife. Today, people come here not only to work but to experience life in what is now considered an exciting city."

To some extent, Dublin's swagger and newfound self-confidence reflect a broad revival in Irish culture that also began in the 1990s. *Angela's Ashes,* Frank McCourt's Pulitzer Prize–winning memoir, stayed on the best-seller lists for two years. Author Thomas Cahill told us *How the Irish Saved Civilization.* Nobel Prize winner Seamus Heaney's soul-searching poems and the music of Van Morrison, the Corrs, and Sinead O'Connor captured international audiences. Filmmaker Neil Jordan achieved glowing praise for *The Crying Game*, which won him an Oscar for best screenplay. And *Lord of the Dance,* choreographed by Irish-American Michael Flatley and Jean Butler, made Irish folk dancing seem hip.

Despite Ireland's cultural vibrancy and its more cosmopolitan turn, nearly everyone I interviewed had mixed feelings about the new prosperity. Some worried that the Irish elite would rob the country of its special charm. Others feared that the Celtic Tiger had produced a legacy of ostentatious young Irish people, whom writer Kevin Courtney calls "Flash Paddys" or "Celtic Cubs." For others, boom times led to housing shortages, crowded roads, underfunded health-care services, and immigrant workers.

Increasingly, these concerns weigh heavily on returning émigrés, who often cling to a romanticized vision of Ireland. Poet Heaney likens this idealized Ireland to "a mythologically grounded and emotionally contoured island that belongs in art time, in story time, in the continuous presence of a common, unthinking memory life."

Several studies have shown that the country's new, faster pace has caused serious adjustment problems for repatriates. "They have difficulty in acquiring reasonably priced housing, commuting times are considerably longer and more frustrating than they had anticipated, and there is less time than they had hoped to enjoy a social life," says sociologist Corcoran.

During the mid-to-late 1990s, property prices climbed steadily at more than 20 percent a year. Despite the recent economic tailspin, more Irish returnees with more money have been competing for fewer properties. Consequently, prices are continuing to grow at 8 percent to 10 percent a year. In a country short on rental properties and with the highest percentage of home ownership (82 percent) in the world, the frustrations for those coming home are high. The problem has become so acute that some employers (Intel, for example) reportedly are considering providing company housing for returning professionals.

But reentry problems occur on many fronts. "I miss the service culture that I experienced in New York City," bemoans hotelier Denneny. "There, you can get whatever you want twenty-four hours a day. It's changing here, but it's still not the same." Another former New Yorker turned Dubliner, Anthony O'Neill, finds Dublin insular and confining and, despite its recent makeover, not nearly as vibrant as the Big Apple. Rising costs, too, are a problem for the U.S.-trained market researcher, who complains that "our standard of living and purchasing power were actually higher in the States."

For book publisher David Givens, the small size of the domestic market poses the stiffest challenge. "A best-seller in this country is 1,500 to 2,000 copies in paperback," says Givens, an Irish-American

with previous experience at the Harvard Business School Press and
the San Francisco–based Institute for Contemporary Studies. "With
such limited scale, it's extremely difficult to turn a profit."

Also, the Ireland many came home to has a decidedly different face. With an acute labor shortage, the country has been importing as many as 30,000 workers a year from outside the European Union, principally for low-paying service jobs

> **Expand the Workforce**
>
> Faced with an acute labor shortage, Ireland has been poaching 30,000-plus workers a year from outside the European Union.

in fast-food chains and hotels. "You can go into any restaurant and
find Latvians, Poles, Lithuanians, and whatever," says Prime Minister
Ahern. "But nobody gets too excited about it."

In reality, many Irish, long accustomed to a white society, have not
behaved well toward newcomers, who represent 160-odd nationalities.
Widespread incidents of racism are directed at the growing number of
immigrants. This can be very upsetting for émigrés who have lived in
a multicultural world. One visiting repat told me how disappointed he
was to hear his father chastise a "darkie from Jamaica" who had refused
to offer him his seat on a public bus. "A real shocker," the son said.

Resettlement is not as easy as anticipated. "Irish people returning
home should be prepared for a culture shock because things have
changed dramatically," says Eugenie Houston, author of *Working and
Living In Ireland*. "It's not the same quiet place that it used to be."

As the flow of homing pigeons increases, the Irish government and
business groups have been trying to ease their landing. For several
years now, Ireland's Department of Social Welfare has published a
primer for its native born: *Thinking of Returning to Ireland?* Returned
Emigrants is one of a number of private entities revving up the welcome wagon; it provides a support network for those seeking jobs,
accommodations, or simply a shoulder to lean on.

From all reports, the assimilation process is much harder on rank-
and-file returnees. Typically older and less educated, they tend to feel

left behind by the economic renaissance. At the working-class level, jobs do not come easily or pay well. My cab driver, home two years from New York where he had worked for several years in the hotel industry, claimed that he couldn't find comparable employment in Dublin. "They don't want to pay an Irishman fair wages," he lamented. "All of the hotel jobs are filled with foreigners. I'm taking my family back to the States next year."

Reentry poses a different challenge for the professional and managerial class. "These folks are also caught in a bind," says professor Corcoran. "Ireland's exemplary economic performance in the 1990s made the dream of return possible, but the economic miracle of the Celtic Tiger is predicated on the very practices and values that the returnees are trying to escape." Simply put, the demands of working in a more modernized and globalized Ireland threatens the kind of intimate lifestyle that returnees seek. Yet, Corcoran insists, "Irish core values haven't been eroded."

John Hegarty agrees. Reflecting on his own homecoming, the Trinity College provost recalls waking up one Saturday morning in a cold sweat wondering what he had done. But what was sobering "was the fact that Ireland itself hadn't really changed all that much since I'd left. I had changed a lot having gone to the States," he says, "but I came back and found that Ireland had not changed."

Despite the pressures of postindustrial society, the Emerald Isle has not lost its soul. If anything, its emotional pull seems even more powerful today. The continuing search for *grá,* the easygoing Irish heart, the promise of a better quality of life for children, and the value of friendship have made this tiny island the New Promised Land. Last year, the *Economist,* in its annual Intelligence Unit Report, cited Ireland as the country with the best quality of life.

That the republic prospers should be celebrated, not lamented. The lessons for Americans should be equally clear. The United States is, in its own way, an insular nation. "We do not realize the extent to which other nations like Ireland are moving rapidly ahead with innovations and development in areas in which we have enjoyed dominance and leadership," says Virginia Commonwealth University president Eugene P. Trani, a longtime Ireland observer. "This should be a wake-up call to the U.S. that it also can no longer rest on its laurels."

In the meantime, "Ireland also cannot rest on its laurels," says Notre Dame's Whelan. "The challenge is how to handle the novel politics of prosperity. At the moment, we are on the cusp, at the turning point. The key issue is sustainability."

How will the Irish Republic cope with this challenge? As before, the answer lies in pragmatism. "My vision is to build a better Ireland," Prime Minister Ahern tells his countrymen. "And it is set out in practical steps to deal with the real issues faced by real people. I am working to deliver practical solutions that improve people's lives. That is the real and practical standard that I have set for myself."

Perhaps "The Spike" is emblematic of Irish pragmatism and resolve. Built in the center of Dublin's O'Connell Street, the $4.6 million tower replaced Nelson's Pillar, the architectural landmark highlighting the British naval hero that was blown up by Irish republicans in 1966, deliberately timed to mark the fiftieth anniversary of the 1916 Easter Revolution. The gleaming, stainless steel needle, 396 feet high, reflects the towering aspirations of the Irish today and reminds us, as one of the country's most celebrated bards, George Bernard Shaw, once did, that "an Irishman's heart is nothing but his imagination."

miracle **on ice**

The Icelanders are staunch Protestants and,
by all accounts, the most devout, innocent,
pure-hearted people in the world.

—LORD DUFFERIN,

Governor General of Canada

Letters from High Latitudes, 1856

Iceland, the "Land of Fire and Ice," is perhaps best known to Americans for its geothermal springs; its luminous pop music; and its hardened lava, verdant sheep-grazed hilltops, thrusting mountain peaks, and jagged coastlines. Throw in the gnomes, elves, fairies, and dwarfs of local lore, and what you have is the stuff of legend. Cold, isolated, and windswept, with poetry reading and coffee klatches apparently the pinnacle of social life, Iceland would not seem to be the most desirable place to live and work.

Yet, miraculously, this subarctic island of 290,000, Western Europe's poorest nation a century ago, now ranks, per capita, among the world's seven richest countries. Iceland also boasts a thousand-year-old legislative assembly (called the Althing), universal literacy, extremely low infant mortality and unemployment rates, and much more. In retrospect, it would seem that Leif Eriksson, the Viking explorer who sailed from Iceland and discovered Greenland, got the names backward. It is Iceland that is bidding to become the world's greenest country.

Over time, Iceland has become an especially humane and prosperous place. Like Italy's old city-states, Iceland has thrived by trading freely with neighbors and defending itself against bigger states. In the 1940s, it got the United States to defend the island during World War II and, later, signed free-trade deals with the European Free Trade Area and the European Economic Community. Meanwhile, the government increased funding for education and public services, diversified the economy, privatized industries from alcohol to banking, solicited foreign investment, and slashed corporate taxes.

Between 1999 and 2004, Iceland's economy grew an average of 4.5 percent annually—nearly twice the European Union average. Though it has marked time recently, it looks set to expand again in 2005. Today, Iceland is the envy of its European competitors.

Icelanders, though fiercely proud, have always been acutely aware of their country's natural limitations. "It was always my belief that we're on a rock in the North Atlantic and the only way to grow was to find opportunities outside the country," says one corporate executive. "There were limited opportunities for wealth creation amid such a small population." Looking outside was what many of the best and brightest did. By going abroad, they were following the tradition of their forebears, the Vikings. But, in a recent migration reversal in common with émigrés from a number of other countries, these modern-day adventurers are coming home to participate in nation building.

Several years ago, the country suffered a shock when DNA tests suggested that Icelanders might be of Celtic, rather than Norse, stock. Researchers believe that the first inhabitants were Irish monks who came a century before the Norse. They arrived in 795, the same year the Vikings sacked Dublin. An unknown number of friars followed the monks, in keeping with their search for a far-distant island where they could contemplate God in peace. Their solitude, however, was short-lived; when the Vikings landed, they tossed the monks and friars out.

The first known Nordic would-be settler, a Viking named Flóki Vlgerdarson, arrived from Norway with his family and livestock around 860. However, the cruel winter killed his animals, and the disheartened adventurer decided to return home. Before departing, he named the territory *Ísland,* meaning "ice land," to discourage other potential settlers. Eventually word leaked out that Iceland, far from being a frozen wilderness, was a plentiful land replete with salmon-thronged rivers and lush green meadows. In fact, a shipmate of Vlgerdarson claimed the country was so fertile that "every blade of grass was bedewed with butter."

Ingólfur Arnarson, the country's first permanent settler, landed in 874. Like the other Vikings, he was a pagan. He had brought with him as tribute to the god Thór the "high seat" pillars of his house in Norway. As his ship lay in sight of land, Ingólfur followed the approved traditional practice and threw the pillars overboard. They washed up on the southwest coast, which steamed with hot springs. Ingólfur named the spot *Reykjavík,* meaning "smoky bay" in Old Norse. There, he built his homestead.

Once discovered, this island, slightly larger than Ireland and roughly the size of Kentucky, did not remain empty for long. By 930, most of the habitable land, particularly in the south, had been claimed. The early pioneers grew to number perhaps 70,000 by the end of the eleventh century. Almost without exception, the newcomers were farmers. To their dismay, what at first appeared to be a bountiful land proved quite the opposite.

Iceland is almost wholly volcanic, with soil that crumbles easily. The early settlers found it almost impossible to grow vegetables; the only indigenous edible plants were angelica, moss, and tiny berries. Hunger became a constant companion, and starvation was not uncommon. Oddly enough, rich sources of food remained untapped, waters that teemed with shellfish—shrimp, lobsters, clams, mussels, scallops—and squid. "But the Icelandic farmer, isolated, cautious, and conservative, would have none of these bizarre creatures," writes Pamela Sanders in *Iceland*.

To worsen matters, the Icelanders were confined to the island. Once the masters of the sea—fierce warriors who had reached North America, Russia, and Byzantium in swift longboats—they soon found themselves stranded in this unforgiving land. They had depleted most of the native birches for housing and firewood, leaving no timber for ship repair or building. The loss of tree and plant cover created the erosion that, in turn, led to further devegetation and famine. Today, the country remains nearly treeless.

Iceland's poor soil, harsh climate, short growing season, and active volcanoes made it difficult for settlers to survive. Natural disasters, time and again, reduced the population. In the early fifteenth century, the Black Plague wiped out almost half the country. Another 9,000 people died of famine following a volcanic eruption two hundred years later. In the eighteenth century, a smallpox epidemic killed 16,000. In 1783, following another major volcanic eruption, one-fifth of the population died of famine and disease. Each eruption was followed by a severe winter and heavy snowfall. The following springs brought destructive flooding. In addition to nature's assaults, pioneers also had to fend off a constant stream of marauding pirates, who saw Iceland as a vulnerable target.

The island was ruled first by Norway and later by Denmark, with the same kind of neglect that England lavished on Ireland. Treated as stepchildren by both colonists, Icelanders remained poverty stricken, socially undeveloped, riddled with superstition, and technologically backward. Danish doctors who traveled around the country in the nineteenth century were appalled at the lack of cleanliness, the poor food, and the high disease and death rates. In 1853, one visiting physician was moved to ask if there were ever a war so bloody that over 10 percent of the population was killed every three years.

Hardships continued: unseasonably cold weather in the mid-1800s, followed by another major volcanic eruption in the northeast, caused

Icelanders to consider abandoning the country. Most lived in poverty as tenant farmers. Religious and political oppression, along with severe restrictions on home ownership and marriage, made emigration a tantalizing option.

In 1855, five Mormon converts sailed to America, settling in Spanish Fork, Utah. Later, they were joined by other Mormons, bringing the total to about 370. Some 40 or 50 Icelanders set sail for Brazil in the 1860s, although many didn't stay. Iceland's first serious wave of out-migration occurred in 1873, when the Canadian government offered newcomers what seemed an unimaginable prize: free land, even a separate settlement. The designated area, called New Iceland, sat on the western shore of Lake Winnipeg in Manitoba Province. Only sparsely populated by Native Americans, it attracted an estimated 10,000 Icelandic immigrants. However, many of them found the barren territory even less hospitable than their homeland and quickly departed. Within a few years, the town of Winnipeg, much farther south, had become the largest settlement of Icelanders in North America.

Although New Iceland failed, those who stayed, the *Vester-Íslendingar* (or West Icelanders, as they are still called back home), retained many of the vestiges of their culture. Five generations later, there are still Icelandic societies, congregations, and newspapers in Canada. Other Icelanders emigrated to the United States; large Icelandic communities sprang up in North Dakota, Minnesota, and Washington. From

> **Dust Off the Welcome Mat**
>
> A century ago, Icelanders who left the country were considered traitors—with no chance of ever returning home.

1870 to 1914, an estimated 14,000 Icelanders emigrated to North America, roughly 15 percent of the island's population. As with the Irish emigrants, those who left home had no thought of returning. Among other things, they were strongly condemned by Icelandic nationalists, who viewed emigration as treason against the motherland. As a result, "many people no doubt left the country with a feeling of guilt, which may have made immigrants of Icelandic origin more attached to their old country than others," writes historian Gunnar Karlsson.

Today, the island nation jealously preserves its Viking heritage. Iceland puts up a spirited defense of its language, which is closest to the Old Norse once spoken across northern Europe. Its vivid centuries-old sagas were passed down orally until the eleventh and twelfth centuries, when they were written on calfskin using the Latin alphabet and ink made of berry juices. Today, these sagas are still read to children and studied at school. Because of the pressures to preserve the Icelandic language, special committees go to great lengths to avoid absorption of foreign words. When a new concept or invention is imported into the country, the relevant committee sets about producing the Icelandic equivalent of its name. "We see our culture as a kind of linguistic monument," says Audur Hauksdóttir, a leading linguist.

Iceland's nomenclature testifies to the people's allegiance to their history. The majority of Christian names are as old as the sagas. When a child is born, he or she is given only a first and, perhaps, a middle name. The surname is, in Iceland, a patronymic—it simply tells who the father is. A boy takes his father's first name plus *son;* a girl, *dóttir.* Telephone numbers are listed in the phone book by first names. People are not permitted to take a new family name, nor can they adopt the family name of their spouse. Even immigrants must take Icelandic names before they can attain citizenship. The only exception ever made was for Soviet pianist Vladimir Ashkenazy.

Iceland prides itself on being a sanctuary of Nordic culture. Given their country's size, history, and homogeneity, it is not surprising that Icelanders will go to great lengths to deflect outside influences. During World War II, they resented the presence of American troops (there were 60,000 of them— equal to half the country's population at that time). Eventually, they came to appreciate the military's economic benefits, in particular jobs. When a U.S. airbase was established at Keflavík in the 1950s, the Icelandic government insisted that no black servicemen be stationed there. (That agreement is no longer in effect.)

Unlike in Stockholm or Copenhagen, the streets of Reykjavík are still full of the fair-haired, blue-eyed descendants of Norse farmers, fishermen, and traders. Non-Europeans represent less than 1 percent of the population. Hence, one wonders how the volatile and eccentric chess icon Bobby Fischer will assimilate to his new sanctuary.

The close-knit nature of Icelandic society gives people a personal stake in one another's affairs. The country's minute size has a major influence on local attitudes. In a community so small, almost everybody is famous in some way, and it is nearly impossible to avoid the scrutiny of one's neighbors. Says Martin Wilhelm, a German molecular biologist working for a local biotech company, "People can't be anonymous here. They live in a fishbowl and are always under surveillance. If they mess up, they'll bring great disgrace to the family, and that's simply not tolerated." These social safeguards help explain the minuscule crime rate (the country reported its first bank robbery in 1995).

Iceland's transformation from one of the poorest nations to one of the richest began in 1944 when the country attained independence from Denmark. Fishing remains the mainstay of the economy, accounting for nearly 70 percent of exports. Iceland uses an innovative scheme of transferable quotas that give fishermen a stake in protecting their grounds. These quotas can be traded among firms, enabling the strong to grow and the weak to pull out of the business, if they choose. Iceland has thus preserved its stocks; its fishing industry is the envy of the world.

Recently, the country has sought to reduce its dependence on fishing. Tourism has grown quickly, reaching 350,000 visitors annually—more than Iceland's population. So have energy-hungry industries eager to harness the island's untapped reserves of geothermal power and hydropower. A $2 billion hydroelectric system and aluminum smelter, which will be built with the help of an Italian company, should provide a further economic boost. Reykjavík businesses are going global, acquiring—among other things—a prosthesis business in California, a large Russian brewery, Swedish and Danish banks, and stakes in some of Britain's major retailers. Also, the island is fast becoming a thriving hub for all kinds of technology ventures: genetic research, biotech, software, telecommunications, and filmmaking.

How Iceland's miraculous economic turnaround will play out depends, in part, on returning émigrés. Unlike Ireland, Iceland is not an emigrant country: excepting the fifty years prior to World War II, the number of people leaving the country roughly equaled those arriving. Annual net emigration is often less than one hundred. As a result, there are no specific government programs to repatriate Icelanders, although officials at both the Trade Council of Iceland and the Invest in Iceland Agency concede that a more aggressive approach may be in order. As we shall see, returnees are having a major influence on the nation's economic renaissance.

• • •

On a brisk autumn day, I set off to meet Kári Stefánsson, Iceland's most famous homing pigeon (better yet, "homing puffin," in honor of the national bird). Stefánsson's company, deCODE Genetics, has been on a tear recently, identifying genes involved in many of the world's most common diseases. Only a month before my visit, the Reykjavík-based firm had discovered the first gene ever linked to various forms of stroke. A global leader in population genetics, deCODE has found sixteen variant genes implicated in thirteen diseases, from obesity to schizophrenia. Its chief: the mercurial Stefánsson, whose driving ambition is to put Iceland on the map as the epicenter of genetic discovery.

Trundling through the wind and morning darkness, I approach deCODE's ultramodern headquarters. Perched on a petrified lava field on the fringe of the University of Iceland campus, it is home to three hundred leading scientists and researchers from more than twenty countries. I am greeted warmly by Stefánsson, who gives me the obligatory plant tour and quickly gets down to business. "I want to cure every major disease," he begins, demonstrating his penchant for grand plans and bold talk. "I want to use this incredible technology with

Iceland's unmatched database to unlock mysteries that will lead to profound improvements in human healthcare."

Setting such titanic goals is the norm for the fifty-six-year-old medical entrepreneur. One of five children, Stefánsson was heavily influenced by his father, one of the country's best-known radio personalities, a widely published author, and a longtime member of Iceland's parliament. "My father wanted me to be a writer," Stefánsson recalls, "and he was disappointed when I went into medicine and later science." He confesses that his heroes —in keeping with the nation's self-image as a literary enclave where poetry is the most admired of professions—were W. H. Auden, William Butler Yeats, and the national icon, Nobelist Halldór Laxness. Indeed, Iceland has more statues honoring poets than politicians. A local saying claims that it is better to go barefoot than without books. More books per capita are published in Iceland than in any other country. A remarkable number of Icelanders are published authors; amazingly, 10 percent of Icelanders will publish a book in their lifetime!

> **Target the Best Minds**
>
> When Stefánsson traded in Harvard for Reykjavík, Iceland's stock of scientific talent soared enormously.

"I look at myself as a failed writer," Stefánsson told the *New Yorker*. "A successful man is a great writer." Yet he studied medicine at the University of Iceland, graduating first in his class. However, he soon came to sense the limitations of traditional practice. "Medicine is so anachronistic," he claims. "It doesn't make use of any technology. It's utterly ridiculous." Recognizing the power and potential of genetics, he switched course. "Genetics provides a marvelous opportunity to study disease," he says. "I am first and foremost a physician, concerned with how to cure and prevent diseases. I am secondly a scientist, trying to find an explanation for diseases in the hope that it will lead to new ways to treat and prevent diseases. I am convinced that genetics provides the best tools to discover the nature of human diseases and new ways to treat and prevent them. These are the reasons I became a geneticist."

But to realize his dreams, Stefánsson had to leave the country. "At the time, the U.S. was the only place to go," he told me. In 1978, he was off to the University of Chicago, where he trained in neurology and neuropathology, joining the faculty a few years later. "I loved being there," he recalls. "It was a great university, small, cohesive, and very scholarly." For the first time, the fiery-tempered Icelander found that he could vigorously disagree with his superiors without threat of retribution. "That simply wouldn't have happened here." Stefánsson also came to appreciate the openness of American society. "I felt incredibly privileged to live and work in the States. I was never treated like a foreigner. America is extraordinarily generous," he said, carefully interjecting "*if* you have something to contribute."

After fifteen years at Chicago, Stefánsson moved to Harvard Medical School in 1993, where he served as professor of neurology and pathology. Later, he also did a three-year stint as director of neuropathology at Beth Israel Hospital in Boston. Despite his academic accomplishments, Stefánsson continued to feel the tug of his home country and its unique human database. "I saw where science was heading. It was becoming increasingly obvious that to shine the spotlight on important diseases, you needed scale," he says. "The only way I was going to make any headway was to access a large population base. And Icelandic society contains unrivaled [genetic] information dating back to the ninth century."

Yet there was more to this homecoming than simply making scientific headway. "This cold, wet, barren place is where I fit," he confesses. "You can't underestimate its importance in my decision. For 1,100 years, my family had lived here. This is where I felt I belonged."

In early 1996, Stefánsson and Jeffrey Gulcher, an American colleague and former doctoral student, developed a business plan and secured $12 million in American venture capital. That August, deCODE Genetics was born. Although the company was incorporated in the United States, its headquarters and primary research laboratories would be in Reykjavík. Four years later, the firm raised an impressive $172.8 million through an initial public offering on the NASDAQ.

Today, deCODE is owned primarily by Icelandic investors and employees, but it maintains important links to America, where 150 people are employed in Woodbridge, Illinois; Bainbridge, Washington; and Waltham, Massachusetts.

In many respects, this gene-tracking enterprise is binational. "Everything we do here is deeply rooted in U.S. entrepreneurial soil," Stefánsson explains. "But our subject matter, our species, is extraordinarily Icelandic."

Encourage Dual Loyalties

With its incorporation in the United States and command post in Iceland, deCODE enjoys the best of both worlds.

While connections to the Icelandic government and, to a lesser extent, to local universities would be essential in getting deCODE off the ground, Stefánsson felt that forming a private corporation was the only way to go. "I didn't spend fifteen years at Milton Friedman's university [Chicago] for nothing," he says. "I'm absolutely convinced that a partnership with the government, let alone a partnership with this lethally bad university in Iceland, would have been disastrous. They had no idea how to create value."

The geneticist turned entrepreneur enjoys being outrageous to make his points. His provocative, straightforward style reminds many of James Watson, the Nobel Prize–winning geneticist who unlocked DNA's structure fifty-two years ago and, in his seminal book *The Double Helix,* wrote, "A good number of scientists are not only narrow-minded and dull, but also stupid." Stefánsson seems to delight in poking his scientific peers with the same sharp elbows he displays on the company basketball court. "I am besieged by little people," he told the *New Yorker,* in describing his colleagues. "But these people are scared of change and are unwilling to lose their standing in the scientific community . . . and they will lose."

To mollify his detractors, Stefánsson first had to lure a number of world-class biologists, chemists, and business professionals to Reykjavík. "It was a tremendous challenge," said company spokesperson

Páll Magnusson. "How in the world were we going to attract full-fledged scientists from their tenured positions at prestigious universities around the world—people who were way overqualified for the University of Iceland—to this Mickey Mouse company?" Yet in a matter of months, streams of brilliant young Icelanders began returning from Harvard, Chicago, and MIT. For the first time in the country's history, there was something to come home to.

> **Celebrate Science and Technology**
>
> "We have the opportunity to participate in genetics at the leading edge," says deCODE's Stefánsson. "Iceland is the best place in the world to do advanced molecular research."

"I didn't find them. They found me," brags Stefánsson. "But Icelanders always want to come back. Like me, their roots are here. Of course, you need a good concept, good science, to attract outstanding talent. These people recognized that we were offering an unparalleled opportunity to participate in genetic research at the leading edge. Iceland is the best place in the world to do advanced molecular research."

The potential benefits of accumulating a critical mass of first-rate scientists were not lost on Iceland's public policymakers. They reckoned that deCODE's success in this youthful discipline might halt the brain drain, enticing bright Icelanders to stay home rather than seek opportunities in the United States and Europe. Another plus: a healthy biotech industry could help reduce the nation's overdependence on fishing.

And so, in the summer of 1996, Stefánsson—with his family in tow—returned home a hero. Fellow Icelanders seemed primed to create the conditions under which his ambitious start-up could succeed. But what this *stórfiskur* (big fish) needed most was unlimited access to the country's meticulous genealogical records, which date back to the ninth century.

Until recently, the understanding of human disease was fairly limited, confined to such classic single-gene mutations as those found in cystic fibrosis, sickle-cell anemia, and hemophilia. However, most common diseases such as stroke, heart disease, and Alzheimer's result from the interplay of multiple genes and environmental and health factors. Finding the genes that underlie these more complicated diseases was the central justification for the Human Genome Project at the U.S. National Institutes of Health. With the project's contributions in DNA sequencing and mapping technologies, scientists around the world have become more proficient at tracking genetic variations among individuals. Genetics now combines molecular biology with digital manipulation to create genomics—and, in turn, a potentially large industry built on gene diagnostics and gene therapies.

The hunt for disease genes begins by choosing a target disease such as osteoporosis, whose genetic combination is unknown. Family groups are identified in which the disease is statistically more prevalent than in the general population. Blood samples are collected from these people, and their DNA is analyzed to identify regions of the genome that are linked to the targeted disease. Unraveling this complexity requires the ability to gather and correlate details on disease and genetic variations across the largest group possible. It also requires accurate and comprehensive genealogical records.

Here, Iceland's population provides special advantages. Icelanders are probably the most genetically similar people on Earth. For over a thousand years, immigration has been negligible, and virtually every Icelander living today is descended from the Vikings who first inhabited the land in the ninth century. Thanks to two well-documented annals, the *Ísledingabók* (The book of Icelanders) and the *Landnámabók* (The book of settlements), there are records of nearly all the 700,000 people who have inhabited the country since then. Therefore, researchers can track diseases in hundreds of current patients, as well as in their forebears several generations back. In addition to Iceland's genetically homogeneous population and its extensive genealogical records, the country has one of the world's most comprehensive, uniform healthcare systems, with detailed medical records dating from 1915.

Together, these factors make the business of searching for genes and their mutations much easier. But to access what has been described as "the richest national genetics laboratory on earth," Stefánsson still would need government support. Shortly after his return to Iceland, deCODE's chief began lobbying to secure exclusive rights to Iceland's medical records. One of his first and most influential converts, Davíd Oddsson, until last year Europe's longest-reigning prime minister, saw the potential benefits not only of diversifying the economy but also of bringing high-paying biotech jobs to the country.

Yet, a heated debate raged as Iceland's scientists and doctors, as well as medical ethicists from around the world, voiced their concerns about issues ranging from the risks of privacy invasion to the wisdom of offering one company unrestricted access to the national database.

> **Know Thy Competition**
>
> "There's no genetic operation that can compete with us," boasts Stefánsson of his country's prowess. "No one can match us."

In December 1999, deCODE prevailed and received an exclusive twelve-year license to access the medical records of all Icelanders. However, the Althing insisted that the company build in strong third-party protections for individual privacy and that all processing of the database be done locally. The company, in turn, agreed to allow other Icelandic researchers free use of the information as long as they were not working for a competing firm.

"There's no genetic operation that can compete with us now," Stefánsson said, in celebrating his victory. "For a thousand years our nation has suffered because of its isolation. Now, at last, modern science will enable us to take advantage of our isolation."

With government cooperation, deCODE researchers can track disease in most of the country's citizens and analyze DNA samples for affected family members. By comparing genes of those who have the disease with those who are healthy, they can isolate the location of a specific gene. Using extremely sophisticated technology, DNA sequencers, and automated gene-hunting equipment, deCODE's scientists sort billions of pieces of individual data like a jigsaw puzzle. Today, the Reykjavík facility generates 30 to 40 million genotypes a month—more than the rest of the world put together. The second-largest genotyping lab, Marshfield Clinic in Wisconsin, processes about 8 million a year.

Three billion. That's the approximate number of DNA "letters" in each person's genome. Therefore, despite its high-velocity detective work, gene hunting is an arduous and laborious process. "It's like looking for a single typing error in a very large book," says one deCODE researcher. Nevertheless, by marrying state-of-the-art technology with the special features of the Icelandic population, deCODE Genetics has taken a substantial lead in tracking down the variant genes that underlie common diseases.

In July 2002, after a three-year search, the company pinpointed a gene for schizophrenia. Called Neuregulin-1, it affects about 30 percent of patients with the disorder, including Stefánsson's brother. At the time, Stefánsson described the finding as "the most solid piece of work in the genetics of complex diseases so far." Subsequent breakthroughs led to a series of landmark discoveries. The September 2003 identification of PDE4D, the stroke gene, was called "highly, highly significant" and a "tour de force" by Jonathan Rosand, a leading stroke specialist at Massachusetts General Hospital. A month later, a team of deCODE scientists decoded BMP-2, a gene that triples people's risk for osteoporosis and related bone diseases. Lawrence G. Raisz, chairman of the National Osteoporosis Foundation's scientific advisory board, conceded that much larger studies would have to be done to substantiate these results. "But it's exciting," he told the *New York Times*. In February 2004, the deCODE team located a gene that doubles a person's risk of having a heart attack or a stroke, and, perhaps even more significant, a drug that might block the gene's ill effects.

Even Stefánsson acknowledges that further studies should be conducted in each of these areas. Though disease genes found in Iceland are always relevant elsewhere, he admits that the local population tends to have fewer variants of each gene. To capture such differences, deCODE is engaged in collaborative efforts to confirm its findings in several other countries.

"Genetics doesn't tell you the answer," says Jonathan Knowles, director of global research for Switzerland-based Roche Pharmaceuticals. "It tells you somewhere in here an answer lies." The end game for gene-hunters is the hope that by accurately identifying how and where a disease process begins and continues, DNA-based diagnostic tests can be developed that lead to protocols to treat the disease. "It sounds a bit Orwellian to think of testing that way," says Stefánsson. "But it's no different than running cholesterol tests to see whether you'll get heart disease."

As with other biotech start-ups, deCODE has weathered a long period of financial losses and wild gyrations in its stock price. Now it must deliver. "There are two ways of sustaining ourselves," says Stefánsson. "One is to bring in partners who take most of the risk but who also get most of the upside when a drug hits the market. The other is to sell our proprietary clinical tests and software systems."

DeCODE is playing it conservatively on both fronts. Thanks to its gene-hunting prowess, the company has established a wide range of alliances with big pharmas such as Bayer, Roche, Pharmacia, Merck, and Wyeth. The Roche deal, for example, gives deCODE up to $200 million if it manages to identify genes for several major diseases. On the contracting side, deCODE has been selling its medical and chemical expertise to Applera Corp., Applied Biosystems Group, and others. While hedging its bets, the company is also devising its own limited array of proprietary drugs and diagnostic products.

Its recent string of breakthroughs has propelled deCODE into the upper echelon of the scientific community. "We are by a wide margin the best," beams Stefánsson. "No one else can compete with us. But our success lies entirely in our people. Of course, you need a good science. But most important, you also need outstanding people with creativity and energy. We have that. The scientists who work here are as good as anyone in Boston, San Francisco—anywhere."

Among deCODE's most prominent repatriates are Hákon Gudbjartsson (VP, Informatics), Hannes Smárason (EVP and senior business officer), and Hákon Hákonarson (VP, Clinical Services). In 1996, Gudbjartsson, holding a doctorate from MIT, left Boston's Brigham and Women's Hospital to join the company. About the same time, businessman Smárason, with two degrees from MIT, traded in a consultancy with McKinsey & Co. in the United States for some home cooking. Then, in 1998, with both M.D. and Ph.D. degrees from the University of Iceland, Hákonarson returned home from the faculty of the University of Pennsylvania School of Medicine. This cadre of homegrown talent complements imports such as Hong Kong–born Augustine Kong, a Harvard Ph.D. who served on the University of Chicago faculty before directing deCODE's statistics unit. Add to this mix a platoon of brainy commuters—including Stefánsson's right-hand man, company cofounder, and research chief, Jeff Gulcher, who also taught at Chicago and Harvard—that can be found shuttling between Reykjavík and deCODE's U.S. facilities.

Working in this global melting pot is both challenging and demanding. Yet the company makes every effort to ensure that its employees' professional skills are maintained. "We couldn't have made those assurances before the Internet," says Stefánsson. "But today we can. I expect our people to be well ahead of their peers around the world. And the day that doesn't happen, we'll close this establishment down."

As far as their socialization, Stefánsson professes disinterest. "I look at deCODE like a ship," he says. "I don't care what goes on off the ship. If someone has a problem on the outside, that's for them to solve." But when pinned down, he admits that both his returnees and foreigners are "warmly received by the community" and "have an easy time adjusting" to Iceland. In fact, the company sponsors various clubs and activities: costume parties, white-water rafting, and Friday beer fests. DeCODE also offers an attractive compensation package, including stock options—a rare benefit for most Europeans. However, the company's major attraction remains the opportunity to participate in cutting-edge genetic research.

Despite deCODE's victories, unlocking the secrets of genomics is a tall order. A few short years ago, there were seemingly boundless promises that gene-hunting technology would lead to a cornucopia of amazing new drugs. However, researchers around the world underestimated the cost and complexity of sifting through thousands of genes to pinpoint the tiny minority suitable as drug targets. As a result, only a trickle of genomics drugs has reached human trials.

At deCODE, Stefánsson's best bet is a diagnostic test for assessing the risk for osteoporosis, which is scheduled to hit the market later this year. Most of the company's gene-based products are still years away from the market. Stefánsson, however, remains convinced that deCODE can unlock genetic secrets that will lead to cures for common diseases. Perhaps the brash scientist is somewhat more guarded, sobered by the challenges ahead. Yet he never questions his decision to return home to harness the power of genomics: "Never, not for a minute."

Pioneers like Kári Stefánsson think big. Small-mindedness didn't lead Lewis and Clark to conquer the Rocky Mountains or Jonas Salk to discover the vaccine for polio. Less than a half-mile from deCODE's headquarters sits another idiosyncratic scientist, Bragi Árnason. Nicknamed "Professor Hydrogen," you may have caught him on National Public Radio, CNN, or the BBC. As head of chemistry at the University of Iceland's Science Institute, Árnason believes that, in thirty years, his homeland can become completely powered by hydrogen, with water vapor the only emission. "Using

> **Celebrate Science and Technology**
>
> In hydrogen engineering, Iceland is leading the way toward a pollution-free environment.

hydrogen from renewable geothermal water in Iceland is really only the first step toward a pollutant-free environment," he says.

Iceland is, in many ways, the perfect laboratory for hydrogen technology. It has had a long history of using alternative fuel: almost 90 percent of its electricity comes from geothermal springs or hydroelectric power, a proportion unmatched by any other country. Approximately 87 percent of all homes are powered by geothermal energy at less than half the cost of comparable fossil fuels. That's only the start. In a bid to create the world's first hydrogen economy, Árnason hopes to make Iceland totally self-sufficient.

Professor Hydrogen greets me in his modest office at the Science Institute. Árnason, though one of the world's foremost scientists, does not take himself too seriously. His nickname, he says, used to be a way of poking fun at him. "But that changed," he explains. "You see, in the earliest days, when we were talking about converting Iceland to a hydrogen economy, many people said, 'Well, maybe it will come, but it's too distant. It's too expensive and we don't need to think about it now.'"

But Árnason, who earlier had developed a reputation for his work in geothermal energy, would not be deterred. In 1978, he delivered his first paper on the possibilities of creating a hydrogen highway. "I talked about my ideas to my old friend and mentor, a physics professor here at the University of Iceland, and he said, 'If you think that something will happen . . . you should do it now.'" Árnason also knew that it often took fifty years to convert from one energy system to another—for instance, from wood to coal or from coal to oil.

In Iceland, clean electricity is almost as abundant as clean water. Furthermore, just 17 percent of the country's available electricity is consumed by its small population, suggesting that Iceland may one day be able to export energy. However, the immediate challenge is to reduce Iceland's dependence on expensive imported oil. Today, in a country that has more cars per capita than anywhere else in the world, a full tank of gas costs more than $100. Worse yet, the nation's biggest industry, fishing, guzzles millions of gallons of gas a year.

Despite the enormous challenges of creating a cost-effective hydrogen economy, the government fully supports Árnason's ground-breaking work. As former prime minister Oddsson put it, "If our cars . . . utilize this environmentally friendly fuel, everyone will be able to see that Iceland is an environmental paradise."

In Stuttgart in the 1990s, German automaker Daimler-Benz had joined forces with Canada's Ballard Power Systems to develop hydrogen fuel cells for buses. After visiting Dr. Hydrogen's labs, they formed a partnership to test-market hydrogen power in Iceland. Later, Norway's Norsk Hydro, Royal Dutch Shell, and several Icelandic investors joined the team. The European Union also contributed $3.1 million of the $7.7 million cost of the venture, called New Iceland Energy. "I think Daimler-Benz and the foreign energy companies really became the driving force," says Iceland's president Ólafur Ragnar Grímsson. "When we realized that they were serious, we opened ourselves up to this form of cooperation."

> **Act Now**
>
> Sensing the urgency to create a hydrogen economy, former Prime Minister Oddsson pulled out all stops to see that Iceland became an "environmental paradise."

In April 2003, New Iceland Energy opened the world's first commercial hydrogen vehicle filling station, just outside Reykjavík. It is designed for vehicles powered by fuel cells in which hydrogen reacts with oxygen from the atmosphere to produce electricity. From the outside, the station looks like a typical gas station—complete with the distinctive yellow Shell logo—except that one wall facing the street bears an enormous light blue sign that reads, "the ultimate fuel." The hydrogen, in gas form, is dispensed via a thin tube.

At the end of August, the first hydrogen-powered Daimler buses arrived in town. Able to go 125 miles without refueling, the buses run out of a central depot. Similar projects are being launched in ten other cities, nine in Europe and one in Australia. Eventually, the government hopes passenger cars will follow suit. Today, several auto companies have developed models as demonstration vehicles and plan to have many more in service by the end of the decade. (Two years ago, President George W. Bush pledged support to the alternative-energy movement, committing the U.S. government to spending $1.7 billion to fund hydrogen fuel cell research.)

The newfound respect for hydrogen is tempered, though, by constant challenges, and no one expects overnight success. "The hydrogen business is a mixture of hype and hope," admits Chris de Koning, spokesman for Shell Hydrogen. "But we are in this for the long haul." Perhaps no one is more realistic about the prospects of the first fossil fuel–free society than Dr. Hydrogen himself. "A true hydrogen economy is probably thirty years away," Árnason concedes. "But my children will watch the whole transformation. And when my grandchildren are grown up, we will have this new energy economy in Iceland."

In the interim, Árnason wants to turn Iceland into a hub of high technology. Like many others, he left home for his graduate work. "I went to Munich at the end of World War II," he says. "Back then, Germany was the magnet, especially for those of us interested in the sciences. Later, the United States became the favorite spot for advanced studies, largely because of its generous research grants. But many of our people never came back."

Recently, however, he has seen a reversal of this trend. "Although I should probably only comment on my field, chemistry, in the last few years there have been more and more bright people returning in genetics, solid-state physics, molecular biology, geology, and computer science." In his department, Árnason cites two brilliant, tenured, full professors—Hannes Jónsson in physical chemistry and Snorri Thor Sigurdsson in organic chemistry, both from the University of Washington—as emblematic of the migration turnaround.

"It's definitely not for salaries or facilities," he says. "We still can't match those found at leading foreign universities." According to Árnason, many Icelanders believe that their homeland is well on its way to becoming world class in selected disciplines.

Family, too, plays a prominent role in the decision to repatriate. Icelanders, by and large, have a strong sense of family. "Children help with chores and, despite increased affluence and satellite television, there is a marked absence of the teenage conflicts that affect other European nations," writes Richard Sale, a longtime observer of the country and author of *The Xenophobe's Guide to The Icelanders.* "Perhaps this is because family life is less frantic and there is more time for social life. One of the joys of Icelandic society is that there is no fear that kids will be harmed by anyone. Icelanders view societies in which children cannot play outside for fear of being molested as very sick indeed."

"Talented professionals and scientists today have more choices, more options," Árnason adds. "They can afford to be more mobile. Today, Icelanders living in the States are asking themselves: Where do we want our kids to grow up—in Iceland or the United States? The answer invariably is Iceland."

Echoing Kári Stefánsson's sentiments, Dr. Hydrogen believes the Internet is working to Iceland's advantage. "Our parents were isolated; not us," he says. "Perhaps it's the threat of isolation that has made us so plugged in. But technology keeps us connected—that and the huge number of cooperative arrangements we have with leading universities around the world."

"In America, you can just hop in a car and drive to another state or country, but we're stuck," says Daddi Gudbergsson, a returnee who worked in New York and San Francisco and later cofounded Web site distributor GM.is. "People feel less isolated because of the Net. Whether it's the Bay Area, Israel, or Stockholm, we make sure we're aware of what's happening."

Former prime minister Oddsson sought to guarantee that his countrymen would never be disconnected. In 1996, he signed legislation that ensured a portion of the $500 million raised by privatizing banks and other state businesses went for computers in the classroom and to assist anyone interested in a high-tech career. Four years later, Iceland had the highest Internet usage per capita in the world, according to the OECD.

Icelanders are infatuated with technology and electronic gadgetry. It is not unusual to find automobiles outfitted with fax machines, televisions, CB radios, and satellite navigation systems. "We're very tech-conscious," says Ebba Thora Hvannberg, a computer science professor at the University of Iceland. "Something comes out, and we want to grab it."

Icelanders are among the most IT-savvy people on Earth. They use the Web, mobile phones, and broadband with the same gusto as the technology-obsessed Asians. Toddlers play computer games almost before they can walk. As a result, the tech-crazy citizenry is making Iceland a major player in information technology. The World Economic Forum recently ranked it as the fifth most tech-ready country in the world—after Finland, the United States, Singapore, and Sweden. On its "digital access index," the United Nations' International Telecommunications Union scored Iceland third, behind only Sweden and Denmark.

Much of the credit for Iceland's high-tech takeoff goes to its education system, which was recently voted third out of forty-nine countries by the *World Competitiveness Yearbook*. Free compulsory education starts when children are six and continues through age sixteen, after which they typically attend high school until age twenty. Approximately 25 percent of Icelanders go on to university. Roughly one out of every six of them study abroad, with some 90 percent returning home at some point in their career.

> **Reform Public Education**
>
> After overhauling its education system, Iceland now boasts schools that rank among the world's top three.

Another émigré instrumental in the country's tech transformation is Ebba Thora Hvannberg. She teaches in the University of Iceland's computer science department, where enrollments have skyrocketed in the past few years. An expert in human-computer interaction and distributed processing, Hvannberg also actively consults for the tech communications and air traffic control industries. Although on sabbatical, she returned to campus to meet with me and describe her professional journey. In 1983, Hvannberg left Reykjavík for Rensselaer Polytechnic Institute in Troy, New York, where she earned her master's and doctoral degrees in computer science. "My husband, who's also a computer scientist, and I were getting very comfortable there," she recalls. "There were lots of opportunities, and we were involved in some very exciting projects, but eventually we recognized that we didn't want to live in the U.S. forever. So we decided to take the jump."

In 1991, they came home to careers in industry and academia, respectively. "My husband got a good job with a company almost immediately," Hvannberg says. "But it took me a while longer to reestablish myself professionally."

Once she had settled in, Hvannberg found Iceland to be "more open, more outward-looking, and more open to new ideas" than it had been in the 1980s. The economy, too, was on the rise, fueled in part by the growing presence of multinational companies such as Microsoft and LM Ericsson. University enrollments were mushrooming, particularly in the sciences and technology. Iceland's participation in the European Research Framework also "made it a lot easier to conduct serious research with a variety of foreign universities." In addition, Hvannberg noticed a shift in campus culture from theoretical to applied research. For years, it had been all too easy to dismiss her colleagues as abstract academics who lacked the interest and discipline

Nourish the Halls of Ivy

Recently, the country has actively encouraged its universities to focus more on practical research.

to bring their ideas to market. Now, professors were actively encouraged to engage in more practical research. "Since then, there have been quite a few commercial spin-offs from our faculty," she says. "And that's viewed as a good thing."

Hvannberg confesses to some frustration over her country's snail-like acceptance of women in science and engineering. "In electrical engineering and computer science, progress here has been minimal," she says. "It's somewhat better in industrial, civil, and environmental engineering. But it's still rather slow."

Iceland's software industry boasts more than 350 companies. The country's well-educated techies are gaining international recognition, particularly in multimedia and Internet applications, medical software, and e-commerce. Exports of computer software have grown exponentially in recent years, and 4 percent of the GNP comes from the computer services sector. In a 2002 study of comparative costs, KPMG consultants estimated that Iceland's data centers and advanced software facilities were two to three times more profitable than their American counterparts, and ranked at the top in the ten-country survey.

Icelanders are expanding tech-based businesses in a variety of sectors, from pharmaceuticals to fishing. Seven-year-old Prokaria is developing medicines from the thermophilic bacteria around the country's many hot springs. Its major shareholder: deCODE's Kári Stefánsson. U.S.–owned Columbia Ventures's high-tech aluminum smelter, located north of Reykjavík, taps Iceland's abundant hydroelectric and geothermal resources. Nickelodeon Television is relying on the country's computer-animated filmmakers and television programmers to produce its children's series "Lazytown." Icelanders go to more movies, on average, than any other people in the world, edging out Americans (second place) and Australians (third), film industry data indicate. Islandssimi, a local telecom provider, and Sweden's Ericsson have been laying miles of fiber-optic cable around Reykjavík to test a system that compresses voice, data, and video into a single line. Marel manufactures sophisticated fish-processing equipment marketed in thirty countries. Eimskip, whose ships first left Iceland for the high seas eighty-seven years ago, stands at the forefront of multimodal transportation. The list goes on.

Despite these successes, Icelandic entrepreneurs continue to voice their frustration in attracting much-needed venture capital. The country's isolation and small size make it a struggle to secure deep-pocketed investors. Software developer OZ.com had to incorporate in San Diego to attract start-up financing. Although founder Skuli Mogensen says he "will go back to Iceland eventually," he now runs the company out of Montreal, largely because of its easier access to funding and major markets. Says Daddi Gudbergsson, "Access to venture capital is basically zero. After the dot-com bust, local banks got badly burned and shut the door. It's very hard for anyone here trying to take an idea from scratch to commercialization." However, Gudbergsson has no regrets about returning home. "It was an easy decision," he told me. "It may sound cheesy, but I was 'called back.' I actually felt very much like one of the old Vikings who'd been sailing the seas but wanted to come home with the knowledge acquired in his travels."

Perhaps no one can articulate the pluses and minuses of repatriation better than Sveinn Valfells. His family spans five generations of homing pigeons. "Each one has a different story to tell," says the thirty-six-year-old entrepreneur. "Why they went to the States. Why they returned. And how they tried to use the best of both worlds."

In the 1870s, Valfells's great-great-grandfather, Jón Olafsson, was convicted of slandering the Danish king. So Olafsson, at twenty, fled Iceland for America. Several years earlier, in 1867, the United States had purchased Alaska from Russia for $7.2 million. Political leaders were keen to establish a pro-American presence in the newly acquired territory, largely to reduce Russian influence there. Thanks to his friendship with an influential senator, Olafsson was commissioned to explore Alaska and report back to Congress on how an Icelandic settlement might be created. His 1875 monograph, *Alaska lysing a laudi og lands-kostrum* (Alaska, description of the land and its conditions), is now in the U.S. Library of Congress.

After Olafsson presented his findings to President Ulysses S. Grant, Congress authorized funds to relocate Icelanders to Alaska. Olafsson, having received clemency from the Danish crown, returned home and began lobbying Icelanders to emigrate. However, the landed gentry, fearful that the country would lose its base of tenant farmers, thwarted him at every turn. As time passed, the U.S. authorization for funding lapsed.

In 1890, Olafsson again set out for North America, going first to Winnipeg, where he worked as a publisher, and later to Chicago, where he served as a manager at the Newberry Library. In 1897, he went home and established himself in the Althing. There, he helped develop the country's parliamentary rules, which are still in effect; helped codify the separation of the executive, legislative, and judicial branches of government; and championed the temperance movement. He translated John Stuart Mills's works into Icelandic, authored the first business textbook in the country, and founded Iceland's first commercial college. Olafsson died in Iceland at sixty-six. Subsequent generations, while less colorful, made their own marks on both sides of the Atlantic, from industry to academia.

Valfells grew up in Pittsburgh, where his father was studying at Carnegie Mellon University. After some years in Iceland, he returned to America in 1987. Subsequently he earned his bachelor's degree in physics at Columbia University, followed by a doctorate in physics from Boston University and a master's degree in management science and engineering from Stanford.

"I really wanted to stay in Silicon Valley," Valfells told me, "but I got an offer from this unique biotech start-up back home. It was simply too good to miss." In 1998, seeking to leverage his U.S. experience in physics and high tech, Valfells joined deCODE Genetics as its director of operations. After a year, he decided to strike out on his own, forming Islandssimi Ltd. (now part of Og Vodafone), the first full-service telecom company competing against the state-owned enterprise. Then, following a stint as an independent consultant, it was on to a job as CEO at a local software company for Internet users. "The experience I gained in the

> **Encourage Dual Loyalties**
>
> For five generations, the Valfells have tried to blend the best of both worlds: Iceland and the United States.

States on how to run and sustain a viable high-tech business was crucial in helping us survive the IT bubble," he says. But after three years
as CEO, Valfells set off "looking for fresh trouble."

For the physicist-cum-entrepreneur, the information revolution
offers almost unlimited opportunities. "Until the recent tech boom,
there were very few commercial prospects outside fishing, agriculture,
and heavy industry," he says. "Iceland was simply off the radar screen.
But that's all changed because of advanced telecommunications and
less expensive travel. The country's now much more sophisticated,
much more connected to the global economy, than it was when I left."

Valfells represents the new entrepreneurial generation that has
pepped things up. Like his adventurous forebears, he wants to leverage his overseas experience "to create more value-added businesses in
Iceland." Yet he fears that his country may not be fully exploiting its
strategic location, halfway between Silicon Valley and Europe.
"Unless we really change our culture, Iceland could be left behind
places like Ireland and Finland, which have been much more proactive
in building knowledge-oriented businesses," he warns. "The powers
that be in both business and government are often indifferent or apa-
thetic to high-tech start-ups. Launching a company here can be like
running with one leg amputated." Valfells contends that those in the
traditional business establishment have "limited horizons" when it
comes to exploring emerging industries. Government, too, "has a long
way to go. They're often out of touch with the times. There's almost a
Stalinist approach here. There's too much focus on large infrastructure
projects [hydroelectric ventures, for example] at the expense of budding industries in technology." The spoils of wealth, he believes, are
not being evenly distributed.

Reykjavík, located midway between the Old World and the New,
is where the majority of Iceland's new-generation leaders are fulfilling
their dreams. The world's northernmost capital, only five hours flying
time from New York and three from London, it is no less vibrant than
other major European cities. Home to 178,000 people (61 percent of the
country's population), it exudes the sophistication of Oslo and Helsinki.

Not so long ago, Iceland's capital was an economic and cultural backwater. As late as the 1980s, dogs and beer were banned, and potatoes were the only fresh vegetable on supermarket shelves. Not so today. Thanks to the country's recent economic upswing, Reykjavík is much more cosmopolitan. Boasting chic hotels, posh restaurants, and sizzling night spots, not to mention art museums, theaters, an opera house, a symphony orchestra, a national ballet, and music for every age and taste, it is beloved by residents and visitors alike.

Ringed by splendid mountains, the city is bordered by the open sea and Reykjavík harbor, its historic economic lifeline. Breathtaking natural wonders—geysers, waterfalls, naturally heated pools, and black lava badlands—pristine beaches, challenging golf courses, and a network of footpaths throughout the capital and along the coastline make this the perfect setting for outdoor enthusiasts.

Against this backdrop of nature, Reykjavík seems a natural showcase for classical Nordic virtues: cool beauty and elegant restraint coupled with an absence of pretension. "It's somewhat rustic and innocent," says actor and singer Egill Olafsson, of his hometown. "But at the same time, it's wild!"

Reykjavík has been called Europe's hottest capital. Slick advertising campaigns champion the city's famed nightlife, featuring energetic clubs like Pravda, Sirkus, and Grand Rokk. In October, Iceland Airwaves, reputed to be the best rock festival in Europe, comes to town, drawing hundreds of visitors and music enthusiasts from abroad. For pub crawlers, there is Gaukur á Stöng, birthplace of Iceland's famous vodka-spiked beer; the huge Tungliō, frequented by the young, fashionable, and skimpily clad; and

> **Adapt—or Die**
>
> Once an uninteresting backwater where dogs and beer were banned, Reykjavík has become one of Europe's most cosmopolitan cities.

many others. Likewise, discerning diners have unlimited options: from Italian and Mexican to Thai and Icelandic specialties, featuring ocean-fresh seafood, highland lamb, and unusual varieties of game. One can dine, for instance, on traditional fare—fresh lobster or smoked puffin with orange vinaigrette—at Laekjarbrekka or sample a fusion of French, Asian, and Cuban cuisine at Sjávarkjallarinn—both in the heart of the city.

With limited sprawl, traffic congestion, and pollution, Reykjavík is one of the world's most livable cities. To live there is to enjoy a healthy life. Those seeking relief from the grind of work can relax in of one of seven thermal pools and baths or in the man-made Blue Lagoon, a forty-minute drive from the city center. Famous for its healing powers, the lagoon encompasses an enormous pool of hot, mineral-rich water, the salty effluent from the geothermal plant that generates Reykjavík's electricity. Every year, it is visited by thousands of people from around the world.

Downtown Reykjavík, better known by its postal code 101, is home to a wide range of coffeehouses, kiosks, boutiques, and bookstores. Nestled among them are quaint, corrugated-iron houses with brightly colored roofs, winding back alleys, and hidden private gardens. Also close to the center is Hallsgrimskirkjá Church, the city's tallest building and one of its most enduring landmarks, as well as the green-stoned Althing, open year-round to the public. A few minutes' walk away is a picturesque toy lake, the Tjörnin, which is partially heated in the winter months for the comfort of the geese and swans. And one of the world's cleanest salmon rivers, the Ellidaar, flows through the city center.

"Reykjavík offers big-city sophistication with small-town virtues," says fifty-year-old Edda Sverrisdóttir, who returned home after ten years in San Francisco and Copenhagen. "Everything you'd want is right here, from diverse restaurants to a pristine living environment." How about the weather? "I love it. It's never bad," she answers. "You simply have to dress for it." For most, however, Nordic winters are something to be endured, not enjoyed. Icelanders suffer through months of pitch-blackness, accompanied by endless wind and fog. From November to March, the city "resembles a small town in Siberia," writes novelist Hallgrímur Helgason. But with the summer comes all-night sunshine—party time, as people plunge into nonstop celebration.

"It's all one world, there are no islands anymore," anthropologist Margaret Mead once observed. Once remote and isolated by virtue of its location and daunting geography, Iceland has shed its insularity and catapulted into the economic mainstream. Icelanders today are more assured of wealth, political stability, generous welfare, low crime, and a good life than are citizens of most other countries. It's small wonder that, according to various polls, more Icelanders declare themselves happy than any other people in the world. The island ranks as one of the best countries in which to live. Next to the Finns and New Zealanders, Icelanders are rated the least corrupt; they have one of the best growth prospects in the world; their longevity, along with Japan's, is the highest; and the list goes on. As one returnee puts it: "We live in idyllic circumstances in terms of security, living standards, and domestic politics. In a way, it's unbelievable."

4

india **rising**

Lo, soul, seest thou not God's purpose from
the first? The earth be spann'd, connected
by network . . .

—WALT WHITMAN
"Passage to India," 1871

"It looks like India is the place for global IT," says Sean Narayanan, an
Indian-born U.S. citizen. "I had to get experience here." So in 2002, he
quit his job with Booz Allen in northern Virginia and, with his Indian
wife, Yamini, an economist working for a U.S. computer company,
went to work in Bangalore.

For decades, India watched thousands of its top students and scientific and technical talent emigrate to the United States. Today, there
are some 2 million Indian Americans in the United States, and they
have the second-highest income of any ethnic group. India is second
only to Mexico in terms of legal migration to the United States. More
students (roughly 70,000) have come here from India than from any
other country. Many of these newcomers ended up in Silicon Valley,
Boston, Seattle, and Austin, where they started their own businesses

and served as an important catalyst in America's high-tech ascent. But with the downturn in the U.S. technology industry, along with a booming economy back home, India's brain drain days may soon be over.

In a dramatic reversal, the United States is becoming India's gateway to advanced technology. For more than a decade now, Indians and nonresident Indians (NRIs) have been going home to bootstrap the economy and reestablish cultural roots. According to India's software trade body, the National Association of Software and Service Companies (NASSCOM), about 5,000 technology-savvy NRIs with more than five years of work experience have repatriated from the United States in the past two years.

> **Dust Off the Welcome Mat**
>
> "There is a clear trend of a reverse brain drain beginning to manifest itself," writes the *Business Standard*. "It could be hugely positive."

These include people holding U.S. work visas and green cards, and even U.S. citizens.

"Professionals are writing us directly," says Vishal Bali, vice president of operations for Wockhart Hospitals Limited, a subsidiary of India's third-largest drug company. Yet he discourages NRIs from making a hasty relocation decision based on a brief visit or home leave, when nostalgia often masks reality. The proper stay, he believes, should be a year or two. "But the homeward-bound trend is very real now," he contends. "In the last four years, we've attracted fourteen highly trained physicians specializing in cardiology and neurology." No doubt, Wockhart's three-year-old partnership with Harvard Medical International—the only one in India—carries special appeal. "There used to be a tremendous disparity in medical science between India and the United States," says Bali. "But today, we're only months—not years—behind the standards practiced at [Boston's] Massachusetts General and Beth Israel hospitals."

"There is a clear trend of a reverse brain drain beginning to manifest itself," reports India's *Business Standard*. "While still early, this could be hugely positive were it to continue gaining momentum."

Most recent émigrés such as the Narayanans and the Wockhart doctors are experienced professionals in their thirties and forties. For the most part, they are being lured back by the same thing that attracted foreign investors after the country began to liberalize in the 1980s—a huge potential market in one of the world's fastest-growing economies combined with improved living standards. Many returnees are launching their own companies, bringing with them the management and scientific expertise and global perspective needed to stimulate India's economic development. Others are seeking their fortunes in a host of foreign and domestic companies. Still others are advising businesses, universities, and government ministries on how to adapt to the global scene. With few exceptions, these returnees have highly marketable skills—the entrepreneurial, market-driven savvy acquired in America that translates to economic success.

Even those on the sidelines sense that something special is happening on the subcontinent. "There is a buzz that permeates daily life now," says NRI Sumant Anand, thirty-seven, after a recent visit to New Delhi. "There's a sense that we are on the verge of something big. If you talk to people my age, nobody wants to leave India." Anand is content to make his home in the United States—at least for the time being. "When I left India thirteen years ago, all anybody could talk about was 'I want to go to the States,'" he adds. "Now, nobody talks about that. If India was then what it is now, I probably wouldn't have left."

> **Target the Best Minds**
>
> "I'm living my dream," says talented software engineer Despa Paranjpe.

For an increasing number of India's well-educated, well-skilled workers, the adventure is at home. They sense that high-tech centers such as Bangalore, Hyderabad, Chennai (formerly Madras), and New Delhi offer the same promise Silicon Valley offered ten years ago. For software engineer Despa Paranjpe, twenty-five, a graduate of the Indian Institute of Technology in Mumbai (formerly Bombay), the globalization of technology offers power and riches right in her own backyard. Unlike members of previous generations, she is happy to make her career in India. "I'm living my dream," she says.

• • •

"At the stroke of the midnight hour, when the world sleeps, India will awake to life and freedom." With these words on August 14, 1947, Jawaharlal Nehru, the first prime minister of independent India, announced the arrival of a new nation, born after more than a century of British rule. Injecting a note of caution, Nehru continued, "The achievement we celebrate today is but a step, an opening of opportunity, to greater triumphs and achievements that await us. Are we brave enough and wise enough to grasp this opportunity and accept the challenge of the future?"

At the time, the challenges seemed almost insurmountable. Six decades later, a new optimism and pluck are blossoming with India's emergence as a land of opportunity. Some 1.1 billion people—one-sixth of the world's population—live in a country one-third the size of the United States, speak more than a thousand languages and dialects, and are poised to reap the benefits of the fifth-largest economy in the world. The Indian middle class, miniscule at the time of independence in 1947, is now nearly as large as the total population of the United States—roughly 260 million people, who are determined to seize their share of the good life for themselves and their children. Most do not yet have the comforts enjoyed by their counterparts in the West, but their growing number represents a revolutionary change in Indian society.

India has finally arrived on the global scene. Its economy is expanding at almost 7 percent annually, making it one of the fastest growing in the world. The bounce is being felt across nearly all business sectors. For the first time in the past several decades, agriculture, manufacturing, and services—the Indian trifecta—are showing signs of simultaneous revival. At $120 billion, foreign currency reserves are also peaking, and India's foreign debt received its first investment-grade rating in early 2004. A gradual upturn in the world economy is expected to bring even greater bounty. Despite political and labor opposition, India's government is also loosening its stronghold on various industries, through the privatization of state-owned companies.

A major sell-off of the country's industrial holdings, most notably the giant Oil and Natural Gas Corp., is fueling foreign interest. Insular India is giving rise to open India. Over the past fourteen years, New Delhi has slowly liberalized the economy, easing regulations and opening doors to overseas inves-

> **Adapt—or Die**
>
> Slowly, India has evolved from British-based Fabian socialism and central planning to a more open, free-market economy.

tors. The government has also lowered import tariffs and granted generous tax breaks to offshore businesses. Political leaders have made important progress in overhauling a once notoriously slow, bloated, and dysfunctional bureaucracy. "Government efficiency and infrastructure in the last four years have gone from a level 4 to a level 6 on a scale of 1 to 10," says Mumbai-based Partha Iyengar, vice president for research at Gartner, the technology consultants.

These sometimes slow, yet bold reforms have bolstered the expectations of foreign investors, who like what they see: a secular state; a free press; a decent, if imperfect, legal system; and one of the largest consumer classes in the world. "Business has become much easier in all sectors," concludes Monsanto spokeswoman Ranjana Smetacek. India leapt up the ranks of the world's most attractive destinations—from fifteenth place to third place—two years ago, according to management consultants A. T. Kearney. "Right now, it's a good period to go to India," says Michel Leonard, chief economist of Aon Trade Credit, which maps political and economic risk for multinational companies.

India is squarely placing its bets on gaining greater access to the world economy. "India has finally shed its traditional defensiveness: that the British ruined us, that the U.S. was out to get us, that multinationals were just exploiting us," according to Columbia University economist Arvind Panagariya, in a *USA Today* interview. "The idea now is that openness is good, that foreign companies can do good things for us. The ones on the defensive now are the antiglobalization people."

An open India did not come easily. Prime Minister Nehru admired British-bred Fabian socialism and central planning. *Swadeshi* (self-sufficiency) was the official order of the day. India was determined to go it alone. This led to a highly regulated economy with sharp controls over private investment by Indian companies, many license requirements for even the smallest economic steps, high tariffs and other import barriers, and little interest in exports. Foreign investment was negligible, while government-owned enterprises proliferated. As a result, Indian per-capita income grew at only a little over 1 percent per year until the mid-1980s—"a wounded civilization," in the words of novelist V. S. Naipaul.

In 1991, a balance-of-payments and national solvency crisis, caused by skyrocketing world oil prices, prompted a far-reaching change of heart. As important, India also became concerned about the economic progress of its powerful neighbor and rival, China, which had begun reforming in 1979. New Delhi, still controlled by Nehru's Congress Party, shifted direction thanks to its then-finance minister and current prime minister, Manmohan Singh, the Oxford-trained economist who dismantled the old system—moving away from socialism and toward more open, free-market policies. The result was a dramatic acceleration of GNP growth to about 6 percent a year since 1991, among the fastest of any nation. Subsequent governments, under the Bharatiya Janata Party (BJP) and, more recently, the Congress Party, have been extending these reforms.

Nonetheless, India is still a developing and largely poor country. Despite its resurgence—and 61,000 millionaires—some 223 million Indians live in hunger, consuming less than 1,960 calories per day, says the U.N. Development Program. India suffers widespread and inescapable poverty: high unemployment, 40 percent illiteracy, an

AIDS crisis, and a crumbling infrastructure of clogged roads, over-crowded housing, poisonous water, and frequent power outages. The country's recent gains have been confined primarily to a handful of high-growth urban centers: New Delhi, Mumbai, and the southern stars—Bangalore, Madras, and Chennai. Many important sectors, par-ticularly small-scale farming and manufacturing, and populous rural areas, most notably Orissa, Bihar, and the northeastern states, have experienced no improvement in their well-being. Agriculture, on which almost 70 percent of the population depends for a living, requires bountiful monsoons that are unpredictable at best. These imbalances, in large part, contributed to the shocking upset of the rul-ing BJP coalition in the 2004 parliamentary elections.

Politics in India is considerably risky. Just six months after inde-pendence, a Hindu extremist, angry about Mahatma Gandhi's support of Muslims, shot and killed him. Nehru's daughter, Indira Gandhi, served as prime minister for sixteen years; in 1984, she, too, was assas-sinated. Her son, former prime minister Rajiv Gandhi, was killed by a terrorist in 1991. The record of violence persists today and may help explain why Italian-born Congress Party leader Sonia Gandhi, Rajiv's widow, declined the top post in May 2004. Also, India's volatile rela-tionship with neighboring Pakistan, though improved in recent months, led the two nations to the brink of nuclear war just a few years ago.

Yet, for much of the middle class, India is rising. Its prospects are improving fast. The challenge, then, is for the country to bring all its people—in their full ethnic, religious, and political diversity—to the table of economic success. Here, India is pinning its hopes on human capital.   .

More than half of India's 555 million people are under age twenty-five. That sort of demographic bulge typically produces explosive growth. It's the reason India is expected to become one of the world's three largest economies—surpassing China—within thirty years. India is also the only country in which the population will continue to grow for the next fifty years, and the proportion of working-age residents will increase well into the 2020s. These demographics, along with India's English-speaking tradition and strong education system, suggest that the country's exuberance is well grounded.

Credit the British with introducing the building blocks—language and education—of India's economic resurgence. Policy decisions made by British administrators from 1831 until Indian independence in 1947 endure today. The national language became—and remained—English. The British also built on India's rich tradition of scientific learning, including more than a millennium of achievements in mathematics, and supported the development of a first-rate system of higher education.

In the 1950s, the postindependence government sought to strengthen the country's reservoir of engineering and scientific talent. Prime Minister Nehru made technical education a priority, starting an elite cadre of universities: the renowned Indian Institutes of Technology, which are more difficult to get into than MIT, Yale, or Harvard. Hundreds of lesser-known engineering schools also emerged to teach young people whose culture views mathematical and scientific expertise as a prerequisite to economic advancement.

> **Nourish the Halls of Ivy**
>
> Under Prime Minister Nehru, India launched an elite cadre of universities that together form the renowned Indian Institutes of Technology.

Playtime ends early in twenty-first-century India. Parents send their children to rigorous cram schools so they will qualify for even ordinary preschools. The growing pressure to make it educationally and then obtain high-paying technical or scientific jobs has created fierce competition from a child's first step into the classroom. In elementary school, children master algebra; on completion of middle school, many have acquired a far better grounding in math and science than the average high-schooler in the United States.

As a result, India has a seemingly endless stream of high-caliber, English-speaking techies. The country produces 2.1 million college graduates a year, a number expected to double by 2010. The number of engineering colleges—now cranking out about 300,000 graduates a year—is slated to grow 50 percent, to nearly 1,600 in three years. In addition, there are India's six Institutes of Management; three of them—Bangalore, Calcutta, and Ahmedabad—are considered among the top business schools outside the United States. Then add the three-year-old Indian School of Business in Hyderabad, with ties to the Wharton School and North-western University's Kellogg Graduate School of Management and a first-class faculty lured primarily from the United States.

Reform Public Education

Another Nehru-inspired initiative transformed the school system, with special emphasis on math, science, and English.

Taking advantage of the tradition of using English in business and the excellent education system, companies began tapping the country's talent base in the 1970s. Local software firms such as Tata Consultancy Services, Infosys Technologies, and Wipro sent programming teams to the United States to work on projects for American companies. Over time, they convinced their clients that they could accomplish the same tasks back home using Indian talent at one-fourth the cost. Because India is on the other side of the world, Indian subcontractors could also work in the evening and exploit the twenty-four-hour workday. Foreign multinationals soon began setting up facilities in India to take advantage of high-skilled, low-wage engineers and programmers, whose tasks initially were confined to business processing, call-center operations, and minor software repair. Later, Indian knowledge workers mastered a range of more sophisticated services, from designing chips to research and development.

India's recent push to the frontiers of cyberspace stands at the heart of the current outsourcing debate. Last year, the country exported $17.3 billion in technology and back-office services, mostly to the United States. The volume is said to be growing almost 30 percent a year. NASSCOM, the trade body of India's software and services companies, forecasts that by 2008 industry exports will exceed $50 billion and IT will employ 2 million people, up from the current estimated 770,000, and will create another 2 million jobs indirectly. Many of these techies will be working for U.S. firms—Intel, 3,000; Oracle, 6,000; Hewlett-Packard, 10,000; Accenture, 10,000; and IBM, 15,000. In the past four years, an estimated 300,000 high-tech and engineering jobs have moved to India, as multinationals continue to bulk up their operations. At the same time, the U.S. Bureau of Labor Statistics reports that 234,000 American IT professionals are unemployed. And that's the rub.

Shifting U.S. jobs overseas remains an emotional hot button. In 2004, Democratic presidential candidate John Kerry chastised "Benedict Arnold CEOs," who favored foreign over American employees. Then-secretary of state Colin Powell, dispatched by President Bush to New Delhi, countered by saying that outsourcing was "a reality of the twenty-first century" but that India should do more to offset the loss of U.S. jobs by opening its market to American goods.

But don't dismiss the gains in productivity and competitiveness to U.S. business and the jobs that are created as a result of outsourcing. The rule of thumb is that each Indian employee represents an annual savings to American employers of $20,000 to $30,000. The cost of transmitting work offshore is expected to plummet by as much as 60 percent in 2005 thanks to new undersea cables. While such savings are a big draw, quality of work is a close second—and gaining in importance. The skills of India's computer scientists, for example, are unsurpassed. The Capability Maturity Model, or CMM, developed by the Software Engineering Institute at Carnegie Mellon University, has been used to evaluate the software development processes of hundreds of companies. Software teams receive a rating of 1 to 5, with 5 being the highest. A decade ago, only Motorola's unit in Bangalore achieved a 5 rating. Today, 387 Indian companies are so accredited. Therefore, multinational enterprises are getting more complex work done on the subcontinent—not just in IT but in fields ranging from financial services to biotechnology.

Clearly, corporate America can no longer be lulled into thinking it is immune to Indian competition. "The globalization of white-collar services has become mainstream," says Nandan Nilekani, CEO of Infosys, India's IBM. The country's unforeseen leap into the top ranks of global technology refuted conventional development theory, which predicted that India and other poor countries would follow the same long, slow path Western industrial nations had followed—from agriculture to manufacturing to high technology. India's devel-

> **Know Thy Competition**
>
> "Every company aspiring to be global has to have an Indian strategy," says Infosys CEO Nilekani.

opment shortcut made it the first Third World nation to use its brainpower, not natural resources or low-wage labor, to propel its entry into the economic big leagues. "Every company aspiring to be global has to have an Indian strategy," says Nilekani.

This does not mean the United States will repeat the fall of the Roman Empire. "Offshoring is not a zero-sum game," says Diana Farrell, director of the think tank McKinsey Global Institute. "It creates value for individual American companies and frees U.S. resources for activities with more value added." Infosys's Nilekani agrees: By working together, both India and the United States win. "You have this whole ecosystem [that constitutes] a crucible for innovation," he told the *New York Times*. "The whole process where people get an idea and put together a team, raise capital, create a product, and mainstream it—that can only be done in the U.S. It can't be done sitting in India. The Indian part of the equation [is to help] these innovative [U.S.] companies bring their products to market quicker, cheaper, and better, which increases the innovative cycle there. It is a complementarity we need to enhance."

While Americans fret over Third World competition, half a world away in Bangalore engineers are hard at work writing software for the latest telephones, designing next-generation microprocessors, and developing wireless broadband technology that they hope will transform homes around the world. By some estimates, there are more IT engineers in Bangalore (150,000), India's self-proclaimed Silicon Valley, than in its California counterpart (130,000). In this southern city once known as "pensioners' paradise" for its mild weather and slow pace, you'll find the landscape blazoned with famous corporate logos: GE, Intel, Cisco, IBM, Philips, AOL. More than half the U.S. Fortune 500, as well as leading European, Japanese, Chinese, even Pakistani companies, have a significant presence here—all using Indian brainpower.

Today Bangalore, India's fifth-largest city with 6.5 million people, is the center of the country's booming IT industry, which has mushroomed from about $20 million in sales in 1988 to $22 billion in 2005, according to NASSCOM. But India's technology pool extends far beyond software and chip development. At General Electric's John F. Welch Technology Center on the city's outskirts, 1,800 engineers— about 450 of them with doctorates—are designing turbine-engine blades and scrutinizing the molecular structure of polymers. They are part of a worldwide research and development team digitally connected to other GE centers in Munich, Shanghai, and Schenectady, New York.

A conspicuous class of high-tech entrepreneurs has also emerged in Bangalore, running firms such as Infosys, Wipro, and MSource, which have made them instant multimillionaires. Secluded in serene, orderly, state-of-the-art campuses as modern and efficient as anything in America's Silicon Valley, these highly skilled professionals are taking the lead in colonizing cyberspace.

The growth of more sophisticated R&D opportunities is encouraging the repatriation of native sons and daughters who have been working in North America and Western Europe. "Bangalore is thriving the way Silicon Valley was in 1999," says Laxmikant Mandal, a refugee from Nortel Networks, Cisco, and Cypress Semiconductor. Although currently completing his MBA studies in Canada, the twenty-eight-year-old engineer plans to return to Bangalore after graduation to start his own company. "First-rate talent is moving back and helping bridge cultures, bootstrap new work, and build skill sets in organizations," according to Vijay Anard, managing director of Sun Microsystems's India Engineering Center in Bangalore, in an interview with the *New York Times*.

That this southern Indian jewel, once a favorite retirement venue for senior colonial officers, would trigger India's leap into the top ranks of global technology is no accident. Prime Minister Nehru forged a unique vision for the city. Calling Bangalore India's "City of the Future," he sought to turn it into the nation's intellectual capital, a place where scientists could shape the ideas and programs that would guide the country's ambitions for economic and military self-reliance.

Nehru and subsequent governments, eager to mute British influence, poured money into the city, transforming it from a popular destination for retirees and pleasure seekers into a serious scientific and technological hub. Over fifty years, they built a comprehensive infrastructure including the nation's most sensitive military and space research facilities. Today, the city has three universities, hundreds of engineering and polytechnic schools, and a plethora of research institutes devoted to science, technology, the environment, and more. Public-sector giants—including Hindustan Aeronautics, Bharat Electronics, Indian Telephone Industries, Hindustan Machine Tools, and the Indian Space Research Organization—are all located in Bangalore.

Vivek Kulkarni, a career bureaucrat turned high-technology entrepreneur, credits the city's cosmopolitan traditions and openness to private education as important factors in its economic evolution. Compared with other Indian regions, the state of Karnataka, where Bangalore is located, has seen minimal religious and ethnic violence. As the area has prospered, Indians from many different states speaking widely diverse languages—from

Dust Off the Welcome Mat

"Other states have been highly discriminating," says Vivek Kulkarni. "But in Karnataka, we've attracted not only Indians but also foreigners."

Bengali to Punjabi to Tamil to Hindi—have come to the city and been accepted. Marriage between members of different castes and religions is less of a taboo. "This is highly unusual," Kulkarni told me. "Other states have typically been highly discriminatory. But [here] we've traditionally been liberal and nonsectarian. That's made it a lot easier to attract not only Indians but also foreigners."

As important in fulfilling Nehru's desire for modernization was the state government's decision to license private engineering colleges in the 1970s. "Before that, the socialists wanted to restrict education to the public sector," says Kulkarni, a Wharton School grad who headed Karnataka's IT efforts and is credited with much of its success. "There were many obstacles, strikes and the like. It was an extremely difficult period. But, today, our 127 private schools are churning out about 38,000 engineers a year, roughly half the number produced in the entire United States."

These forces have contributed greatly to Bangalore's metamorphosis. The economy is growing 10 percent annually. By 2010, Kulkarni predicts Bangalore will pass Mumbai as India's wealthiest city. "The euphoric mood in the economy is backed by solid signs," he says. Convinced of the country's bright future, Kulkarni, forty-six, left government service in late 2003 to found B2K, a Bangalore-based technology-support company providing analytical services to American clients such as Citigroup and Capital One. He hopes to increase from 200 employees today to 1,000 in the next two years.

There's a definite Indian-first hiring strategy at B2K. "My country is spending roughly $1.2 billion every year sending over Indian students to the States for an education," says Kulkarni. "If we can keep them home or at least bring them back, that's a tremendous savings. And we're now finding it much easier to recruit NRIs in the U.S., especially after 9/11. They want to come home. The country's experiencing a wave, and they want to be part of it."

However, many Indian professionals want to have a foot in both India and the United States. That was the conclusion of Sudhakar Kosaraju and Nags Nagarajan, cofounders of 24/7 Customer, based in

Los Gatos, California. The five-year-old start-up provides call-center operations and data analytics for corporations needing technical support and telemarketing. The company has almost 4,000 employees in three centers—Bangalore, Chennai, and Hyderabad.

"It's simply much easier to build a major multinational company in America," says COO Nagarajan. "There's a cachet, a legitimacy, a credibility that goes with being defined as an American company. Besides, we never would have secured the level of venture capital and board guidance in India." He is referring to 24/7's investor, Sequoia Capital Partners, and his fellow director, Michael Moritz, whose previous winners include Google, Yahoo, Flextronics, and PayPal Software.

> **Encourage Dual Loyalties**
>
> "It's simply much easier to build a major multinational company in America," says 24/7 Customer's Nagarajan. "There's a cachet, a legitimacy, a credibility that goes with being American."

Since the great majority of the firm's employees are Indian, the cofounders have a special interest in returnees. "Recruiting them has gotten much easier, especially after the jobs dried up in the States and work visas became harder to come by," says Nagarajan, who did stints at Princeton and Austin. By one estimate, there are 35,000 returned nonresident Indians in Bangalore. Nagarajan especially covets their "global skills and competitiveness" gained from working abroad. "You often don't get that here," he contends. As for government's role in the process, "They have nothing to do with it. In fact, Delhi seems much more interested in continuing to receive [financial] remittances from NRIs living abroad."

Infosys Technologies sits in the center of Bangalore's high-tech Electronics City Industrial Park. Its thirty-five-building, fifty-five-acre campus—billed as the world's second-largest software campus after Microsoft—is full of enthusiastic young engineers who write code, build software, and maintain computer systems for a host of multinational corporations including Cisco, Aetna, Boeing, Airbus, and JC Penney.

Founded in 1981, Infosys saw revenues hit $1.57 billion in 2004, a 50 percent gain over the previous year. Almost three-fourths of its sales come from the North American market. The company earned $419 million in that same year. That's 30 percent more than the second most profitable offshoring player, Wipro. For these reasons, NAS-DAQ-listed Infosys has the highest market value among its rivals: $11.26 billion at the time of this writing. To keep pace with its explosive growth of nearly 30 percent a year, the company has recruited and hired extensively. In 2004, it received 1 million résumés for 9,000 openings, with many inquiries coming from NRIs.

One of the firm's brightest twenty-somethings, Bhavna Mehra, gave me a golf-cart tour of the lush green campus and its crown jewel: the ultramodern, wood-paneled, corporate conference center. A wall-size, multiscreen TV allows Infosys to conduct simultaneous meetings with its overseas offices and multinational clients. "We can have our whole global supply chain on the screen at the same time," boasts Mehra. The company's virtual command post serves as a useful reminder to visitors of India's prowess in globalizing technology.

Two years ago, Microsoft's chairman, Bill Gates, received a standing ovation in this room. The world's wealthiest man got a firsthand look at the new generation of Indians who have vaulted into the new India. Addressing 1,000 Infosys employees, he told the audience that India was "the world's next IT superpower. . . . There is a very interesting energy here around taking technology and making it relevant to all citizens, much more than I've seen anywhere in the world."

Enhancing productivity and competitiveness is a top priority at Infosys. "The only way to raise the standard of living is to improve productivity," says CEO Nilekani, who has set his sights on the business consulting arena dominated by Accenture, EDS, IBM, and others. The preferred way to do this rapidly is through acquisition; Infosys has taken a first step by purchasing Expert Information Systems, the Australian IT service provider, and hiring 330 locals. Nilekani also frets about foreign competition, especially from the Philippines and China. To counter these threats, Infosys has established more than twenty-five overseas offices, including a software development center with two hundred employees in Shanghai.

Infosys also has been expanding in the United States, driven by a desire to be closer to top clients and to stem political pressure over the outsourcing of American jobs. In April 2004, the company set up a fully owned subsidiary, Infosys Consulting, in Texas with an initial investment of $20 million. Headed by Stephen Pratt, a twelve-year veteran of Deloitte Consulting, the new venture plans to hire five hundred people within three years. "We are creating jobs in the U.S. and that should help us counter some of the anti-outsourcing sentiment," says Kris Gopalakrishnan, chief operating officer of Infosys.

Going multinational requires staff with global expertise. Hence, the company has been heavily recruiting Indian émigrés. "Until quite recently, we were only getting onesies and twosies returning home," says Infosys cofounder and head of worldwide customer delivery, S. D. Shibulal. "More recently, it's been much, much easier to woo them back." Ironically, though, he cautions returnees not to get too comfortable back home. "In the new India, people—especially high-potential people—can't stay home. Just the opposite. They'll be expected to travel and live abroad extensively. So they'll have to be much more adventurous."

In a parallel move, Infosys has also been attracting non-Indians to India. One such recruit is American Josh Bornstein, formerly an investment banker in Los Angeles, who moved to Bangalore in late 2003 to co-manage business planning for Infosys. "I would highly recommend such a move for new college graduates and people with one to three years' experience," he says.

If information technology is India today, biotechnology may be India tomorrow. Many believe that BT is even hotter than IT. They hope the country's two hundred embryonic biotech companies will grow into full-blown pharmas as their technologies develop, creating jobs for the nearly 500,000 Indian students graduating each year in the biological sciences. Given this vast pool of skilled resources, the country appears poised to create a globally competitive stronghold.

"India can be at the forefront of biotechnology," says Labji Singh, director of the prestigious Center for Cellular and Molecular Biology in Hyderabad. "We have the potential. But we need to work on that potential. We need to go on 'mission mode'—the way we took our space and nuclear defense programs on mission mode." By some estimates, biotechnology has the potential to generate $5 billion in revenues and 1 million skilled jobs over the next five years. This would propel India into the biotech big leagues.

> **Celebrate Science and Technology**
>
> "India can be at the forefront of biotechnology," predicts Labji Singh, one of the country's most noted scientists.

In many respects, the revolution has already begun. Leading the charge in this high-stakes field is Kiran Mazumdar-Shaw. The fifty-two-year-old scientist turned entrepreneur has been heralded as "India's biotech guru" (*Economist*), "the mother of invention" (*New York Times*), and "the face of modern India" (*Business India*). Last year, *BioSpectrum* honored her as "Person of the Year" for her entrepreneurial spirit and leadership in driving the nation to seek its rightful place in the global biotechnology arena.

Mazumdar-Shaw's success story is almost without equal in India. In the 1970s, she started a small enzyme company—and India's biotech industry—out of her garage in suburban Bangalore. Over the next twenty-six years, she transformed it into the country's largest and most powerful biotech enterprise. Today, she is a chairwoman and managing director of the company, Biocon India Ltd., which employs nearly nine hundred people in many diverse areas—from worldwide patents to cutting-edge R&D, from enzymes to biopharmaceuticals, from custom research to clinical trials.

"The difference lies in our DNA," shout Biocon's advertisements. That difference describes both the company and its founder. Growing up in the 1950s, Mazumdar-Shaw wanted to be a brewmaster like her father, "Mazzy," and he encouraged her. "My father had great respect for professional women," she says. "He was way ahead of his time. He had no gender bias, no religious bias. But most of all, he had great reverence for technology—he was an unconventional brewer receptive to new ideas and technologies and always eager to experiment with them. On reflection, I guess I owe my own unorthodox ways to my father's genes."

After obtaining a B.S. degree in zoology from Bangalore University, Mazumdar-Shaw left India in 1970 to train in Australia. At Ballarat College, she specialized in malting and brewing technology. Returning home in 1975, she found making headway in the male-only brewing industry extremely difficult. "Those were very trying times," she recalls. "I realized it wasn't going to be easy for a woman." Although she was a practicing brewer for the next three years, "the men who led the industry couldn't believe that a woman could ever handle the difficult tasks of union negotiations, dealing with government, and handling equipment breakdowns. Still, I was very committed to making a career in brewing."

Out of the blue, she received an offer to work in the industry in the United Kingdom. "It was a great opportunity. Things were basically closed here," she says. "So I was prepared to go anywhere to work in brewing."

But before she was even out the door, a chance encounter with Leslie Auchinclaus of Biocon Biochemicals in Ireland led her in a different direction. "[Auchinclaus] knew of my background in brewing and fermentation, and wanted to start a joint venture to manufacture enzymes, a rich source of raw materials, here in India," Mazumdar-Shaw recalls. "I knew there were a lot of parallels, a lot of similarities, between brewing and enzyme production. So, I figured, why not take a chance? If I failed, I could always accept the U.K. job."

> **Act Now**
>
> "I knew there were a lot of parallels between brewing and enzyme production," says Biocon's Mazumdar-Shaw. "So I figured, why not take a chance?"

Relying on "foolish courage," Mazumdar-Shaw plunged into the uncharted waters of biotech in 1978. In a small shed in Kormangala, on the outskirts of Bangalore, she launched Biocon India Ltd. with $10,000 and a plan to extract two enzymes—papain and isinglass—from papaya and catfish. In the 1980s, Biocon India began manufacturing industrial enzymes through solid-state fermentation, a difficult process dominated by Japanese technology. By 1991, the company had leapfrogged Japan with its novel reactor, the Plafractor, patented in several countries including the United States. The invention was a resounding success and played a key role in the company's production of immunosuppressants—critical drugs for organ transplant recipients.

Three years later, Biocon India took on additional challenges. Leveraging the R&D skills acquired in the customized enzymes business, the company set up a subsidiary, Syngene, to provide targeted research for multinational pharmaceuticals and biotech clients. Today, Syngene performs complex analogy and molecular biology research, enabling Biocon India to transfer its fermentation expertise from enzymes to drug molecules. It produces fermentation-derived small molecules (statins and immunosuppressants) and recombinant proteins such as human insulin. With 225 biologists and chemists, Syngene has been a major player in the company's ascent.

To exploit these exciting initiatives, Biocon India first had to break from its parent company, Biocon Biochemicals, which by this time had been acquired by Unilever. In 1998, John Shaw (whom Mazumdar married that year) orchestrated a buyout of Unilever's 25 percent stake in the Indian operation for $2 million. Mazumdar-Shaw retained the naming rights and, more important, the ability to expand beyond the company's historical focus on enzymes. "Until then, we were really struggling to grow the business," she recalls.

In 2000, Biocon expanded again, launching Clinigene, a clinical trial company for testing new drugs. Performing longitudinal lab tests in India is not only economical but fast. India's vast, genetically diverse population provides enormous clinical research opportunities. Every possible health problem, from tropical diseases to lifestyle-related ailments, is present. In addition, among the many English-speaking physicians and nurses are some who are well-grounded in international clinical trial practice. Hence, Western drug companies are increasingly drawn to conducting research in India.

Clinigene is poised to corner a sizeable chunk of the global clinical trial market. It was the first Indian company to receive accreditation from the College of American Pathologists, the industry's "gold standard," enabling it to service large global pharmas such as Astra-Zeneca, Pfizer, and others. These facilities have also allowed Biocon to conduct a clinical development program for recombinant human insulin and other new products.

Since its independence, Biocon has seen sales grow by 56 percent annually and after-tax profits by 102 percent. The company's net profit margin of 25 percent far exceeds that of its competitors. Anji Reddy, chairman of the highly regarded Indian pharma Dr. Reddy's Laboratories, acknowledges, "Biocon has [transformed] itself from an enzymes company into a serious biopharmaceutical company with strong roots in the manufacturing of active pharmaceutical ingredients that are not the run-of-the-mill type but those requiring strong research capabilities."

Mazumdar-Shaw's ambition has always been to build an integrated biopharmaceutical company of world-class competence. Unlike the many Indian pharmas that focus primarily on the domestic market, Biocon has set its sights overseas. Today, approximately 60 percent of its sales come from abroad—a testament to its global prowess. Bill Harris of the Science Foundation of Ireland (see chapter 2), of which Mazumdar-Shaw is a founding member, says, "I have no doubt that Biocon is a serious biopharmaceutical company. It has first-rate facilities comparable to what I have seen in the best global players."

A visit to Biocon's campus on Honsur Road, just a half-mile from the Infosys headquarters in Electronics City, reveals a business in serious need of room to expand. A dozen or so buildings are crammed into a thirty-acre compound that is bursting at the seams. In 2005, the company will move to a ninety-acre site three miles away. Biocon Park will house world-class fermentation facilities (three times the current capacity), a biological plant for mammalian cell culture, and state-of-the-art research labs.

To fund this expansion, as well as potential acquisitions, Mazumdar-Shaw took Biocon public in early 2004. The much-anticipated IPO, touted by investment bankers as the Infosys of biotech, was oversubscribed by thirty-three times, making Mazumdar-Shaw—with a 40 percent stake in the company worth roughly $450 million—India's richest woman.

A critical ingredient in Biocon's evolution to an industry power-house is the treasure trove of intellectual capital in the area. The state of Karnataka aims to make Bangalore "The Biotech City." In 2001, it initiated its Millennium Biotech Policy, shaped in consultation with industry leaders such as Mazumdar-Shaw, to ensure the availability of frontier researchers. To complement the renowned Indian Institute of Science (founded in 1909), local politicians recently created the Institute of Bioinformatics and Applied Biotechnology and the Agribiotechnology Institute. These new institutes will join Bangalore's Nehru Centre for Advanced Scientific Research and National Center for Biological Sciences, as well as a bevy of private institutions providing postgraduate talent in fields ranging from genomics to molecular biology.

Over the years, Mazumdar-Shaw has successfully recruited many locals and émigrés. "There is a huge reservoir of scientific talent here and abroad. We have been able to attract many of them, women in particular," she says. "A significant number of our employees worked in the States before returning to India, bringing with them much-needed international exposure and a global work culture." She believes that enticing brainpower home has become much easier in

> **Expand the Workforce**
>
> "There is a huge reservoir of scientific talent here and abroad," says Mazumdar-Shaw. "We have been able to recruit many of them, women in particular."

the past few years: "India used to be viewed as a hardship post. The compelling reason to return was to care for one's aged parents. No more. There's a definite shift in the mind-set of overseas Indians. Success begets success. As our economy improves and jobs open up, people want to come back to be a part of the exciting story of nation building."

No doubt Mazumdar-Shaw's unusually open and participative management style helps. Among other things, she opens her home, on acreage near the corporate office, for official business. "Glenmore," as it is called, is where Mazumdar-Shaw holds all major meetings and company celebrations. Company executives are encouraged to bring their visitors for dinner.

"From day one, I figured that management was all about handling people's emotions, their egos," says Mazumdar-Shaw. "I think women are particularly effective at handling these emotional issues. In the biosciences, especially in our company, where the average age is twenty-eight, you need to create a vibrant, campuslike environment where ideas can be freely shared. And, above all, people must have fun!"

Warm and outgoing, Mazumdar-Shaw eats lunch regularly with employees in the cafeteria and decorates the company walls with her personal art collection. "I have never seen a company with such an open culture," says her husband, who as vice chairman helps infuse leading-edge management systems into Biocon's relatively unstructured world. Shaw worked for thirty-two years as a senior executive for the British textile company Coats Viyella. Others, too, soon sense that there is something truly special in Biocon's DNA: a shared commitment to build a life sciences giant. Performance-based compensation and generous equity participation reinforce the esprit de corps. People rarely leave the company once they join. Annual staff turnover is below 3 percent, and most of the senior management team have been together for fifteen years. "I can't think of working for another company," says longtimer Nirupa Bareja, who heads human resources and holds a doctorate in marine biology. "It's either Biocon or nowhere."

Capitalizing on its rave reviews, India's flagship biotech company is attracting both homing pigeons and people who ordinarily might have contemplated leaving the country. Arun Chandavarkan, for example, earned his master's and doctoral degrees from MIT and was expected to accept an offer with Unilever. Instead, Mazumdar-Shaw convinced him to join Biocon, where he heads manufacturing. Earlier, she swayed Shrikumar Suryanarayan, a graduate of the prestigious Indian Institute of Technology, to trade doctoral studies in America for an opportunity to start Biocon's research and development function. "Why don't you do your research here and start an R&D unit for me?" she asked him twenty years ago. Suryanarayan agreed and has been directing Biocon's research arm ever since.

Mazumdar-Shaw has also recruited an international board, dominated by independent directors, and a powerful group of scientific advisers. For example, Charles Cooney, professor of chemical and biochemical engineering at MIT, sits on both boards. The advisory panel includes heavyweights like Sam Pasternak, a leading international patent attorney, and Anthony Allison, former research vice president at Syntex and inventor of the immunosuppressant micophenolate mofetil.

Target the Best Minds

One of Biocon's winning strategies was to develop an international board of directors and a first-rate team of scientific advisers.

Besides transforming her company from a small maker of enzymes into an integrated biopharma player, Mazumdar-Shaw has been in the forefront of developing India's life-sciences industry. In launching the Association of Biotechnology-Led Enterprises, she has undertaken a tireless crusade to lure back the country's scientists. "We have this wonderful pool of talent. Fifteen percent of scientists in the U.S. are NRIs; faculty, too," she says. "If we can get just a fraction of them to return, we can do wonders. We can build a huge biotech industry here."

So far, she contends, the government has not played a major role in the recruitment process. "But today, political leaders are at least talking to the business community. Now, you can actually criticize the national government. That never used to happen." Mazumdar-Shaw has been an outspoken critic of New Delhi, calling access to the capital "inadequate" and the regulatory environment "slow if not a veritable nightmare."

In the meantime, Mazumdar-Shaw and other business leaders are the country's primary talent scouts. "The private sector's doing it," she explains. "For the first time, ordinary people like me, the founders of Infosys, and other first-generation entrepreneurs are proving that you can start from scratch with nothing, with no family or government connections, and create a world-class company. We're all driven by a similar passion and determination. Frankly speaking, we're the role models who are attracting people back to India."

Nonetheless, she knows that the payday for biotechnology is much farther off than it is for information technology. Even for companies with pockets deep enough to wait, there are limits to investors' patience. It will be roughly ten to fifteen years before a vibrant industry is established, Mazumdar-Shaw predicts.

Outside the well-ordered self-sufficiency of Electronics City and other glitsy industrial parks are the dusty, polluted, traffic-clogged streets of Bangalore. The city, often touted as a showcase for the benefits of globalization, suffers obvious shortcomings. The biggest is infrastructure. Bangalore lacks an international airport, good highways, sewage and water treatment facilities, and a mass transit system. Like most of India, it is short on electricity—requiring most major complexes to generate their own, more expensive power.

Fortunately, business leaders understand the damage poor municipal services can do to the city's reputation as a world-class technology hub. Four years ago, the state government established the Bangalore Agenda Task Force to improve the city's infrastructure and standard of living. However, it was Infosys's Nilekani who spearheaded the effort—with a personal contribution of $1 million. To date, the private–public-sector coalition has tackled everything from reforming property taxes to buying 1,000 new air-conditioned buses.

Other concerned citizens are also pitching in. Five years ago, urban designer Swati Ramanathan, forty, moved back to India with her husband, Ramesh, a managing director at Citicorp in San Francisco. "We grew up in Bangalore and always had plans to come back," she says. "It was an emotional decision that had to be made." However, their hometown had changed, and there was a dearth of information on how to solve everyday problems in the more frantic, faster-paced city. Wasting no time, Ramanathan compiled *Participatory Planning,* a coping manual for Bangaloreans. The book identifies hassles—from garbage to lack of water and electricity—and clever ways to solve them. Her user's guide has been a huge hit with both locals and fellow homing pigeons.

> **Act Now**
>
> To forge a permanent place in the high-tech hubs of the world, Bangalore must quickly solve its many infrastructure problems.

To some extent, Bangalore is a victim of its own success. Rooms are in short supply at the city's five-star hotels—the Leela Palace, Taj Western, and Oberoi—where rates jumped 40 percent last year. The same is true for the luxury-service apartments that cater to the surge of well-heeled expatriate and NRI visitors. Cybercafés and restaurants, too, are packed. Bangalore's easiest ticket and biggest draw are its two hundred–plus pubs. "Every day it feels more like Silicon Valley to me," says Indian American Hans Taparia, thirty-two, an MIT graduate who runs a technology consulting business in Bangalore.

Amid this hectic activity, the city offers an ideal base from which to explore the fascinating and culturally rich state of Karnataka: the ruins of the once-powerful Vijayanagar empire, the sculpted wonders of Belur and Halebid, the awesome mausoleum of Bijapur, and much more. And it offers extensive shopping opportunities, a rich variety of cuisine, and world-class entertainment. Although Bangalore can never regain its former reputation as a "pensioner's paradise," it offers the best urban working environment in India.

Nevertheless, coming home is not easy. Indian returnees face serious adjustment problems. Staggering poverty, garbage heaps, clogged roadways, pollution, and wandering cows can tear at the heart of émigrés from the United States. And then there's the country's chronic inefficiency. "The American system is so well organized," says Wockhart's Vishal Bali. "You take so many things for granted—installing a phone, getting a driver's license, dealing with school admissions. Those things can be an absolute nightmare here. They're extremely irritating."

Perhaps more difficult to deal with are the pressures of balancing two cultures—Indian and American. "Indians yearn for a more spiritual, religious, and family-oriented environment. That's generally missing in the U.S.," says 24/7's Nags Nagarajan. "Consequently, we generally have a tougher time assimilating to the States than other immigrant groups. Crunch time comes when you've got a daughter getting married. Most Indians simply don't want her hooking up with an American, unless, of course, it's a prearranged wedding with a suitable Indian American."

• • •

Underscoring Nagarajan's point, I came across one of many "Brides Wanted" advertisements in Mumbai's *Asian Age:* "High-status physician—NRI family in USA seeks match for their 31-year-old medical doctor son. Doctors and dentists welcome. We only desire that the girl should be homely, gracious, and willing to relocate to the USA."

Similarly, Anand of New York wrote to Dr. Aruna Broota, India's Dear Abby: "I live in the U.S. with my son and daughter, but am planning to return to India for two reasons. One, my daughter has imbibed American values and is not in good company. Two, my 20-year-old son has an American girlfriend and doesn't have interest in studies. I am really worried about my children." The counselor responded: "Learn to accept change. Do some yoga. It will help you cope with the situation." But she also cautioned the distraught parent not to force her children to return to India against their will.

When I recounted this story to M. P. Singh, managing director of Alpenstock Consulting, over lunch in Mumbai, he was not surprised. "These cases are actually quite familiar," said the well-traveled executive, who has lived and worked in the United States, the United Kingdom, and Eastern Europe. "Deep down, most Indians want to come home, but frequently their Indian American kids won't let them. After all, it's quite natural for these kids to covet the same kinds of things—the social life and living standards—that their American peers covet."

Later that evening, in the departure lounge at Mumbai International Airport, I witnessed a raging dispute between an NRI father and his two teenage daughters. The New Jersey–based engineer was trying to persuade the girls to accompany him back to India later in the year for a family wedding. "Never again!" they shouted, reflecting the cultural shock of spending two weeks in a Third World country. Put off by the dust, the flies, the heat, and the pervasive odor of cow dung, U.S.-born children are invariably reluctant to accompany their parents on their annual trips to India, much less move there permanently.

A number of wealthy NRIs contemplating repatriation have built replica homes in their ancestral hometowns. In rural Punjab, for example, there are sprawling, palatial residences with names like Orlando House, Vancouver Villa, White House, and California Farm. "The idea is to have the same comfort level as one is used to abroad," says Devinder Singh Sandhu, thirty-five, who returned after fifteen years in Canada and is running the family's consulting business. But the main objective is to lure their foreign-born offspring to join them. "The children are more keen to stay here now," says Anjna Mann of Piara Farm, a swanky, one-acre estate with an indoor swimming pool, a fifteen-foot-high waterfall, a home theater, a fitness center with sauna, and central air conditioning. "It was a small price to pay to attract them to their roots," husband Kamal agrees. The Manns' California-style dream house mimics their $3.5 million home in San Francisco.

Of course, the returnee movement will always have stops and starts. However, the shift of human capital back to India is starting to take hold. "The worm has turned and our time has finally come," says one business leader.

"Elephants do not gallop," Rudyard Kipling once wrote. "They move . . . [at] varying rates of speed. If an elephant wished to catch an express train, he could not gallop, but he could catch the train." In the years following independence, India was something like that elephant. Ponderous. Often outpaced by faster rivals. But moving forward, nonetheless.

Quietly, but now with breathtaking speed, the new India is beginning to edge out the old. The dream of a prosperous India—"the opening of opportunity," as Nehru put it fifty-eight years ago—may soon be fulfilled. True, the country's transformation is still a work in progress. But rarely has India enjoyed such favorable prospects, as reflected in its evolving superpower status. At home, there is newfound confidence. Unlike the generation before, young Indians feel a sense of optimism that the country hasn't experienced in decades. Empowered by their exuberance, they are no longer obsessed with the nation's past, but with its future. They are India's rising hope.

5

home to
the world

Singapore is everything we could desire,
and I consider myself most fortunate in
the selection; it will soon rise in importance.

—SIR STAMFORD RAFFLES

1819

Although Singapore (from *Singa Pura,* or Lion City) was discovered in the third century by Chinese sailors, the island on the southern tip of the Malay Peninsula remained relatively uninhabited until 1819, when Sir Stamford Raffles of the British East India Company arrived on the *Indiana.* Landing at the mouth of the Singapore River in January of that year, Raffles was under orders to create a strategic base to refit and provide protection for the British fleet, as well as to forestall any advance in the region by the Dutch. He immediately recognized Singapore's geographic significance, located between the trading countries of the East and West. "By far the most important station in the East," he described it, "and as far as naval superiority and commercial interests are concerned, of much higher value than whole continents of territory."

Raffles established a British trading post on the island. Word spread quickly throughout the archipelago, and within weeks hundreds of Indonesian and Siamese vessels were anchored in the harbor. Soon the settlement was teeming with immigrants from around the world. Six months later, it had expanded to nearly 5,000 inhabitants, including Malays, Chinese, Arabs, Indians, and Europeans. By 1824, just five years after its founding, Singapore had drawn merchants of every variety, as its population doubled to 10,000.

Today, the tiny island, about the size of Rhode Island, is one of the world's great economic successes. Once a humble fishing village, surrounded by swamps and jungle and populated by tigers until the 1930s, Singapore has transformed into a pulsating business hub. Skyscrapers and shopping centers have replaced the colonial town Raffles designed. Modern expressways cover the cart tracks that once led from the harbor to the commercial district and the countryside beyond. Hills have been leveled, swamps filled, and the city expanded through extensive reclamation projects. Adjacent islands house parks, refineries, and military bases. The harbor has evolved into the world's biggest and busiest port.

Modern Singapore, home to 4.3 million people, is a model of efficiency. It is envied for its prosperity, cleanliness, social order, great shopping, and world-class dining. Asia's Mr. Clean is the kind of place anyone would want to live in—in other words, a home to the world.

Newcomers feel welcome the moment they arrive at the spotless, award-winning Changi Airport. In a matter of minutes, they are whisked through immigration to a fleet of taxis lined up outside. After a drive along the palm-lined East Coast Parkway, with beaches on the left and high-rise condominiums on the right, they reach the central business district in less than thirty minutes.

Verdant, peaceful, and prosperous, Singapore is one of the world's most livable cities, a regional financial center, and home to 7,000 multinational corporations. English is the language of business. International phone calls can be dialed as quickly as in the United States. Telecommunications and broadband Internet access are first-rate. No litter mars the city streets. Every block has trees and flowers. The island's entire east coast, facing the South China Sea, is a string of parks and beaches. Only half an hour from downtown are a nature preserve and charming semirural areas. Food-handling guidelines are strict, and multiethnic menus abound. Rules are predictable, and government officials are helpful, if somewhat officious. Simply stated, Singapore works.

For years, this tidy outpost of prosperity was stereotyped as repressive, smug, and dull—a place where the papers are full of good news, and chewing gum and *Playboy* magazine were banned. "Disneyland with the death penalty," writer William Gibson called it. According to Amnesty International, Singapore has the highest execution rate in the world relative to its population. Drug offenses carry the ultimate penalty. Certainly the pro-business government, nicknamed "Singapore, Inc.," loves to make rules. The walls are plastered with them, warning everyone what they can't do: spit, litter, forget to flush, engage in oral sex. Notorious for such rigid controls, this never-naughty nation has recently loosened up.

In 2004, Singapore removed its ban on bar-top dancing and chewing gum (although only sugarless varieties are allowed), eased free speech rules, gave the thumbs-up to bungee jumping, and authorized all-night operations at some bars and nightclubs. The public sector even started to employ gays as civil servants. These liberalization efforts are intended to help the country reestablish its global competitiveness by making Singapore more attractive to expatriates and homegrown professionals. As the government tweaks its social policy, political leaders are attempting to redefine the city-state in the face of radically shifting conditions while still maintaining a visible hand in day-to-day affairs. One thing is clear: Singapore has to stay ahead of the game if it is to maintain its hard-earned prosperity.

One of Asia's earlier tiger economies, Singapore was enjoying heady days just a decade ago. With regional economic growth roaring along, spurred by electronics and pharmaceutical manufacturing, oil refining, and shipping, this country with no natural resources competed fiercely to keep the boom going. But by 1997, a recession

began to unfold. A downturn in the economies of its nearby trading partners—Indonesia, Malaysia, and Thailand—hurt the export-
dependent nation, particularly its electronics sector. Its competitive
advantage began to erode as manufacturers looked to neighboring
countries for cheaper, more plentiful labor and land. The technology
meltdown in the West, the effects of 9/11, the war in Iraq, the SARS
outbreak, and the bird-flu crisis also took a toll. Economic growth
went negative in 2001 and was relatively flat in the two subsequent
years—2.2 percent in 2002 and 0.9 percent in 2003.

The country's long-standing reputation as a safe haven was also
called into question. Particularly chilling was the discovery of an al-
Qaeda plot to blow up American interests in Singapore, including the
U.S. Embassy. Government officials became increasingly aware of the
nation's vulnerability in a region rife with economic, social, religious,
and ethnic tensions.

In 2002, then-prime minister (now senior minister) Goh Chok
Tong launched a "Remaking Singapore" project. "We need to go beyond economics," he said. "The third generation of post-indepen-
dence Singaporeans has different
aspirations from the founder [Lee
Kuan Yew] and the second generation." Goh expressed his desire to
position the country "as a learning
nation, a renaissance nation. We
want it to be highly differentiated,
intellectual with excellent scientific
and technological capabilities—
creative, innovative, and vibrant." Today, the challenge is to build a
more well-rounded citizenry, transforming Singapore into a more con-
genial place for free-thinkers and entrepreneurs.

Adapt—or Die

After the economic downturn in the
late 1990s, Singapore transformed
itself into a more vibrant, creative,
and innovative city-state.

The goal is to move up the value chain into such intellectual arenas as applied research and development, advanced information technology, biotechnology, and nanotechnology. Government planners
hope to boost knowledge-based industrial output to 40 percent of the

nation's gross domestic product by 2010. The plan also calls for attracting top foreign universities to conduct cutting-edge research. "By having prestigious institutions here, we will be in a better position to cater to the needs of a knowledge-based economy," says Philip Yeo, co-chair of Singapore's Economic Development Board (EDB) and one of the most powerful figures in the state industrial sector.

Becoming a mecca for knowledge-intensive fields requires an infusion of foreign talent. The cache of local citizens simply isn't up to the task. Recruiting foreign professionals and enticing Singaporeans home is "a matter of life and death," says Senior Minister Goh. "If we don't top up our talent pool from the outside in ten years' time, many of the high-valued jobs we do now will emigrate to China and elsewhere."

The country's hunt for global brainpower has widespread public support. In a recent survey, two out of three Singaporeans agreed that recruiting foreign professionals is necessary for Singapore's continued development. Singapore Inc. is also helping current residents make the difficult transition from an industrial economy to an innovation economy. Several comprehensive government programs are available to help older and less-educated workers learn new skills and find new jobs. In addition, Singapore is overhauling its education system, with a new emphasis on creative, critical thinking, which is crucial to high-tech industries.

Historically, public schools rewarded concentrated attention to school work, getting good grades, and spending after-school hours preparing for exams. Recently, however, a government panel recommended developing fewer geeks and more "resilient people," who have perseverance, focus, discipline, creativity, and a healthy lifestyle. In response, the Education Ministry trimmed the primary and secondary schools' curricula by one-third to give students more time to relax and think creatively.

Some see sports as the answer to developing a resilient population. In addition to injecting more athletics into the school curriculum, the government recently created a $44 million Singapore Sports School to fast-track its most promising athletes. It then recruited Australians to teach swimming, a Chinese coach to teach table tennis, an Indonesian to oversee badminton, a Briton to lead soccer, a German to coach track and field, and a South African to build strength and conditioning.

The country is also working to convince students from an early age that science and math are cool. Steps are being taken to improve the quality of these critical subjects at the secondary-school level—a move, it is hoped, that will ultimately nurture local doctoral candidates. The government has set aside more than $250 million in scholarship funds for students who want to study science and math, either at home or abroad. These efforts are paying off. The latest Trends in International Math and Science Study ranked Singapore first in the world.

Reform Public Schools

Recently, the government began focusing its education system on providing the creative, critical thinking needed in the innovation economy.

Singapore's state-supported Raffles Junior College is a stepping-stone to the Ivy League. In 2004, more than 40 percent of its 820 graduates were accepted by top U.S. universities—about half by the elite Ivies. Cornell alone accepted 90. More than half of Raffles's America-bound grads are on government scholarship.

No doubt, elevating public education and improving the skills of its people will aid Singapore's makeover. But developing a knowledge-based economy means opening the door even wider to outside talent. For example, the government plans to double the number of foreign students to 150,000.

Fortunately, Singapore has always been a city of immigrants. Throughout its history, it has never succumbed to the fiery nationalism and xenophobia seen in neighboring Malaysia, Indonesia, Vietnam, and Burma. Upon his arrival in 1819, Stamford Raffles established a policy of welcoming foreigners who had the commercial, financial, and technical skills to help develop the area. Fortune-seeking settlers from Malaysia, India, and China transformed Singapore into a flourishing seaport. By the turn of the twentieth century, the country had become a kaleidoscope of cultures.

That pattern of openness gained new meaning under Singapore's charismatic modern leader, Prime Minister Lee Kuan Yew. Rising from a legacy of divisive colonialism, the devastation of World War II, and the resulting poverty and disorder, Lee secured the nation's independence in 1965. At the time, few gave Singapore much chance of survival. But Lee had a vision of building a multiracial, multilingual society that would be unified, while retaining a uniquely Singaporean identity built on "brain services."

"We had to create a new kind of economy, try new methods and schemes never tried before anywhere else in the world, because there was no other country like Singapore," Cambridge-educated Lee explained in his autobiography, *From the Third World to First.* "We had to be different."

Lee soon recognized that "trained talent is the yeast that transforms a society and makes it rise." During the sixties and seventies, the country experienced the inevitable leakage of its best and brightest. "Many middle-class, professional Chinese, Indonesians, and Malaysians migrated permanently to Australia, New Zealand, and Canada because their careers in Singapore were not advancing rapidly enough," recalls Lee. "To get enough talent to fill the jobs our growing economy needed, I set out to attract and retain talent—entrepreneurs, professionals, artists, and highly skilled workers." Slowly, Singapore Inc. began to reverse the brain drain and replenish the nation's human capital.

> **Dust Off the Welcome Mat**
>
> "To get enough talent to fill the jobs our growing economy needed, I set out to attract and retain talent," recalls former prime minister Lee Kuan Yew. "Without foreign talent, we would not have done as well."

During Lee's reign, which ended in 1990, Singapore boomed. Lee and his team rapidly modernized the nation's infrastructure to attract foreign investment and help Singaporean businesses compete in world markets. Nothing escaped the prime minister's watchful eye—from restoring the historic Raffles Hotel to unabashedly persuading Singaporean men to marry women as well educated as themselves and encouraging young couples to bear more children. Despite his heavy hand, Lee, now mentor minister, remains unapologetic for the country's stern dictates: "If this is a nanny state, I am proud to have fostered one."

Lee also concedes that outsiders were his stalwart partners in creating this prosperous First World country: "Without foreign talent, we would not have done as well. They are the extra megabytes in Singapore's computer. If we do not top up with foreign talent, we will not make it into the top league."

The country's liberal policy of attracting outsiders is still in place today. In the 1990s, the number of foreigners working in Singapore more than doubled to roughly 720,000. They now account for more than one in five residents, and they are increasing in number nearly twice as fast as the native population. Although many foreigners are engaged in low-paid grunt work—mostly in construction and domestic service—almost 100,000 are highly skilled professionals and managers who have put down roots. More than anywhere else, Singapore has tapped an army of Chinese researchers, engineers, and technicians. An estimated 60,000 mainland Chinese nationals work there; many are permanent residents. They play a crucial role in keeping the country's technological wheels turning.

"Attracting talent is a crucial policy, which must continue," echoes the current prime minister, Lee Hsien Loong, the elder son of Lee Kuan Yew. The son is tasked with extending his father's welcome to newcomers, while putting his own stamp on the country. He wants "to raise the quality of foreign workers who come here to help Singapore compete for global investments." To that end, the government has liberalized foreign employment rules by speeding up approvals for work permits, making it easier for spouses to work in Singapore, offering subsidized state housing, and providing tax rebates to cover relocation and recruiting expenses.

To create a home to the world, "Contact Singapore" was created in the late 1990s. Like Enterprise Ireland, its mission is to locate and poach global talent interested in working in Singapore. With offices around the world, the agency means business. In 1998, it assisted the Development Bank of Singapore—Southeast Asia's largest bank—in hiring American John T. Olds as its CEO. Olds, formerly the managing director of J. P. Morgan & Co., was given free rein to shake up the bank, positioning it for the twenty-first century. In short order, he replaced entrenched civil servants with first-rate foreigners. This was exactly the kind of bold step many felt was needed to raise the country's banking standards. The bank is now run by another talented outsider, Jackson Tai, a Chinese-American who also came from J. P. Morgan.

"We're selling dreams," says David Tan, director of Contact Singapore and head of the Ministry of Manpower's International Talent Division. "Our branding studies show that Singapore is primarily known for its world-class efficiency. Hence, the need to sell the soft side—a place where dreams are made." Tan, thirty-five, holds degrees from the University of Melbourne and Harvard Law School and previously worked at McKinsey & Co., Development Bank of Singapore, and several local companies. Working out of the treasury, he is currently targeting overseas Singaporeans and foreigners in a range of high-value, high-growth sectors, from biotechnology and nanotechnology to broadband and software sensors. But unlike Enterprise Ireland, "we really don't have a good handle on the numbers—how many people are out there and who they are," he admits. Therefore, Contact Singapore is rapidly building its worldwide database of potential recruits.

In the interim, Tan presses on. "Since 9/11, things have gotten a lot easier," he claims. "We've attracted thirty leading scientists and professionals in the past six months, primarily [as a result of] safety and security concerns in the States. They tell us they don't want their kids riding on public buses. Nor do they want them being raised in the MTV generation." The city's world-class infrastructure and multicultural character are also major attractions. As for the downside, Tan points out that, unlike multinational companies operating in-country, local firms generally pay 25 percent to 30 percent below world standards. The government's perceived heavy hand scares off others. Then, there is the steamy climate. "Life in Singapore is like living in a warm bath," says one returnee, longing for the variety of four seasons. But on balance, Tan believes the pluses far outweigh the minuses—a message he constantly stresses in wooing knowledge workers.

Like many other countries, Singapore is pinning much of its future on life sciences. The government views biotechnology, pharmaceutics, medical equipment, and healthcare services as critical complements to its strengths in electronics, chemicals, engineering, transport, and financial services. Its goal is for the country to be home to fifteen world-class life-sciences companies by 2010. With little homegrown expertise, Singapore has set out to import what it cannot produce.

> **Celebrate Science and Technology**
>
> Singapore wants to be home to fifteen world-class life-sciences companies by 2010.

In biotechnology, the government has earmarked $2.3 billion for investments, grants, and other incentives. "Over the last twenty years or so, we've built up manufacturing technology," says Beh Swan Gin, second director of biomedical sciences at the Economic Development Board (EDB). "Biomedical sciences will add an anchor to that. We expect to reach our target of S$12 billion [US$7 billion] in biomedical output by 2005." (Reports indicate that objective was reached a year ahead of schedule.)

To support its expanding biotech industry, Singapore recently built a $294 million medical-science park, Biopolis, as part of the One North complex (referring to Singapore's location one degree north of the equator), which will house a collection of knowledge-based industries. The five-hundred-acre One North cluster will take fifteen years to complete and will be a self-contained city with its own apartments, schools, entertainment centers, and monorail system.

• • •

When I visited the complex in 2004, workers were putting the finishing touches on The Genome, one of Biopolis's several state-of-the-art research buildings designed to meet the needs of 2,000 scientists. I met with one of the country's most famous recruits, Edison Tak-Bun Liu, a recipient of awards from the Susan G. Komen Breast Cancer Foundation and the American Association for Cancer Research. In March 2001, Liu left his scientific directorship at the National Cancer Institute in Bethesda, Maryland, to become executive director of the Genome Institute of Singapore (GIS).

"GIS is a unique place for scientific discovery," said Liu. "We believe that a future in biology lies in the fusion of highly comprehensive and massively parallel genomic and computational approaches with cell and medical biology. We'll be providing the genomic infrastructure for Singapore, training new talent in these emerging fields and attracting international talent to work in the country." By 2004, Liu had recruited 170 scientists, trainees, and staff to his team, with the ultimate goal of 280. About 85 percent of his senior people came from abroad, including the entire gene-sequencing team, which moved from Paris.

For Singapore's homing pigeons, the opportunity to have their children reconnect with their roots is a powerful incentive. For Westerners, the excitement of doing leading-edge research in one of the world's most vibrant regions has been a huge plus. "It's been easier for me to recruit here than in some of the institutes I've worked at in the States," says Liu. "The resources and infrastructure here [are] as good as anywhere in the world. And there's the promise of doing something new."

Undoubtedly, GIS has a lot to offer. Singapore's location makes it an ideal spot to study tropical diseases endemic to the region, in addition to contemporary illnesses such as heart disease and cancer. Its advanced telecommunications and computing resources allow scientists to sort through billions of genetic combinations. Singapore also offers opportunities to participate in stem cell research (stem cells can be taken from aborted fetuses and human embryos to be cloned and kept for up to fourteen days). By cracking the mysteries of human genetics and unraveling the secrets of human existence, Liu sees himself as a principal player in the creation of a brave new world.

The welcoming climate lured not only Liu but a host of other scientific luminaries. Top researcher Sir David Lane, who in 1979 discovered the cancer tumor suppressor gene p53, came from Scotland. "I'm fascinated by the possibilities of interaction with the other institutes at Biopolis," he said. "It's an amazing opportunity."

Yoshiaki Ito is another recent recruit. An alumnus of Kyoto and Duke Universities, he is a leading global authority in cancer research. As a visiting guest speaker at a scientific symposium a few years ago, Ito was impressed with the rich talent pool, strong research capabilities, and ample funding that accelerate the discovery of new cures. "That's why I took the post as director of the Oncology Research Institute at the National University of Singapore," he says.

In 2002, Singapore also poached Alan Coleman, the Scottish scientist who helped create Dolly, the world's first cloned mammal. When research funding in Europe tightened up, he moved to ES Cell International, a joint venture of Australian investors and EDB. "I was just seduced by the enthusiasm for building scientific infrastructure and putting money into biotech," Coleman said.

> **Target the Best Minds**
>
> "I jumped because, on a scientific level, Singapore is where I wanted to be," says Stanford-trained superstar Edison Liu.

In Edison Liu's case, the primary attraction was the thrill of "green-fielding a new social culture—multicultural, multiracial, multidisciplinary—based on teamwork, but without diminishing individual effort." He was also drawn to the country's vision of using biology not only to advance medicine but as a tool for economic activity, and the chance to make an impact in Asia. "I jumped because, on a scientific level, it's where I wanted to be," he told the *Far Eastern Economic Review*. The Hong Kong–born Liu emigrated to the United States as a youngster with his parents, both physicians, grew up in the San Francisco area, and trained at Stanford. "Unlike many Chinese who either migrate or return here, I never bought into the victim mind-set of many minority groups. I always felt that we overseas Chinese—like the Jews—were an adopted people and, in many respects, a harbinger of world peace." Therefore, he feels especially proud to be a partner in Singapore's efforts to socially engineer a multicultural society.

"Except for maybe Hawai'i, there's no other spot on Earth that's done as good a job at building a polyglot society," he told me. "The human species is extremely fragile, and a place like Singapore can play an important role in ensuring world peace and stability. It can be a microcosm of what the rest of the world could become."

When Liu moved to Singapore, he gave his fifteen-year-old son a cell phone. "I told him, 'Take it—you're on your own. Wander around town freely. If you have any problems, just call me.' Can you imagine doing something like that in New York or Chicago? It never would happen. In the United States, parents—especially in big cities—are constantly concerned about their kids' safety and security. Not here." As a result, Liu chafes at criticism of Singapore's orderly, buttoned-down government. "They've got it right," he insists. "Newcomers accept the restrictions. They're actually comforted by them."

Another high-profile outsider is James P. Tan, dean of the School of Biological Sciences at Nanyang Technological University. Over the past twenty-five years, the University of Wisconsin–trained Tan established himself as a leading scientist in microbiology, immunology, and biochemistry. Attracted by the availability of funding and the ease of doing research, the Hong Kong–born U.S. citizen took a leave of absence from Vanderbilt University.

On the last day of the Lunar New Year in 2004, I met Tan and his wife for dinner. "Recruiting top scientific talent is extremely competitive," he explained. "Every country is after the same limited pool of people." Since arriving in Singapore in September 2001, Tan has recruited 70 percent of his faculty from abroad. He has had particular success with Taiwanese and Korean scientists in the United States who were interested in returning to Asia but feared that their children, raised in America, would be unable to adapt to life back home or compete in the local school systems. "Children are often the dominant factor in the relocation decision," says Tan. "Fortunately, in Singapore, we're able to offer them excellent subsidized international schools where foreign-born kids fit in quite easily."

In addition, Nanyang Technological University permits faculty members to develop and commercialize their research on school grounds. While the university has first call on intellectual property, a faculty member typically receives 70 percent to 75 percent of the royalties. This practice differs markedly from that of the United States, where professors generally are prohibited from setting up companies on campus.

Despite these incentives, Tan has found it difficult to lure Singaporean scientists away from America, with only two to his credit. "Don't underestimate the United States," he warns. "There's a major prestige factor there, which is extremely important. And as far as the money side goes, the U.S. still has a huge advantage in funding scientific research."

Therefore, Tan has been recruiting doctoral students, primarily from China, India, and Southeast Asia. Yet there is the constant danger that many of them will use Singapore as a bridge to North America, Western Europe, and Australia. "You hope a certain percentage will stay on, but if we lose 70 percent, we'll still keep 30 percent," he says stoically.

> **Encourage Dual Loyalties**
>
> Leading microbiologist James Tan oversees the School of Biological Sciences at Nanyang Tech, while maintaining a position at Vanderbilt, where he keeps his primary lab.

As for himself, Tan is hedging his bets. He spends roughly 60 percent of his time at Vanderbilt, where he maintains his primary laboratory. "Our permanent home is in Nashville," adds Mrs. Tan. "Although we're empty-nesters, it's very important for us to keep in touch with our two adult children back in the States."

For microbiologist Lan Kong-Peng, coming home was an easy decision. Born in Singapore, he was trained at the University of Minnesota, Columbia, and Germany's University of Cologne. In 1998, he turned down job offers from Columbia, the University of California at Berkeley, and the University of North Carolina. "My wife, who is also from here, and I didn't want to deal with the stress and crime [of the U.S.]," he says. "But the professional opportunities and government support of life sciences here won the day. In the States, junior faculty members typically spend their first year or two doing nothing but drafting research proposals. Not here. From day one, I was able to engage in research full time. That convinced me to come home."

EDB's Beh believes that his countrymen, by and large, are more inclined than people of most nationalities to become homing pigeons. "Only a small number of people make emigration a one-way trip," he claims. "Good ideas quickly get recognized in Singa-pore. You don't get lost here. There's always the feeling you can make a difference—and be rewarded for it. And that's a major incentive to come home." Beh also contends that, "coming from a small country, most overseas Singaporeans bond easily. The desire to reconnect with their roots, their country, is quite powerful." He credits the country's compulsory two-year national service for men with fostering these strong ties. "There's absolutely no opting out of the military. Every male does it," he says. "In fact, many Singaporeans return just to make sure their sons experience the required two-year military stint. We've even had a number of foreigners living here volunteer for national service as a sign of their commitment to the country."

> **Reconsider National Service**
>
> "There's absolutely no opting out of the military," says Beh Swan Gin. "Every male does it. We've even had a number of foreigners volunteer for national service."

That said, can Singapore realize its life-sciences dream? As we have seen, the country is not alone in targeting this sector as a new growth industry. India, China, South Korea, and Taiwan also want to climb on the bandwagon. Singapore has already attracted big-name manufacturers. Six of the top ten pharmas and many leading medical technology companies produce their wares there. Eli Lilly, Schering-Plough, Novartis, and other drugmakers have established major research labs in Singapore. The country also has one of the highest standards of medical care in the region and a strong record of protecting intellectual property rights. This has enabled local institutions to partner with big-time players in biomedicine: Johns Hopkins, Stanford, MIT, University of Chicago, and Sweden's Karolinska Institute.

Most pundits believe Singapore can successfully compete with other bioscience hot spots. "Singapore will succeed in life sciences," predicts GIS CEO Liu. "Small, smart, and nimble is what we are and what will be our formula for success. By being outward-looking and global in reach, we can multiply our prosperity and ensure an exciting life for our children."

When Ron Frank agreed to lead Singapore Management University (SMU), it proved to be a wonderful experience. "It's been a rebirth, a dream," he told me. Frank and I taught together at the Wharton School thirty years ago. After teaching at Harvard, Stanford, and Wharton, he went on to serve as dean of the business schools at Purdue and Emory universities. When the call came asking him to become president of Singapore's first private university, Frank seized the opportunity.

Nourish the Halls of Ivy

The country tapped highly regarded American Ron Frank as president of its first private institution, Singapore Management University.

SMU opened its doors in January 2000. Spearheaded by the EDB and the Education Ministry, it was the first local university with business education as its focus. "Most countries only want to build their own universities," Frank says. "Few are willing to attract and welcome other leading schools." But under a five-year partnership with the Wharton School, SMU is quintessentially American.

"If you look at the way we compensate both faculty and staff, we're much more similar to what U.S. multinationals do than to what other educational institutions, particularly in Asia, do," says Frank. Nor is there any Old-Boy network—so familiar to the region—in the hiring process. "We're looking for first-rate professionals," he insists. "I don't care where they come from; they just better be highly qualified."

Roughly half of SMU's faculty of 110 came from other Singaporean institutions, the balance from abroad. Among the more notable recruits are world-renowned marketing scholar David Montgomery from Stanford, Wharton econometrician Roberto Mariano, and hands-on business executive Steven Miller from IBM Global Services. SMU's faculty is generating leading-edge research in a number of exciting new fields, including wealth management. Today, 2,200 undergraduate students from twenty-one countries attend the university. Eventually, the student body will ramp up to 6,000 undergrad and graduate students at SMU's new campus, now under construction, in the heart of the central business district.

"What's the difference between SMU and a Wharton or Harvard Business School?" I ask Frank. "Most of all, it's the lack of cynicism," he replies quickly. "It doesn't exist here. In the States, faculty often impute evil motivations every time you or someone else make a decision. Thank God, I don't have to deal with that here. There's a real can-do attitude in Singapore." He attributes this difference to the country's "social integration—it's a real strength, a major asset."

Frank will do whatever it takes to rally community support for his young university; he is famous for calling attention to SMU. Although government aided, the institution relies heavily on outside resources. Here, the seasoned educator excels. In 2002, he tapped Hong Kong billionaire Li Ka-Shing for a leadership gift of $10 million, the largest donation ever made to a Singaporean university.

In August 2004, Frank's three-year contract ended. He headed home with "enormous respect for my hosts" and the belief that SMU is well on its way to becoming a magnet for top-tier scholars and students. "In the long run," he says, "this institution should strive to be of the quality of a Wharton, a Stanford, a Chicago."

Forward-thinking imports such as Ron Frank, Edison Liu, and the others are creating world-class learning centers in Singapore. But the country's plans extend far beyond business and technology. "We also welcome creative and artistic talents," says Contact Singapore's Rosa Daniel. "It is not only in high-tech industries, but in a whole range of other sectors that we hope to bring in people who can share their perspectives and expertise." One such talent is Lan Shui. Born in China, he honed his musical skills at the famous Beijing Central Conservatory and Boston University. From there, he went on to conduct the acclaimed Baltimore Symphony Orchestra and Detroit Symphony. In 1997, he became music director of the Singapore Symphony Orchestra. Lan is effusive in his praise of his new home. "Life in Singapore is like an allegro," he says. "Fast, furious, and fun."

Many of the newcomers find themselves featured performers at the Esplanade Arts Center, a stunning $356 million complex on the waterfront. It is affectionately known as "The Durian" because its spiky architectural skin resembles the popular fruit of Southeast Asia. Opened in 2002, the Esplanade has been a magnet for performing artists, including Lan, interested in relocating.

"Singapore has created a dynamic culture and arts scene," says Joanne Blakemore, president of the American Association of Singapore. "Some say they bought it, but so what if they did? They are playing catch-up, and they're doing a good job. They have created a

> **Know Thy Competition**
>
> "It is not only in high-tech industries, but in a whole range of other sectors that we hope to bring in people who can share their expertise," says Contact Singapore's Daniel.

society based on economic success. Now they've got to create the other part." Another boisterous supporter of Singapore's cultural initiatives is mentor minister Lee: "If we continue on this course, we will develop the finer graces of life."

The Lion City's media scene is also heating up. Included in the government's plan are a series of initiatives designed to attract global talent, particularly Asian and Pan-Asian actors and professionals. Bilingual Chinese American actor Allan Wu, a graduate of the University of California at Berkeley, is part of the new breed of foreign talent who are finding Singapore an ideal spot to break into the Asian media scene. "It's a great base for those who are trying to converge in Asia," he says. "I love the buzz and energy here." Today, Wu stars in top-rated Mandarin serials and movies, represents Adidas regionally, and is a bona fide celebrity.

For the same reasons, media pioneer Sunita Rajan chose Singapore as the regional hub for BBC World. After starting up Star TV in India and helping launch Channel V in Hong Kong, the Indian-born Rajan concluded that operating out of one of Asia's most-wired countries made perfect sense. "Singapore is a place of ideas, creativity, and conductivity. It's very exciting to be in the midst of this vibrant and cosmopolitan climate," says Rajan, who speaks eight languages.

● ● ●

In the midst of its skyscrapers, it is easy to view Singapore as a thoroughly Western city, albeit more efficient than most. In truth, however, the city-state's multiethnic influences keep it eclectically Asian at heart.

Singapore's Wall Street is Shenton Way, where the culture, in offices and on the street, is very British. Winding through the business district is the Singapore River, lined with boisterous bistros and fashionable boutiques. Nearby are Victorian government buildings and a cricket field—reminders of the days when Singapore was the British navy's easternmost outpost for refueling and refitting ships.

Ten minutes north of downtown and away from the revitalized waterfront is the older Orchard Road area, where tropical trees and gardens intermingle with shops and cabarets. There you'll find luxury hotels, dazzling restaurants, and funky bars, as well as a statue of the legendary symbol of Singapore—the Merlion, a mythical lion-cum–sea horse.

Farther out, the city's older ethnic neighborhoods offer unexpected backstreet delights. Chinatown evolved around 1821, when the first junks arrived from Xiamen in China's Fujian Province. Today, it boasts beautifully restored Chinese shop fronts with elaborate facades around the Tanjong Pagar Conservation Area, giving way to slightly less tidy but colorful streets, where vendors sell a variety of wares, from traditional herbs to snake wine.

The best time to visit is when Singapore celebrates its Chinese heritage and marks the Lunar New Year, typically in late January and early February. The city comes alive, its markets full of festive goods, a spectacular concentration of lights, and the throbbing drumbeats of lion dances. Mandarin oranges are exchanged for good luck, and children receive *ang pow,* red packets filled with token sums of money. Choose the last night of the Lunar New Year for full effect.

Little India is well worth seeing, too. Indians began settling the area around Serangoon Road in the 1820s, when the British brought Tamil convicts to work the brick kilns. Though new condominiums and subways have encroached in recent years, this busy, noisy, and garrulous enclave still offers a sensory treat: beautiful Indian ladies glide by in colorful saris; a parrot picks out a lucky card and his master tells a fortune. Here, you can buy almost anything that is Indian—from Kashmir silk and pop art posters of Hindu gods to the latest movies from Bollywood.

The Kampong Glam district and Arab Street provide further variety. The Sultan Mosque, Singapore's largest, was built in the early 1820s with a $1,500 grant from Stamford Raffles himself. The current structure, rebuilt in 1928, is a dramatic building with golden domes and minarets that glisten in the sun. The old-fashioned streets in the area form the focal point of Muslim life in Singapore. Nothing beats the bazaar-style shopping, where visitors can haggle over baskets and batiks, camel-skin handbags, and cloisonné boxes.

Singapore's glorious food, however, is perhaps its unequaled attraction. Eating is arguably the national pastime. This melting pot of culinary traditions serves the full range of flavors and spices, from hawker chow to haute cuisine, from pepper crab to pizza.

No sterile ghost town when it comes to nightlife, the city has a watering hole, karaoke bar, or dance club to suit every taste. There's even a comedy club: the Boom Boom Room (yes, there is humor in Singapore).

You can feel the heartbeat of Asia in Singapore. As you mingle with people of different cultures, from different walks of life, you realize that all of them are bound by one common thread—a desire to live and work in one of the region's most vibrant cities. For Singaporeans, this diverse crossroads truly combines the best of East and West.

Working in such a mélange of cultures has given British management consultant Ian Speirs a real edge in understanding the Asian perspective. "Singapore is perfectly positioned to let me enjoy and explore the region," he says. When he's not trekking to exotic locales, Speirs plays a key role in WatsonWyatt's Asia/Pacific operations. His wanderlust has posted him in the United Kingdom, Australia, and a variety of other spots. But he keeps coming back to the Lion City, where he has spent fifteen years, off and on.

Speirs gives Singapore high marks for its pragmatic approach to attracting top-notch international talent and creating a home to the world. "We've got all the right pieces here," he told me. "It's 'Asia for beginners.'" On the one hand, he relishes the multicultural street life of the tropical city. On the other, he cites the constant energy of the place, the sense of a nation going places.

> **Act Now**
>
> "Singapore's perfectly positioned," says WatsonWyatt's Speirs. "Its real challenge is the mounting competition from neighboring economies."

No surprise, then, that he chose to become a permanent resident a few years ago. Now, Speirs keeps his finger on the pulse of important trends in the region. "Singapore's real challenge," he believes, "will be to jump-start its long record of growth in the face of mounting competition from neighboring economies." Especially worrisome are surging India and China. "They want all the chips," he contends. "They want to mimic our success in every way."

As a hedge, Singapore has been using its deep pockets and advanced economy to forge bonds with both countries. For several years, its companies have been expanding into India and buying Indian businesses. For example, government-owned Singapore Telecommunications Ltd. owns roughly 28 percent of Bharti Tele-Ventures Ltd., India's second-largest privately run cellular provider. Singapore's government-owned developer Ascendas Pte. is a co-owner of India's first—and biggest—technology park in Bangalore. Singapore's Temasek, the well-heeled investment arm of the government, and other agencies have invested close to $1 billion in India in less than a year. Likewise, 1,400 Indian companies have offices in Singapore; nineteen of the top twenty Indian technology firms, including powerful Infosys, Wipro, and Tata Consultancy Services, are in town. Government officials acknowledge that Singapore can't battle low-cost India head-on in outsourcing and back-office operations. Hence, its goal: "front-office Singapore, back-office India."

As for China, Singapore has "no wish to become merely an adjunct to the Chinese economy," says Trade and Industry Minister George Yeo. Besides courting mainland Chinese experts, the government has wooed about 160 Chinese companies to the island; it wants to attract at least 100 more over the next three years. On the flip side, hundreds of Singaporean companies have expanded into the People's Republic. One prime example is Flextronics International, the world's largest manufacturer of electric goods. "China is where we will have our biggest footprint," says Michael Marks, chief executive of the Singapore-based giant.

If you can't beat 'em, join 'em. That's Singapore's current strategy in dealing with these two awakening superpowers. Collaboration, suggests mentor minister Lee, "is a way of maximizing whatever [advantages] you have." In an increasingly interdependent world, small states such as Singapore prefer the pragmatic approach of partnering. "This is an unfair world," he explains philosophically. "But the world has never been fair. One tribe is always stronger, has bigger people, more people, better soil, a better climate, and better luck." His son, the prime minister, agrees: "When you are very small, you either hang together or you hang separately."

Singapore is always conscious that it is swimming with much bigger fish. Hypersensitive to perceived dangers, people here typically see disaster just around the corner. The residue of anxiety probably reflects the nation's difficult history of colonialism, Japanese occupation, and long-standing spats with its prickly neighbors. And its vulnerability was heightened recently when cracks in the economy began to appear.

A combination of flexibility and dogged determination, however, has enabled this mini-nation to steer a remarkably steady course though the Asian economic crisis, SARS, and the war in Iraq. Last year, Singapore's fortunes reversed. The country witnessed a whopping economic gain of 8.4 percent. Record export performance made it the world's fifteenth-largest trading economy. According to the World Economic Forum, it is the best positioned country to exploit information and communications technology. Today, the city-state enjoys one of the highest living standards in Asia; its per-capita income exceeds that of many Western countries. Singapore is back on the fast track.

Lee Kuan Yew often speaks of having a long antenna to see what is coming. His mantra: the farther one can see, the better off one is. Taking a long-term view of the world, the eighty-one-year-old father of the city-state and its leader for more than forty years believes the best years lie ahead.

"Singapore is like an aircraft flying at 30,000 feet," he says. "We have to have another 6,000 feet to rise to the 36,000-foot level," referring to the mock altitude of its rivals in the West. "The generation now in their thirties to fifties can take Singapore there in the next fifteen to twenty years," Lee predicts. "The best is yet to come."

the china
syndrome

Let China sleep. When it
awakens, it will shake the world.

—NAPOLEON

The first of October, 1949, Founder's Day of the People's Republic of China (PRC): Chairman Mao Tse-tung stood on the giant balcony of the Gate of Heavenly Peace, the entrance to the five-hundred-year-old imperial palace in Beijing. Before him a sea of red flags waved enthusiastically, held aloft by scores of thousands representing the 650 million citizens of the world's newest nation. Disheveled, robust, and earthy, Mao proclaimed in his harsh Hunanese dialect: "The People's Republic of China is now established. The Chinese people have stood up!"

The celebration marked the end of 2,500 years of struggle against European colonialism, Japanese imperialism, and Soviet adventurism, not to mention infighting among the nation's many feudal warlords. For Mao and his fellow revolutionaries, Founder's Day also marked the end of years spent in filthy jails, hairbreadth escapes, secret meetings, and watery soups. For the next quarter-century, the brutish dictator would be the PRC's unchallenged leader.

Following Mao's death in 1976, China began looking westward. Capitalism became the white knight, communism the white elephant—and ideology gave way to pragmatism. "It doesn't matter whether the cat is black or white, as long as it catches the mouse," said charismatic senior leader Deng Xiaoping. Grand notions of a class struggle with the bourgeoisie soon were eclipsed by a new set of needs: creativity and innovation, access to the latest technology and training, and efficient business enterprises. After watching China sputter through decades of isolation and poverty, Deng began liberalizing the economy in 1978—exhorting the nation that "to get rich is glorious."

At the heart of his "open door" reforms were various initiatives to integrate China into the world. Deng began by eliminating the central government's monopoly over foreign trade and investment. In addition, he established four experimental economic zones: three in Guangdong Province, next door to Hong Kong, the other in Fujian Province, across the straits from Taiwan. These trading areas enjoyed varying degrees of autonomy, as well as tax breaks and other privileges. Beijing pushed vigorously for entry into GATT, adopted copyright laws to protect intellectual property, cracked down on trademark infringement, and took other actions widely heralded by the West. The result: an unparalleled economic boom—transforming the country and tripling its GNP during Deng's reign from 1978 to 1997. So profound, in fact, was China's effort to enter the global economy that historian Arthur Schlesinger Jr. coined an oxymoron to describe it: "capitalistic communism."

Thucydides had it right 2,500 years ago when he said that rising powers challenge the international order. He was talking about Sparta's challenge to Athenian dominance. In the twilight of Maoism, it is the People's Republic of China that now threatens the status quo. If the nineteenth century belonged to Britain and the twentieth century to the United States, then the twenty-first century will surely belong to China. The country's global ascent, more apparent now with its membership in the World Trade Organization, is helping it replace the United States as the dominant force in Asia. This year, the PRC is expected to lead the region with 8.2 percent growth, according to the Asian Development Bank. For the past twenty-five years, its real GNP has expanded at an average of 9.4 percent per year, making China's economy the sixth largest in the world. By 2041, according to investment banker Goldman Sachs, China will overtake the United States as the planet's largest economy. "As the world's economic center of gravity shifts to Asia, U.S. preeminence will inevitably diminish," says economist Jeffrey D. Sachs of Columbia University. *Yu shi ju jin*—look out world, here we come—therefore, seems the appropriate slogan.

> **Know Thy Competition**
>
> "As the world's center of gravity shifts to Asia, U.S. preeminence will inevitably diminish," predicts Columbia's Sachs.

China's twenty-five-year metamorphosis from hidebound communism and faded Marxist-Leninist politics to a furiously competitive brand of "socialism with Chinese characteristics" (as Deng Xiaoping put it) is breathtaking. The country's rags-to-riches makeover has benefited hundreds of millions of Chinese, especially in eastern and coastal China. International trade has skyrocketed, approaching one-fourth of the country's GNP. These days, the People's Republic is a market-driven, consumer-oriented nation in which mobile phones, personal computers, fast food, and designer garb are the standard bill of fare. It is also an investor's dream.

For the past decade, foreigners have been pouring money into the PRC, particularly in the coastal provinces, where 70 percent of foreign direct investment is located. The government reported that overseas investors committed $60 billion in 2004, the largest amount to any country. Microsoft, Intel, Motorola, General Motors, and McDonald's are just a few of the American firms making their mark on the mainland. But the biggest influx has come from well-heeled Chinese businessmen living abroad. Overseas Chinese from Hong Kong and Taiwan (mostly those with roots in Guangdong or Fujian Province) account for more than half of all foreign direct investment. About 1 million of Taiwan's 23 million people now reside in China—half of them *Taishang,* or businessmen, according to the country's Mainland Affairs Office.

Foreign investors are cashing in on China's enormous, skilled, and disciplined labor pool, whose members work for a fraction of the wages their counterparts in the West are paid. The PRC has more than one-fifth of the world's population (almost twice that of the European Union and the United States combined) and a workforce of roughly 744 million. After independence, the country quickly became a cheap-labor workshop for the world, producing everything from widgets to washing machines. But increasingly, multinational companies are looking to China more for its brains than its brawn. They hope to tap the country's huge and rapidly growing stock of technical talent. (China annually educates four times as many engineers as the United States.)

With help from the West, Beijing wants China to become a serious force in Space Age arenas, ascending the technology ladder at an unprecedented pace. It is already an emerging contender in satellite launching. Witness the country's successful manned space flight last year and its commitment to establish a permanent space station within fifteen years. China's next targets are advanced electronics, superconductivity, biotechnology, nanotechnology, optics, and other twenty-first-century sectors. Over the years, the PRC will become "a furiously formidable competitor for companies that run the entire length of the technology food chain," predicts Michael Moritz, the famed Silicon Valley venture capitalist.

> **Celebrate Science and Technology**
>
> China's favorite targets include satellite launching, advanced electronics, superconductivity, biotechnology, nanotechnology, and optics.

Along with many other China watchers, he expects the country's technology-driven leap forward to usher in a new growth spurt.

Capitalism with Chinese characteristics is gripping the nation's leaders as well. Jack Welch's autobiography sold hundreds of thousands of copies in Chinese translation. "I read it and enjoyed it very much," admits one Soviet-trained Chinese official, who prefers to remain anonymous. Only a few years ago, no senior party member would have admitted to being captivated by the life story of one of America's best-known capitalists.

Taking a page out of Welch's book, the PRC is practicing the art of global reach. Its preferred vehicle is the multinational corporation. Actually, China's efforts to build global companies are not new. For years, China State Construction Engineering Corp., the nation's largest building firm, has been sending thousands of its employees abroad to work on projects ranging from highways in North Korea and office buildings in Yemen to schools in South Carolina and subways in Brooklyn. Last year, China's construction companies won international contracts worth $17.7 billion, according to the Beijing-based China International Contractors Association, which represents 1,000 Chinese firms doing business around the world.

Today, PRC companies are involved in an array of overseas projects: shopping malls in France and Thailand, a securities house in the United States, a marketing company in South Africa, a bank in the Cayman Islands, and steel mills in Peru. Powerful global wannabes such as Lenovo (formerly Legend), the world's third-largest maker of desktop PCs, which purchased IBM's PC business for $1.75 billion; telecom force Huawei Technologies; consumer electronics giants TCL International and Konka Group; chemicals conglomerate China Blue Star; and appliance maker Haier—all are holding their own against leading multinationals from the United States, Japan, and Europe.

Thomas Jefferson once suggested that a little revolution now and then was a good thing. While the luster of the communist revolution and of the Maoist figures who won it more than half a century ago is fading away, platoons of eager young expatriate entrepreneurs, scientists, and engineers—and their financial backers—are returning to China to pursue their revolutionary dreams. This new generation is highly valued in a nation where patriotic feeling is a deep well.

Since the late 1970s, when Deng broke with the PRC's isolationist policies, more than 400,000 students from mainland China have left the country to train in the West. Many have stayed there, acquiring a familiarity with cutting-edge academic research and its commercialization. Only an estimated 25 percent to 35 percent have returned home. "When you go into laboratories around the world, some of the brightest people are Chinese," says Juan Enriquez-Cabot, director of the Life Sciences Project at Harvard Business School. Today, nearly 40,000 China-born scientists and engineers ply their trade in the United States, more than in any other country.

The Chinese believe that—irrespective of where people were born, where they live, or what their native tongue is—if they have Chinese blood, they are Chinese. Reportedly, any overseas Chinese individual is welcome and entitled to a PRC passport. So it was understandable that, in the 1980s, Beijing began to tap into what former prime minister Zhao Ziyang called China's "stored brainpower overseas." To reverse decades of exodus, government officials started wooing back the Chinese diaspora. From Shanghai to Guangzhou, local governments today are offering them everything from Western-style salaries and benefits to tax breaks, free housing, and venture capital funding. Chinese businesses are helping spearhead the gold rush for overseas talent. In addition to their special Web sites, TV spots, and print ads, many companies participate actively in job fairs in the United States. Those in Silicon Valley (where Beijing maintains a liaison office) regularly pitch up to 4,000 Chinese engineers, scientists, and professionals keen to explore opportunities in the old country.

Dust Off the Welcome Mat

In the 1980s, the Middle Kingdom began to tap what former prime minister Zhao Ziyang called China's "stored brainpower overseas."

"We're trying to lure the best talent in the Valley to work in China," says Wu Ying, vice chairman of UTStarcom, which makes low-cost mobile phones and generated more than $2 billion in revenues in 2003. With an electrical engineering degree from New Jersey Institute of Technology and work experience at Bell Labs, Wu is the prototypical homing pigeon. In 1985, he arrived in Newark for his studies with just $27 in his pocket. To earn a living, he worked as a porter with Vietnamese refugees and illegal immigrants. Wu returned to China to launch his first business in 1991. Today, his net worth exceeds $150 million—thanks to the success of his NASDAQ-listed telecom equipment company and a first-class management team composed of Chinese nationals, Chinese Americans, and Taiwanese who have worked abroad for many years.

"Over there [in China] people are welcomed with open arms," says Robert Lee, chief executive of two Silicon Valley software companies and president of the Asia American MultiTechnology Association, one of several business associations made up primarily of Chinese engineers from Hong Kong and the mainland. The tens of millions of other prosperous overseas Chinese are tremendous assets in snatching top talent. Asia's richest man, Hong Kong billionaire Li Ka-Shing (a major benefactor of Singapore Management University), aims to entice Chinese scientists and professionals to spend time on or relocate to the mainland. One of his first catches is Soucheng Zhang, forty-one, who holds joint appointments in the physics departments of Stanford and Beijing's prestigious Tsinghua University, where Li has funded a professorship. In addition to his academic duties, Zhang serves as a vice president of Hua Yuan Science & Technology Association, a Palo Alto–based group of 3,000 scientists and venture capitalists who promote exchanges between the United States and the PRC.

Dongping Zhu directs Santa Clara–based Zaptron Systems, a seven-year-old firm that develops and markets data-mining software and services. "Data mining is the development of new knowledge by analyzing existing information," he explains. The prospect of finding hidden treasure inside the foggy bottoms of behemoth companies and government agencies has spurred a wealth of sophisticated technologies. Using projective geometry, pattern typologies, and other space-age techniques, Zaptron is "turning data into dollars."

Zhu was one of 50,000 Chinese students studying in the United States who were granted permanent residency after the Tiananmen Square riots in 1989. He earned a doctorate in electrical engineering from Virginia Tech and worked for InVision, Loral GlobalStar, and Aptronix before founding Zaptron. Then China's booming economy and improved political situation convinced him to return home, where he now spends most of his time.

Like Stanford's Zhang, Zhu is actively involved in China's high-tech development. For several years he has led the Silicon Valley Chinese Overseas Business Association, promoting the exchange of technical know-how, leadership training, and venture capital between the PRC and northern California. "There's much potential in the interaction of the Silicon Valley and Chinese markets," Zhu says. From his base in Beijing, he hopes to realize some of that potential.

Establish Dual Loyalties

"There's much potential in the interaction of the Silicon Valley and Chinese markets," says Zaptron's Zhu, who shuttles between Beijing and Santa Clara.

As the repatriation trend gains momentum, some of those who attained U.S. citizenship or permanent residency are holding onto their American passports or green cards as they test the waters back home. Many business executives and top scientists, including Zhang and Zhu, shuttle back and forth between China and the United States so frequently that they are jokingly called *tai kunren,* or astronauts. Flight capital is no longer a one-way street.

China's bold initiatives, combined with the magnetic pull of a high-octane economy and the hope of greater political freedom, are producing results. The nation's brain drain days appear to be over as the PRC becomes the new land of opportunity. Last year, more than

20,000 émigrés came home, up from 5,800 in 1995. In the last several years, fast-paced Shanghai reports that 30,000 returnees are working or starting their own businesses; 90 percent of them hold a master's degree or a doctorate from foreign universities. Local officials expect the number to grow to 120,000 by 2010.

"It used to be that if you went to the United States, it was, 'Bye-bye, see you when you're sixty-five,'" says Ping Ko, a former professor of microelectronics at the University of California at Berkeley, who runs a high-tech venture capital company in China. "But opportunity now is worldwide. It's no different than working in California and looking for job opportunities in Texas." The environment has completely changed, adds Stanford's Zhang. "People going back really want to be on the ground floor of something very exciting."

The rich seam of brainpower coming home represents the full spectrum of occupations, including lawyers. China's economic modernization is straining its embryonic legal system, and Beijing wants to double its supply of lawyers. (Attorneys were barred from practice as recently as 1979.) So the PRC is looking abroad to expand its legal force—a plan that some Americans consider a mixed blessing. "We've got stacks of applications from star law students and young lawyers—people who two or three years ago were staying in the United States," says Patrick Nolan, a partner at the law firm of O'Melveny & Myers.

Leaving America for China has its drawbacks. Among others, returnees can expect to take a 30 percent to 50 percent pay cut. But increasingly, that concern is muted by other considerations. Some Chinese attribute their homeward-bound thinking to a chillier reception in America after the September 11 attacks. For other émigrés, coming home is a shortcut up the career ladder. Like their Indian counterparts, a number of them experienced an invisible but clearly felt cap on their upward mobility in America. "In the United States, there is a glass ceiling," recalls Ying Luo, an eighteen-year veteran of several U.S. pharmaceutical companies and CEO of Shanghai Genomics. "I don't call it discrimination, but the higher you go, the more political it is. It was difficult for me to merge into business society at the top level." For similar reasons, Cynthia Chen, thirty-eight, left Silicon Valley's venture capital industry thirteen years ago. "In my specialty of investments, cultural connections were especially important," she explains. "My peers had social connections that I didn't have."

Many returnees share a deep passion to remake their country. As chairman of state-owned China Netcom, Ed Tian (see chapter 1) is reprogramming China so that more than a billion people can join the new world order. "We are basically wiring the nation with fiber that will bring limitless opportunities to our people," he says. "With our technology, enlightenment can flow through the taps like water." For others, homecoming simply means getting in touch with their roots. "It's the connections of your heart," investment banker Chen told *USA Today*. "You always have a dream: 'Oh, if I could go back and see how my parents and friends are doing.' You always miss your home."

But, ironically, one of the major obstacles confronting returnees is rejection by family and friends. "The biggest hindrance I had in recruiting top Chinese scientists back to the country was the backlash expressed by their parents, who actually wanted them to *stay* in the States," says Kai-Fu Lee, founder of Microsoft's highly touted regional research lab in Beijing. "Parents told their offspring, 'Look, you've made it in the big time. Why come home?' I know this attitude still persists, although it may be softening a bit."

Obstacles aside, many New China companies are benefiting from the homing pigeon phenomenon, including Intrinsic Technology, a mobile software firm founded in 1999. "When we started recruiting, convincing Chinese to come back home and work here in China, it was like convincing them to work in Africa," recalls Patrick Benzie, one of Intrinsic's founding partners. "Now, people who went

> **Target the Best Minds**
>
> "People who went to Silicon Valley twelve to fifteen years ago are eagerly coming back and bringing the skills needed to run a sophisticated business," says Benzie.

to Silicon Valley twelve to fifteen years ago are eagerly coming back and bringing with them the skills needed to run a sophisticated business."

Actually, these émigrés' greatest impact may be the flow of new ideas into this once-isolated nation. Most of them are in their thirties and forties. Many have prominent positions in the private sector, but more are taking government jobs. This new generation understands how the outside world works and, therefore, helps reinforce Beijing's "go global" reforms. "China needs this top-level talent who not only understand the country but also embrace advanced foreign concepts and technologies," concedes Hu Ping, an official at the Shanghai Pudong Service Center for Returned Overseas Students, one of several government agencies that helps returnees assimilate. "They can help people who haven't left China learn a lot of new skills," adds Hu Jiahuan, manager of the New Hi-Tech Personnel and Labor Bureau for Hangzhou, a city of 6 million people. "They bring a whole new way of thinking."

This cosmopolitan view of the world and fresh perspective are in keeping with the government's efforts to steer the economy away from the entrenched, heavy-handed state policies of the past. For example, professor Hai Wen, a University of California at Davis alum, directs Beijing University's prestigious Center for Economic Research. The entire faculty is Western educated, paving the way for a more entrepreneurial, market-driven, technology-oriented economy. "We're trying to provide an independent view to Chinese leaders," says Hai.

Outsiders also are contributing. Beijing's mandarins believe that infusing foreign talent into the economy will jump-start modernization and entrepreneurship. In March 2004, Jinjiang International Holding Co., China's largest hotel operator, headhunted fifty-four-year-old Christopher Bachran as its new president. The Hawai'i-born hotelier brought with him thirty years' experience in the industry, including twenty years in Southeast Asia.

"I have to admit, I didn't know much about the company," says Bachran. The massive conglomerate, one of Shanghai's most promising state enterprises, runs 128 hotels, including the famous Peace Hotel on the Bund. Beijing hopes this high-level Westerner can raise the chain's level of service, assist its ambitious overseas expansion plans, and secure it a listing on a major foreign stock exchange. Bachran told me that "it will take some time for Jinjiang International to achieve fame in the world market."

Dean Ho took a more circuitous route to China. The third-generation Chinese American, educated at the University of California at Berkeley and Cornell, said aloha to his father and mentor, Chinn Ho, the legendary Hawai'i financier and real estate developer, and hometown Honolulu in 1986. Initially, the younger Ho went to Beijing to oversee the management of the Great Wall Sheraton, the city's first Western-style hotel. Returning to Hawai'i in the late eighties, he immersed himself in Mandarin, a language he had studied in high school and college, in preparation for his eventual emigration.

Today, the sixty-something entrepreneur manages Unison Building Systems, which is involved in construction management and property development in greater Shanghai. The city's breakthrough year, he contends, was 1990, when the mammoth financial and commercial center of Pudong opened. "I was wrong initially," he concedes. "I thought Pudong was a mistake. But, in fact, it was a remarkably well-planned effort—an enormous accomplishment. It represented a sense of grandness that matched the Chinese ego."

Bachran and Ho are modern-day Marco Polos. But these two expatriates—unlike the thirteenth-century adventurer who left the Middle Kingdom with little more than his memories—are likely to return stateside with a sense of accomplishment for having helped transform China from a Third World country into a nation respected around the world.

> **Expand the Workforce**
>
> China has also been tapping a number of foreign expats— modern-day Marco Polos— who can help the country fulfill its economic dreams.

Beijing hopes that these imports, as well as its émigrés, will create additional job opportunities for the nation's vast labor pool. China needs 12 million to 15 million new jobs every year just to keep up with its population growth. Therefore, it is at a critical juncture in economic restructuring and reform. The government believes that attracting the thousands of Chinese who studied or worked in the United States, as well as their foreign counterparts such as Bachran and Ho, can spell the difference between success and failure. Let's examine the two favorite homes for these talented recruits: Shanghai and Beijing.

"Every so often Shanghai cleans itself, like a swan in an oily river," goes a line from *The Shanghai Gesture,* a 1940s B-movie. The city's reputation as a melting pot between East and West arose during the century of Western domination, from 1841 to 1945. Called "Paris of the East" and "Whore of the Orient," Shanghai was considered a foreigner's playhouse—a notorious city of quick riches, ill-gotten gains, and lost fortunes. Its superb coastal location on the Yangtze River delta, limited interference from the central government, and capitalist edge made it China's business hub. Trade and commerce boomed, and by 1850 special settlements had sprung up to house all sorts of foreigners.

At the turn of the twentieth century, Shanghai embraced 1 million people. Textiles, real estate, banking, shipping, and insurance replaced traditional trade in opium, silk, and tea. Compradors oversaw buying and selling, providing a vital link between the natives and outsiders. As the country's most westernized city, Shanghai attracted immigrants from around the world who poured capital and expertise into the burgeoning metropolis. In contrast, its Asian competitors—Tokyo, Hong Kong, and Singapore—seemed like provincial backwaters.

This boisterous, beguiling city became a roiling, boiling stew of clashing interests. Russian émigrés competed with Yankee wildcatters eager to tap the nation's oil wealth. German equipment makers crossed swords with French investment bankers. British griffins, or new boys, fresh out of Oxford and Cambridge, joined the ranks of the great Hong Kong trading houses such as Butterfield & Swire and Jardine Matheson of *Noble House* fame.

Amid the din of honking lorries and trotting rickshaws, foreigners lived in cozy enclaves on quiet, narrow, tree-lined streets in elegant, tile-roofed houses and enjoyed eye-popping privileges and hedonistic pleasures. The common bond between the different nationalities was making money. "Commerce was the beginning, the middle, and the end of our life in China," wrote British trader Charles Dyce. "That is to say, that if there was no trade, not a single man, except missionaries, would have come here at all."

Other than the local warlords and the wealthy merchant class, Shanghainese were excluded from the party. Crippled by hunger and poverty, the Chinese provided the cheap labor that kept the city running. Thousands of workers were exploited in cotton-spinning factories that ran twenty-four hours a day. By the 1930s, life expectancy was twenty-seven years. Starving peasants often sold their children into prostitution, where young girls served as high-class escorts in the clubs of the international settlement, or as *ye yi* ("wild chickens") who prowled the streets and back alleys. Amid this degradation, intellectuals and students led a quiet revolution against foreign domination.

According to most Sinologists, the so-called golden era of Old Shanghai began to dissolve with the first Japanese attack on the city in 1932. Up to then, Shanghai was the most international, romantic, and adventurous post in Asia. Art deco cinemas, hot jazz bands, the latest fashions, even a foreign-run racetrack blended East and West. The city was a place of intense energy where two cultures met and neither prevailed. Chinese girls, dressed in figure-hugging *qipaos* (the Mandarin word for traditional Chinese-style dresses), smoked American cigarettes, while local magazines carried ads for Colgate toothpaste and Kodak film. The best place to watch the swinging city was the glorious Bund, the riverfront strip of turn-of-the-century colonial buildings housing Shanghai's Wall Street. A favorite viewing spot was the Cathay Hotel (now the Peace Hotel) overlooking the Huangpu River, where the guest list included Charlie Chaplin, George Bernard Shaw, and Noel Coward, who wrote much of *Private Lives* there.

By the mid-1930s, Shanghai was the world's largest city, providing a safe haven for more than 70,000 foreigners among its population of 3 million. Its mix of people—from movers and shakers to those on the run—was unequaled anywhere in the world. "Charles Darwin would have found Shanghai as fascinating as the Galápagos Islands," said one observer of the times.

Shanghai's shenanigans came to an abrupt end under Japanese rule, an era of political assassinations and fear. With the establishment of the PRC in 1949, the dour strains of communism further obliterated the city's decadent heyday. There would be no more fashion, music, or romance. "The world has lost Old Shanghai," wrote author Ralph Shaw at the time. "The Leninist-Marxist thoughts of Chairman Mao have swept away the last lingering whispers of a hundred years of sensuality."

For years, the Reds regarded the city as a hotbed of Western imperialist influence, condemning it to an enforced slumber. That changed in 1991, when reformist Deng decided that Shanghai should regain its preindependence glory as the showcase for the country's economic renaissance—aiming to rival Hong Kong by 2010. Since then, this city of 16 million has endeavored to become the center of the New Asia—a fusion of East and

> **Adapt—or Die**
>
> Deng selected Shanghai, once condemned to an enforced slumber, as the showcase for the country's economic rebirth.

West, old and new. In fact, the city government has set a goal of 5 percent foreign residents in order to be a truly "international city."

To restore Shanghai's image as a foreigner-friendly melting pot, city fathers sought to capture a variety of high-profile events that would focus world attention on the capital's new cosmopolitan bent. In 1999, Shanghai hosted the Fortune 500 summit; two years later, the Asia-Pacific Economic Corporation meetings; and, last year, China's first Formula One car races. Buoyed by these successes, Shanghai secured the 2010 World Expo (the world's third-largest event, after the

Olympics and the World Cup). The city is expected to spend $3 billion for the opportunity to showcase its resurgent glory. If all goes well, the Expo will attract up to 65 million visitors.

For almost fifteen years, Beijing has been pouring money into Shanghai. In the mid-1990s, a quarter of the world's building cranes were busy swiveling to and fro on countless work sites throughout the sprawling metropolis. As part of Deng's order to restore the city's former status as a commercial center, the government targeted Pudong, across the Huangpu River from Shanghai. Billions of dollars later, the Singapore-size former agricultural area has transformed into Shanghai's ultramodern financial and business district. Once dismissed as a white elephant, skyscraper-filled Pudong now houses the Shanghai Stock Exchange; Jin Mao Tower, the city's most spectacular and beautiful building; the unmistakable 1,535-foot-tall Oriental Pearl TV Tower; and a sleek international airport, connected to the dome-covered Longyang Metro Station by the world's fastest magnetic-levitation train. Under construction is the world's tallest building, designed by Sandi Pei, son of renowned architect I. M. Pei. Minutes away is the Pudong industrial zone where Intel, Corning, Matsushita, Thyssen-Krupp, Alcatel, and other leading multinationals produce everything from high-end microchips to digital switching systems. Across the river is Fudan University's highly acclaimed Microelectronics Institute, cranking out some of the most advanced semiconductor research in the country. "It's just like Stanford or Berkeley in Silicon Valley," says Tan Tingao, the institute's head.

A few years ago, Beijing designated Shanghai as the heart of its twenty-first-century electronics industry. Already, the city and the surrounding Yangtze delta are home to numerous state-of-the-art semiconductor plants. Chip output may hit $34 billion by year's end, according to researcher IC Insights. In fact, China's Labor Ministry estimates the nation will need 300,000 additional integrated-circuit designers and more than 1,000 senior technical managers by 2010.

Three years ago, James Gao, a Nanjing native, returned to Shanghai after eleven years in the United States to set up Apex

Microelectronics, Inc., an integrated-circuit design firm. He received a modest $12,000 grant from the Shanghai government. But the real attraction was the wealth of semiconductor plants in the area. "Everything comes to Shanghai in the semiconductor business," the thirty-seven-year-old Gao says. "[Even the money] is a sign of support that the government gives returnees."

Hao Min, another homing pigeon, also forsook the United States for hometown Shanghai. In 1998, the thirty-five-year-old electrical engineer with a postdoctoral degree from Stanford returned on the strength of his faith that the city will emerge as a microprocessor powerhouse. Today, he wears two hats, directing the semiconductor lab at Fudan University, one of China's premier institutions, and running Shanghai Hua Hong IC Co., a state-controlled chip designer. In time, Hao believes, many more world-class engineers will move to Shanghai.

> **Celebrate Science and Technology**
>
> Beijing has targeted the software industry as a national priority— hoping to supplant India as the number two producer.

Besides microchips, Beijing has declared the software industry a national priority. It wants to supplant India as the world's second-largest producer of software, after the United States. With 300,000 software professionals and 50,000 new graduates a year, the PRC is closing the technology gap. Also, it has a huge cost advantage: pay levels are a quarter of those in India and one-sixth of U.S. rates. "China's low costs could siphon off high-end work from India, giving Chinese engineers the experience they need to climb the value chain," reports the *Far Eastern Economic Review*.

Ironically, India's Infosys Technologies maintains a software development center in Shanghai, while various Chinese fact-finding delegations regularly visit Bangalore. In fact, China's Huawei Technologies employs seven hundred people, who are soaking up the software programming culture, in its $85 million R&D center in India's high-tech hub. Plans include doubling the workforce in the next two years and moving into a new forty-acre campus now under construction in Bangalore. Conceivably, the PRC could match India by 2006 and become "the next frontier for the offshore market," predicts technology consultant Gartner.

For Chinese policymakers, these high-tech initiatives represent another step up the value chain for the nation's electronics industry, leading to demand for high-skilled, better-paid engineers, particularly those with overseas know-how. What's more, venture capitalists are providing plenty of money to fund new ideas. Thus, China's best technology entrepreneurs are more likely to stay home to launch their new businesses than to head to California or New York.

> **Know Thy Competition**
>
> "The U.S. is falling behind," says Softbank's Son. "For the mass production of electronic goods, China is becoming the new center of the world."

"The United States is falling behind," warns Masayoshi Son, chairman of Softbank, the broadband Internet service provider, and the man often referred to as Japan's Bill Gates. "For the mass production of electronic goods, China is becoming the new center of the world." That was Ling Hai's conclusion. Four years ago, he backtracked from a variety of high-tech jobs overseas to found Sinofusion, a Shanghai-based software services company that competes with American giants Accenture and McKinsey & Co. Its specialty is consulting and high-level designer services for businesses trying to incorporate Internet technologies into their operations. China, however, lacks managers skilled in building such complex businesses. "The problem is finding the middle layer," laments Ling, who is constantly on the lookout for proven middle managers with foreign work experience.

Career opportunities in Shanghai are now the city's biggest drawing card. But it is also easy for émigrés to find a spacious apartment, good Western food, and a Starbucks on every corner. Designed to dazzle, the new Shanghai has something for everyone: Old and New

World architecture, Asia's largest shopping malls, superchic fusion restaurants, minimalist bars, swinging clubs, and the energy and excitement of China's premier business city. "Being in Shanghai is akin to viewing a sociological time-lapse camera on fast play," writes Asiaphile Bradley Mayhew. Small wonder *TIME* magazine recently designated Shanghai "the world's hottest city."

On Shanghai's historic Bund, the sweeping waterfront boulevard, is a string of elegant and carefully preserved buildings now housing top-notch shops and restaurants. M on the Bund, located on the top floor of the 1920s former Nissan Shipping Building, offers salt-encrusted leg of lamb and exquisite Shanghainese goose. Across the road is its newest competitor, 3 on the Bund, a fancy complex with up-market restaurants, including a branch of Jean Georges. For drinks, the in crowd goes to Kathleen's, near People's Square, or Yongfoo Elite, in the former British Consulate Building.

For other dining options, there's the former French Concession, which once housed generals, warlords, rich *tai pans,* and White Russians. Popular Face is perfect for a quiet before-dinner drink, followed by spicy Sichuan food at South Beauty. For Shanghainese cuisine, there is the intimate 1221, the noisier Baoluo Juilon or Yin, near the Jinjiang Hotel. Returning to Pudong, the steak house in the Grand Hyatt offers amazing views from the fifty-sixth floor.

Like Shanghai, Beijing is very much a work in progress. Few cities on Earth have undergone such a rapid transformation, and the changes have many old-timers scratching their heads. Visitors to this boomtown of 12 million see an ostentatious stage set featuring high-rise construction, traffic-snarled junctions, and people trying to make a buck. Forget any visions of Maoist revolutionaries in buttoned-down tunics performing tai chi in the park or bearded old men in thickly quilted jackets with caged songbirds. Today's change agents are stylish, energetic men and women—willing disciples of Adam Smith, not Karl Marx. The younger generation is more interested in Madonna than Mao. Rhetorical slogans from the Cultural Revolution have given way to the lingo of business and the art of the deal.

Progress could not be more apparent. "In Beijing, people hate old things," says thirty-nine-year-old Zhang Xin, the creative force behind SOHO China, one of the city's biggest developers. "The socialist's upbringing did much to destroy tradition, so people have no sense of it. Chinese people are now importing Western traditions—Valentine's, Halloween, everything. But none of it is in the Chinese tradition." Zhang, a confident, polished woman of the world (she went to Cambridge and was an investment banker at Goldman Sachs), returned home to team up with her husband, Pan Shiyi, in the development game. Homing pigeons like Zhang are drawn by the abundant opportunity and emerging buzz of Beijing. They hope to build on a transformation that is well under way, expressing the more international, cosmopolitan, and open city and a society that is quickly and confidently coming of age.

Until recently, Beijing, China's thousand-year-old capital, seemed frozen in time. Developed as a frontier trading post for the Mongols, Koreans, and tribes from Shandong Province and central China, it endured a string of conquerors—from Genghis Khan and the Manchus to the Japanese. After China achieved nationhood in 1949, prospects got no better as the communists stripped the face of the city. Beijing's huge walls—forming the grandest rampart of its kind in urban China—were pulled down, and hundreds of temples and monuments were looted and destroyed. Blocks of buildings were reduced to rubble to widen boulevards. The devastation of Chinese culture continued under Mao's decade-long Cultural Revolution. It was not until Deng Xiaoping's ascendancy that the capital city's fortunes reversed.

During the 1980s and '90s, Beijing awoke from its coma, rectifying the effects of years of damage. The mood today is decidedly upbeat. Party leaders are committed to modernity, at least economically. Political dissent exists, but not unfettered. The government still deletes unfavorable comments from imported newspapers, jams Western TV and radio transmissions, and restricts online access. Nonetheless, Beijing desperately wants to rejoin the community of nations.

Besides pinning its hopes on China's membership in the World Trade Organization, the city's hosting of the 2008 Olympics, at an estimated cost of $20 billion, should be its coming-out party. In addition to the Olympic Park, five new subway lines are slated for development, as well as a Pudonglike magnetic-levitation train to link various athletic venues. This massive effort complements the city's current facelift, which includes new highways, a second international airport, a $365 million world-class theater complex designed by French architect Paul Andreu, and a parade of five-star hotels.

> **Adapt—or Die**
>
> Beijing's planners hope to transform the city into one of the world's great metropolises. Hosting the 2008 Olympics will help.

During the next decade, Beijing's planners intend to propel the city into the heart of the twenty-first century, alongside the world's other great metropolises. Despite the breathless pace of development, the proud capital of modern China has a way to go to catch up with its competitors. Until recently, its Achilles' heel was people, particularly those with cutting-edge skills and international savoir-faire. However, every year thousands of talented overseas Chinese are returning to take advantage of Beijing's economic and scientific opportunities.

China is dotted with districts hailed as this or that city's answer to Silicon Valley. There are more than fifty-five high-tech parks in the country, employing close to 2 million people. The first and largest is Zhougguancum Science Park (ZSP), located in the Haidan District, twelve miles northwest of Beijing's center. Established in May 1988, this Silicon Valley wannabe is a five-mile-long hodgepodge of more than 6,000 tenants: Internet incubators, research institutes, online start-ups, and established high-tech companies. Sutter Hill venture capitalist Len Barker has described ZSP as being "like Silicon Valley in the early days. However, the difference is energy. There's a sense that the fate of a billion people is on the line."

Texas Tech transplant Edward Tian, cofounder of AsiaInfo, the country's first homegrown Internet infrastructure company and the first private Chinese firm to go public in the West, began his reentry in a warehouselike office in ZSP. Following AsiaInfo's success, he went on to found telecom giant China Netcom, where he serves as chief executive. With 22 million new Chinese users joining the Internet last year, the PRC's online population (now 94 million) is expected to outstrip that of the United States by 2006—and Tian is on the ground floor of this boom. Yet Chinese censors, known as "Big Mamas," continue to control the country's cyberspace and freedom of expression. CEO Tian, forty-one, remains positive nonetheless. "We are building our nation so that the people of China will have opportunities they never had before and our nation will thrive," he says. "Imagine what limitless bandwidth can do for China."

Another Internet revolutionary is Charles Zhang, forty, a scholarly entrepreneur with a doctorate in physics from MIT. In 1995, he returned to Beijing and, a year later, founded Sohu.com, the first Chinese-language search engine and directory. The company received $2 million in venture capital from investors, including MIT's digital age guru Nicholas Negroponte and Sloan School professor Edward Roberts, Intel, Dow Jones, and International Data Corp. Sohu, or "search fox" in Chinese, quickly became the country's most popular Web portal, turning a profit of $26 million in 2003.

Zhang attributes the company's success to its ability to mesh East and West. "China is where our roots are and nobody knows it better than we do. We have a perfect balance that blends local expertise and Western management styles." But the climb has not always been smooth. During the dot-com crash, hostile board members and disgruntled investors tried unsuccessfully to replace CEO Zhang. Nor has dealing with the Big Mamas been easy. "We behave as good citizens, so we censor ourselves," he explains. "If you're too confrontational, it's counterproductive. Our best defense is our popularity."

Zhang's dream is to transform his NASDAQ-listed company into the "passport of Chinese into the digital age." Too lofty? Perhaps. But Zhang is not afraid of heights. In 2003, he scaled the face of Mount Everest. "In this business, you cannot rest," he says. Then, taking a page out of Intel legend Andrew Grove's *Only the Paranoid Survive,* Zhang adds: "I'm paranoid all the time."

No less ambitious is Peggy Yu, a forty-year-old MBA from New York University. The Sichuan native left New York for Beijing in 1997, after marrying successful book publisher and future partner Li Guoqing. The couple had monitored the dizzying rise of Amazon.com on Wall Street and dreamed of setting up a similar Chinese-language online bookstore back home. Determined to give it their best shot, they founded Dangdang.com in 1999. (The name comes from the Chinese *xiangdangdang,* meaning "resounding" or "worthy.")

Today, the Beijing-based online retailer sells more than 300,000 different books, CDs, DVDs, and computer games. Co-CEO Yu says they have served more than 2 million customers, with the average order about $10. "We have figured out the basics," she says about Dangdang.com, arguably China's most successful e-commerce venture. As for her best-sellers, six of the top ten books are business titles. Two current favorites are *Who Moved My Cheese?* and *Good to Great.* Chinese soap operas dominate the audiotape market. "This segment is for the more lighthearted," Yu explains.

At the time of Dangdang's launch, though, "we were e-commerce babies," she admits. Unlike the United States, China did not have a national database of book title information, which took the couple two years to compile—a task they compare to building your own bridge to cross a river. In addition, the postal service was unreliable, and few Chinese had credit cards. (Even today, less than 2 percent of retail sales nationwide are conducted with plastic.) The whole thing quickly became exasperating. "It was pretty much a *Mission Impossible* situation," Yu recalls.

The street-smart couple, therefore, shifted to a different strategy, one more in line with a developing economy. They let would-be buyers pay with money orders and old-fashioned cash on delivery. To make sure the packages arrived safely, Dangdang engaged a fleet of delivery boys to zip around China's forty biggest cities on bicycles. The new tactics worked, and the company has never looked back. Indeed, the company's success prompted Amazon to acquire rival joyo.com for $75 million in 2004.

For Yu, the pilgrimage home has never been easy. Besides eliciting the envy of China's stay-at-home women, she occasionally is chided for raising her nine-year-old son, Alexander, with a relatively strong hand, similar to the way she was treated in the sixties and seventies. In urban China today, the country's single-child policy has brought about the "little emperor" syndrome, in which the needs of spoiled children often take precedence. Hence, few people understand Yu's manner. "Everybody says I'm too tough on him," she says.

Undeterred, Yu is committed to fulfilling her dream: to change the way Chinese people think and live. "I don't know if we'll have a massive effect on economic and social life," she says. "But in little pockets, here and there, we can make a difference." There is little doubt that, as tens of thousands of Chinese go online for the first time every day, the country is changing. Thanks to Internet revolutionaries like Yu, China is becoming not only a more attractive place for investors but also a fertile ground for innovation.

Similar optimism abounds at Beijing Genomics Institute (BGI). In 1986, Deng Xiaoping targeted life sciences as a critical future technology. Since then, China's fledgling biotech sector has grown rapidly. There are more than three hundred publicly funded laboratories and roughly one hundred start-up companies, mainly around Beijing and Shanghai. The Science Ministry claims that 20,000 researchers work in life sciences in China, where U.S.-trained Ph.D.s earn about $10,000 a year—one-eighth of their American counterparts. Hence, the government is investing $1.3 billion in biotech between 2001 and 2005 and is aggressively recruiting some of the 20,000 Chinese researchers working abroad.

Beijing has made great strides on the long road to leadership in life sciences. At the five-year-old BGI, not far from the city's main airport, scores of young, ambitious scientists and technicians have produced a string of breakthroughs—from decoding the rice genome, to growing dog-bladder tissue on a mouse's back (a prelude to generating human tissue), to working on a cure for SARS. The institute's director, Wang Huanming, trained in Europe and America before coming home.

China's great leap forward in biotechnology depends on its ability to tap into the tremendous resource base of ethnic Chinese working overseas. "It is very important that so many leading scientists abroad are Chinese," says Jian Wang, a professor at BGI who returned to China after doing postdoctoral work at the University of Washington. "They are the real driving force."

> **Target the Best Minds**
>
> China's leap into biotech depends on snaring gifted Chinese scientists working abroad. "They are the real driving force," says BGI's Wang.

Ultimately, the government wants its ivory towers to become hotbeds of homegrown biotech start-ups. In large part, the nation is depending on Jing Cheng, one of China's most entrepreneurial academics. The forty-two-year-old electrical engineer and molecular biologist, trained in Britain and the United States, has been called "the soul of China's revving biotech machine."

After working in China as a locomotive engineer and a lab assistant, Cheng went to Glasgow, where he earned a doctorate in forensic biology from the University of Strathclyde and gained firsthand knowledge of DNA fingerprinting and other state-of-the-art biotechnologies. In 1994, he headed to America, where he developed automated DNA tests for the predecessor of Beckman Coulter, the scientific instrument maker in Fullerton, California. In the mid-1990s, as a postdoctoral researcher at the University of Pennsylvania, he began experimenting with biochips. This, in turn, led to a job with Nanogen, a biochip pioneer based in San Diego. In 1999, the versatile Cheng cofounded Aviva Biosciences, a San Diego biotech company that employs technology from Beijing's blue-chip Tsinghua University, where Cheng also heads the Centre for Beijing Biochip Technology. As if that were not enough, Cheng runs Capital Biochip, a Beijing-based business that encompasses everything from biochips to dental equipment.

On the whole, returning entrepreneurs such as Cheng would rather have private money than deal with the strings that inevitably come with public funds. Fortunately, more and more Western venture capitalists have been willing to back winners like Cheng who have mastered the art of crossing cultural divides. Still, it will be years before new products start rolling out of PRC labs, and there is no guarantee that the country will ever produce a bevy of blockbuster drugs. "Down the road, maybe in ten to fifteen years, Chinese biotech companies may be able to reach leading positions at the international level," Cheng concedes. "This is not a one-day job. We're really exploring something totally new."

Tsinghua University, long regarded as China's top science and engineering school, is now wooing other disciplines to its campus.

Nourish the Halls of Ivy

In seeking to launch a business school, Tsinghua University reached out to induce Goldman Sachs's John Thornton to join the faculty.

When university officials decided to charter a business school, they tapped John Thornton, president and co-chief operating officer of Goldman Sachs, to join the faculty. Thornton, who remains an adviser to Goldman Sachs, became the first Western business leader to assume a full professorship since the 1949 revolution. "Mr. Thornton's decision to teach here is a treasure for us," says Xia Guangzhi, an executive at the Tsinghua School of Economics and Management, where Thornton, fifty-one, spends most of his time teaching global leadership. "But this is just the start. We hope other high-level foreign managers can also come to work here."

Infusing the university with imported brainpower is inducing many would-be émigrés to stay at home. A decade ago, Tsinghua grads hopped the first plane for the United States or Europe, but no more. "The best Tsinghua students consider going overseas only one option," says Hongjiang Zhang, director of Microsoft's Advanced Technology Center, a division launched in 2003 to accelerate new technologies in the company's global product pipeline. "Ten years ago, it was the only option. I think that's a very positive change." The thirty-ish expert in computer vision, a former research manager at Hewlett-Packard Labs in the United States, returned largely because of China's "investment in education and high-tech push." In just six months last year, Zhang received 10,000 résumés for staff openings at the center. To speed the selection process, his team administered written exams in eleven cities around China. "The biggest challenge is people," says Zhang. "We have to get the right blend of partnership, comradeship, and leadership."

Harry Shum, Zhang's longtime colleague at the world's largest software company, is another U.S. repatriate. Born and raised near Shanghai, he did his graduate work at Carnegie Mellon University and claims he's "still a die-hard Pittsburgh Steelers fan." After a stint at Microsoft Research in Redmond, Washington, the graphics guru returned to China, enticed by the booming economy and the greatly enhanced research and career opportunities. Working with a large pool of well-educated, skilled techies was another draw. "The raw talent here in China is just incredible," says Shum. "Up to undergraduate level, Tsinghua students can compete very well with MIT students. My joke is there are 1.3 billion people in China. Some of them better be smart." Today, Shum runs Microsoft Research Asia in Zhongguan-cum, which houses 150 full-time researchers.

Labeled "the world's hottest computer lab" by MIT's *Technology Review,* Microsoft Research Asia was the creation of another émigré, Kai-Fu Lee. In 1998, the former Carnegie Mellon professor and veteran of Apple Computer and Silicon Graphics moved to Beijing to establish leading-edge technologies for Microsoft's customers. Since its inception, the lab has churned out 750 published papers and hundreds of valuable patents. "There's not a single vice president in the company who doesn't know about the stellar research going on in Beijing," says Lee, now a Microsoft vice president in Redmond. "There's not a single business unit that isn't using the lab's technology."

Microsoft Research Asia's remarkable track record is not lost on Bill Gates, who beams proudly when talk turns to his Beijing bonanza. "People should pay attention to China," says Microsoft's chairman. "It's a phenomenon in every respect."

No question, the People's Republic represents the new wave of scientific and technical know-how. Besides Microsoft, some four hundred foreign companies have recently set up important research centers in China. "It's frightening," admits Ross Armbrecht, president of the Industrial Research Institute, a nonprofit group in Washington that represents large American companies. "But you've got to go where the horses are."

Know Thy Competition

"It's frightening," says Washington-based Armbrecht, of China's ability to woo first-rate brainpower. "But you've got to go where the horses are."

Clearly, China's horses are out of the barn. However, as the PRC anticipates what it feels will be its inevitable domination in Asia, the next generation of thoroughbreds will have to be not only smart but well-rounded. As we saw in India, many primary and secondary schools continue to employ a system of rote memorization, poorly suited to the modern, knowledge-oriented economy. Slowly, efforts to inject more balance and creativity into the school curriculum are beginning to take hold. In the meantime, young urban parents are not taking any chances. They are pushing their offspring to be all they can be. Weekend and after-school classes for three- to twelve-year-olds are a national obsession.

Reform Public Education

Like India and Singapore, the PRC is trading a system of rote memorization for one injecting more balance and creativity into the curriculum.

Schools in Beijing and other big cities offer weekend "math Olympics," advanced math leading to geometry and algebra. Also on the menu are introductory physics, calligraphy, music, karate, and the most popular subject, English. Parents claim their kids need these extras to get into a top middle school, which feeds into a top high school and university. In this supergeneration of high achievers, year-round schooling is the norm.

Beyond the prospects of government-inspired programs to boost the economy and overhaul education, Beijing has changed greatly in the past decade. Ballooning incomes and the crush of visitors provoked a cultural revolution in its restaurant and entertainment scene. Alongside such traditional delicacies as Peking duck and bird's nest soup, Tex-Mex and Cajun cuisines coexist with Sichuan specialties and Indian curry. Many swear by the tasty Hakka fare at Han Cang, one of the city's hottest eateries, or the fusion menu at the chic Green Tea House in Chaoyang. Lip-smacking Italian food can be had at Metro Café; Russian dishes at Moscow Café. Fangshan Restaurant, located in a traditional courtyard villa overlooking Beihai Lake, attracts those seeking elaborate imperial cuisine—from delicately filled pastries to sea cucumber with deer tendon.

While not swinging Shanghai, Beijing has injected new energy into its once-bland nightlife. The bar scene came alive in the late 1980s, primarily in Sanitun Lu in the Chaoyang district. For a cellar of Belgian beer, returnees head to The Hidden Tree. Jazz-ya, a nifty Japanese-style bar, also attracts a hip crowd, as does Charlie's Bar in the cozy Jianguo Hotel. Although the city's discos may not be cutting edge, Vogue, The Den, and Club Banana attract partygoers of every nationality. And for traditionalists, there is always the Beijing opera, regarded as the crème de la crème of Chinese entertainment.

The Chinese have a saying: In Beijing one talks; in Shanghai one shops. Today, as China meshes socialism and capitalism, the demarcation lines between these two great urban rivals are blurring. Bureaucratic Beijing is more entrepreneurial; saucy Shanghai, more buttoned-down.

With a foot in both Beijing (as a Tsinghua professor) and Shanghai (as a technical advisor to Pudong), Stanford physicist Zhang has a unique perspective on China's growing force in the New Economy. "Give the government credit," he says. "They've been building critical mass in science and technology the right way. Instead of trying some massive nationwide scheme to accelerate these exciting new fields, the government's been quite clever—doing things very selectively. They were very smart in targeting Tsinghua, Peking, and Fudan Universities, as well as the Chinese Academy of Sciences. Eventually, the breakthroughs taking place in these elite institutions will spread across the entire country."

Despite its recent rocket ride, China's entry into the economic big leagues is loaded with obstacles. The overheated economy, tensions with Taiwan and Hong Kong, illegal trade practices, and human rights violations are but a few of the signs of challenges to come. After decades of communist rule, China also continues to cope with cronyism and corruption, inefficient state-owned enterprises, and a deeply flawed banking system. Perhaps more worrisome is the yawning gap between the rich and the poor. As in India, the country's economic boom has left many behind. The once-narrow divide between the haves and the have-nots has become one of the widest in the world. In fact, the disparity in income levels today approximates that of prerevolutionary days, when the Reds toppled the Nationalists.

> **Act Now**
>
> To advance China's economic miracle, many serious obstacles will have to be overcome. Most important: narrowing the gap between rich and poor.

China's economic miracle has been confined largely to Shanghai, Beijing, and a handful of coastal cities, such as Guangzhou, and their surrounding industrial belts. For example, Shanghai, the country's wealthiest city, has a per-capita GNP exceeding $15,000—versus the national average of about $1,200. "China still calls itself socialist, and in an odd sense it is," writes Yilu Zhao, former education reporter for the *Times*. "While the income structure has changed, much that was intended to underpin social order has not."

By and large, people living outside the affluent urban areas remain second-class citizens. In the countryside—hardly a workers' paradise—about 800 million people, or 60 percent of the population, remain mired in deep-seated poverty; 200 million are unemployed or underemployed. Consequently, China's poor continue to pour into the big cities looking for work. Called *dagongcai* (slang for "peasants in the city"), this 150-million-strong army of migratory workers labor twelve to fourteen hours at least twenty-eight days a month. Typically, they remit three-fourths of their pay back to their families in the boondocks.

"Manifest plainness. Enhance simplicity. Reduce selfishness. Have few desires," wrote Lao-tzu in the sixth century B.C. The ancient philosopher's advice seems hopelessly lost today in this increasingly materialistic country. Modern China is a land of new money, and new money likes making an ostentatious show. The country's new millionaires—indeed, billionaires—would make Thorstein Veblen, the economist who coined the phrase "conspicuous consumption" one hundred years ago, blush.

City slickers, in particular, define themselves by what they drive, what they wear, where they live. Called *ya pi shi,* or "elegant-skinned beings," the nouveau riche of urban China can't seem to buy enough expensive designer and brand merchandise—from Mercedes-Benz sports cars and Rolex watches to Louis Vuitton handbags and La Perla lingerie. High-end goods are enormously popular, capturing more than one-third of the retail markets in Beijing, Shanghai, and other major cities. These well-to-do urbanites frequent the growing number of huge Western-style supermarkets and fancy restaurants with something tasty for every palate. In their leisure time, affluent Chinese are also discovering golf, banned for many years by the Reds. Now there are almost two hundred golf courses, with as many as a thousand others planned. As for living accommodations, the rich are moving into fashionable American-themed residential developments proliferating in the suburbs: Palm Springs, Napa Valley, Orange County, Long Beach, and Park Avenue.

Obviously, Deng Xiaoping's claim that communism does not equal poverty has captivated China's prosperous city dwellers. No longer hounded as "capitalist roaders," the nation's well-off increasingly are coming out of their shells and declaring their wealth. Celebrity CEO Charles Zhang, the MIT-educated founder of Sohu.com, one of the nation's best-known online portals, boasts that it is "morally uplifting to be a wealth creator." Astonishingly, one-fourth of the Chinese members on *Forbes*'s latest "richest list" are members of the Communist Party. Just don't tell Mao.

Splurging on property, cars, and entertainment causes more jealousy than admiration, though. China's urban wealthy are arousing widespread resentment among the rural population. The so-called "red-eye disease"—the envy of those who are getting more, faster—is reaching epidemic levels in the hinterland. More and more Chinese are expressing anger over the economic disparities between those in the nation's coastal plain and residents of the impoverished inland areas. "The country's rich may enjoy many luxuries," writes the *Economist*, "but peace of mind is not one of them."

The People's Republic must try to avoid becoming a nation with two living standards. Confucius, the Chinese sage who lived 2,500 years ago, eschewed selfishness for selflessness. Unless China returns to its Confucian values, the country may become a faltering dragon.

"Let China sleep," Napoleon once warned. "When it awakens it will shake the world." Clearly, there are numerous obstacles that could set the PRC's experiment back and injure those who've been party to the adventure. But chances are this nation—with one-fifth of the world's population now chomping at capitalism's bit—has gone too far down the road to turn back. Any setbacks will be temporary. Any problems will be solved. And China will be wide awake and roaring once again.

cross-strait
competition

Behind an able man there
are always other able men.

—CHINESE PROVERB

"Any sufficiently advanced technology," wrote futurist Arthur C. Clarke in the early 1960s, "is indistinguishable from magic." Taiwan, officially the Republic of China (ROC), left it to Morris Chang to take the hocus-pocus out of the Digital Age. More than anyone else, this postindustrial impresario has been responsible for leading Taiwan's transformation from an agricultural backwater just a few decades ago to one of the world's high-tech powerhouses today.

In 1985, Chang could easily have retired—or at least slowed down. Born in China, with advanced engineering degrees from MIT and Stanford, he had reached the pinnacle of American industry. After a twenty-five-year career at Dallas-based Texas Instruments in charge of the company's semiconductor business—the largest such operation in the world at that time—Chang was firmly ensconced as president of

General Instrument Corp. in New York. But he wanted a new challenge. If he could lure enough Taiwanese brainpower back from the United States, he saw a wealth of opportunity for developing the semiconductor industry in Taiwan. At age fifty-four, Chang also could no longer defer his lifetime dream of running his own show.

"No matter how high you rise on the executive ladder, your freedom of action is always limited," he says. Chang traded in his executive suite at General Instrument and his swanky apartment in Manhattan's Trump Tower to pursue the "right destiny," helping the island republic build a world-class computer chip industry. The Taiwanese government was happy to help out.

In the mid-1980s, Taiwan had no semiconductor, or integrated circuit, capability to speak of. In 1985, Premier K. H. Yu invited Chang to move to the country to promote its development. As head of the Industrial Technology Research Institute (ITRI), the nation's premier electronics research and development center, Chang quickly shaped a bold vision that would catapult the ROC into a position of global leadership in the rough-and-tumble world of chip making. He reckoned that because Taiwan

Dust Off the Welcome Mat

In a shrewd move, Premier K. H. Yu invited Morris Chang to Taiwan to spearhead the semiconductor industry.

lacked the capital and manufacturing expertise to set up chip fabrication facilities, local companies couldn't compete with Intel, Texas Instruments, and other industry behemoths. "It's too risky to go out and spend money on state-of-the-art chip plants, or fabs, where the minimum investment is $3 billion," he told government leaders. "The barriers to entry are too high."

Chang had a better idea. Why not set up a contract fabrication plant concentrating solely on integrated-circuit wafers and let others control the design process? Taiwan could put up the capital to build a state-of-the-art semiconductor foundry and sell its production capacity to big integrated-device manufacturers and entrepreneurial chip designers. The government bought the plan. In 1987, Chang launched Taiwan Semiconductor Manufacturing Co. (TSMC), a foundry joint venture, with the help of the ROC government, local investors, and Dutch giant Philips Electronics, installing himself as chairman.

Originally capitalized at $220 million, TSMC currently enjoys a market cap of $40 billion. It is the largest silicon chip foundry in the world, ahead of its local imitator United MicroElectronics, Singapore's Chartered Semiconductor, and IBM. With revenues of $7.7 billion, TSMC consistently ranks among the world's highest-margin chip makers.

An added payoff: Chang's foundry concept allowed hundreds of nimble, small- and medium-size Taiwanese companies—the lifeblood of the local economy—to enter the market through the proliferation of so-called fabless designers, the people who draw up the blueprints for the chips. "Taiwan has become the dominant foundry country and the second-most-important design country, after the United States," says Chang, now seventy-three. Today, there are three hundred chip design houses in Taiwan, with combined sales of $23 billion. By the end of the decade, almost 50 percent of the world's chip production should be done by contract, up from 21 percent in 2004. That's good news for the ROC, fondly known today as the "Republic of Computers." It ranks as the world's third-largest computer equipment manufacturer and the number one maker of desktop PCs and peripherals.

Thanks to Chang's clever outsourcing scheme, Taiwan's high-tech industries are being closely watched across the Pacific Rim. China, Singapore, and South Korea, in particular, are examining the Taiwan-ese model of economic reengineering. "Morris Chang's contributions to Taiwan's industrial development are enormous," says Chintay Shih, current president of ITRI. "He's brought a global view to Taiwan. Without him, Taiwan would be far behind the world today."

The recruitment of Chang, along with legions of other China- and Taiwan-born castaways from the United States, has been a boon to national development. The inflow of top talent from abroad helped shift the island's industrial base from textiles and tennis shoes to high-end electronics and computers in less than a generation. After suffering a serious brain drain for thirty years, Taiwan began to attract significant numbers of homegrown scientists, engineers, and businesspeople from America in the 1980s, when the local economy started to improve. The Republic of China, more than any other country I have studied, has scored the biggest gains in wooing back its expatriates. Many, like Chang, hope to set up their own businesses.

Practically everyone wants to be his or her own boss in this country where a technology tycoon like Morris Chang is as much a folk hero as Bill Gates is in the United States. Engineers and scientists who can craft the latest and greatest products are truly stars. "We have a more entrepreneurial spirit," Paul Wang, chairman of Pacific Venture Partners and a former IBM executive, told *Forbes*. Wang contrasts this with Japan: "You don't see many people quitting Fujitsu to start their own companies. There are new ventures set up here every day. It's even more dynamic than Silicon Valley."

To be sure, Taiwan's talent pool of highly skilled techies runs deep. "We stored hundreds of thousands of scientists and engineers in the United States," asserts native son Ta-Lin Hsu, founder and chairman of venture capitalist H&Q Asia Pacific and also an IBM alum. By some estimates, 50,000 Taiwanese engineers and scientists live in the United States, and one-fifth of Silicon Valley semiconductor engineers are Chinese. As these homing pigeons fly home, many of them with impressive résumés, they are transplanting cutting-edge technology, ideas, and the Silicon Valley spirit to Asia's Silicon Island.

> **Target the Best Minds**
>
> "We stored hundreds of thousands of scientists and engineers in the United States," says venture capitalist and native son Hsu.

"When friends visit from afar, is this not indeed a pleasure?" Confucius asked 2,000 years ago. The Chinese philosopher believed that the warm welcome they offered to outsiders was one of his people's greatest virtues. For centuries, this long, tobacco leaf–shaped island—about as big as Massachusetts, Connecticut, and Rhode Island together—proved a safe haven for enterprising émigrés. According to mainstream scientific theory, the country's first inhabitants were not Chinese but aborigines, or Austronesians, from Malay and Pacific Island stock, who arrived between 4,000 and 5,000 years ago. During the fifteenth century, Chinese settlers from Fujian Province immigrated to Taiwan in ever-increasing numbers. In 1517, Portuguese sailors arrived and were so impressed with the mountainous island that they dubbed it *"formosa,"* or beautiful. The name stuck with Westerners, although the Chinese had called it Taiwan for centuries. Later, it was colonized by the Dutch and, briefly, by the Spanish. Then, two Chinese dynasties, the Ming and the Manchu, fought each other for control of the territory. The Manchu won but faced frequent rebellions by the natives.

During the nineteenth century, the British recognized Taiwan's economic potential and advocated its outright annexation. William Jardine of the powerful British trading firm Jardine Matheson told his country's foreign secretary: "We must proceed to take possession of three or four islands, say Formosa, Quemoy, and Amoy [now Xiamen], in order to secure new markets and new footholds in China." However, the Opium Wars between China and Britain dashed those dreams. The United States also showed an interest in the territory. Commodore Matthew Perry was a staunch advocate of annexation. Gideon Nye, a wealthy American merchant and a leading member of his country's expatriate community in Canton, agreed that "Formosa's eastern shores and southern point—in the direct route between China and California and Japan, and between Shanghai and Canton—should be protected by the United States of America."

Trade slowly increased between East and West, and large expatriate communities flourished around Taiwan's port cities. But the increased volume of activity led to a number of violent incidents between foreigners and local Chinese. Leave it to the Rising Sun to restore law and order.

For years, an expanding, imperial Japan had fancied the island. In 1895, after losing the Sino-Japanese War, China was forced to hand it over. The victors built modern schools, hospitals, and industries and upgraded agricultural techniques. But the occupation proved oppressive and unpopular. Tokyo required everyone to adopt a Japanese name and speak Japanese. In effect, Japan tried to remold Taiwan in its own image by forcing the island to sever her ancient Chinese cultural roots. After Japan surrendered in World War II, Taiwan was restored to Chinese rule on October 25, 1945, a date still celebrated annually as Restoration Day.

The Taiwanese were happy to see the war end, but their joy soon faded when Generalissimo Chiang Kai-shek's Kuomintang (KMT, or Nationalist) Party assumed leadership. In the early years, the KMT Party's stewardship was plagued by corruption and incompetence. In 1949, when the Communists took control of China, almost 2 million Nationalists—"elite carpetbaggers" in the eyes of many Taiwanese—fled to the island and established the Republic of China, which it administered under martial law until 1987. The Generalissimo believed that he still ruled China and would eventually resume his authority there. Instead, he remained confined to dictatorial rule in Taiwan. After Chiang's death in 1975, his son Chiang Ching-kuo governed with a velvet glove. The younger, more personable Chiang initiated a series of political reforms, allowing opposition to his KMT Party before his death in 1988.

In 2000, the Kuomintang was voted out of power for the first time in fifty-one years. The citizens elected Chen Shui-bian of the pro-independence Democratic Progressive Party (DPP). In March 2004, in a bitterly contested election clouded by an alleged assassination attempt, President Chen was narrowly reelected by a mere 30,000-vote margin. Nonetheless, the DPP's victories put the majority local Chinese firmly in charge after decades of control by "mainlanders," those who had fled China in 1949 after the Communist takeover.

The presidential and subsequent legislative and special elections highlight a national identity crisis that has hounded Taiwan for centuries and makes patriotism an explosive issue today. The DPP actively courts local Taiwanese, whose roots go back centuries, rather than the mainlanders who came across the Taiwan Strait fifty years ago. The "natives," who make up more than 70 percent of the island's 23 million people—mostly descendants of Chinese immigrants from centuries past—generally see themselves not as Chinese but as Taiwanese. In the latest survey by Taiwan's National Chengchi University, only 6 percent say they are Chinese; almost half claim to be Taiwanese. This growing sense of national identity is based partly on the island's difficult history with waves of opportunistic outsiders and partly on its economic renaissance.

Throat-swelling patriotism and unabashed statements of national duty have profound implications for cross-strait relations between Beijing and Taipei. For more than fifty years, the ROC has been at loggerheads with the PRC, in one of the world's last Cold War struggles. Taiwan, a de facto independent state since 1949, has resisted officially declaring its sovereignty. One reason is the Chinese government's repeated threats to invade should Taiwan do so. In March, Beijing adopted an anti-secessionist law to that effect. What's more, the PRC has amassed an arsenal of more than seven hundred short-range missiles aimed at Taiwan and regularly holds military exercises off the island's coast, making the Taiwanese understandably nervous.

Recently, tempers appear to have cooled somewhat. Money talks, and both sides understand the importance of close business relations. In 2002, China became Taiwan's biggest export market—taking in everything from cell phones to galvanized steel. Taiwanese investments on the mainland exceed $100 billion, representing some 70,000 businesses and employing more than 10 million Chinese workers. Hence, Beijing seems to be toning down its "one China, two systems" rhetoric, a formula that has been used for Hong Kong but was originally conceived for Taiwan. Yet one wonders how conciliatory China's president, Hu Jintao, who also commands the armed forces, can afford to be.

Taiwan's Chen, pressured for moderation by the United States, has adopted a somewhat softer approach as well. No doubt, his narrow

victory and recent polls indicating overwhelming support for the status quo encourage less saber rattling. Chen also knows that his export-
dependent nation is irreversibly linked to the mainland. As China
goes, so goes Taiwan.

Despite the constant threats from its formidable cross-strait cousin
and the diplomatic isolation imposed by the United Nations and a host
of other countries in 1971, the republic has not only survived but prospered. After the fall of China, the Nationalists gave the island's industrious people free rein in the economic sphere, while maintaining tight
political discipline and social order. In the 1950s, Taipei promoted
agriculture through a series of land reforms and, in the 1960s, it
emphasized labor-intensive exports ranging from Christmas tree lights
and shoes to refrigerators and transistor radios. Newly arrived firms
found a low-cost, well-disciplined, strife-free workforce, touted in government ads as "the best bargain in Asia."

Taiwanese businessmen, for their part, were content to copy existing products of Japan and the West. With cheap labor, a weak currency, and an export-or-die philosophy, the country became famous for
its inexpensive knock-off toys and tennis shoes. By the end of the
1960s, pundits heralded Taiwan as one of Asia's "tiger economies."

By the late seventies and early eighties, conditions had changed.
Rising labor costs and land prices—combined with increased competition from Southeast Asia and, later, China—forced the country to
shift strategies. "We had reached full employment, and the labor-
intensive industries could no longer survive," said the late K. T. Li, the
Cambridge University–trained physicist considered the architect
of Taiwan's economic miracle. The government, under Li's watchful eye, began to focus more on capital-
and technology-intensive industries, particularly electronics and
chemicals.

> **Adapt—or Die**
>
> By the late 1970s, Taiwan began
> its shift away from labor-intensive
> to more capital- and technology-
> intensive industries.

In the 1980s, in a stroke of far-sighted genius, Li's lieutenants made a "great leap forward" with the opening of Hsinchu Science-based Industrial Park (HSP), modeled on Silicon Valley. Located on a former tea plantation thirty-seven miles southwest of Taipei, the sprawling complex would become the epicenter of Taiwan's booming electronics industry, serving as a counterweight to the migration of native brain-power overseas. Driving through the park, one can't miss its strategic importance. The aptly named Creation Road winds past a bewildering array of low-slung, California-style buildings, chip factories, and construction sites. With two top universities and leading government research institutes nearby, the campus includes an international school, medical facilities, luxury housing, landscaped gardens, and tennis courts—in effect, all the comforts of home for returning scientists and engineers accustomed to Western living conditions.

> **Celebrate Science and Technology**
>
> The creation of Hsinchu Science-based Industrial Park in the eighties launched Taiwan's steady climb into the world of science and technology.

In addition to these amenities, HSP offers concrete incentives. Investors get tax breaks, low-interest financing, duty-free imports, training support, and efficient administration. Although at first venture capital came slowly, "today there's a stampede," says Ta-Lin Hsu of H&Q Asia Pacific. One of Asia's largest venture capital firms, H&Q has helped many upstart Taiwanese technology companies grow into global manufacturing giants. Currently, 370 firms operate in the park, one-third run by returning Taiwanese and one-third by foreigners—mostly Americans. Together, they generated $25 billion in revenues in 2004 and employed 102,000 people, two-thirds of whom have at least an undergraduate degree. At last count, 4,340 native sons and daughters, most with advanced degrees from the United States, work there—up from 422 in 1980. With thirteen overseas offices (including five in the United States), HSP is constantly adding to this critical mass by tapping the rich vein of Taiwanese engineers and scientists in North

America. Last year, more than 1,500 overseas professionals applied for work in the park.

With such overwhelming popularity, the cradle of Taiwan's high-tech industry has been choking on its own riches. By the mid-1990s, HSP became so crowded that additional facilities were opened in Tainan and Miaoli counties.

Taiwan's economic miracle did not happen overnight. Besides creating Silicon Valley–inspired settings, government leaders liberalized the economy, lowered trade barriers, slashed bureaucratic red tape, and overhauled the infrastructure. More important, they revamped the country's education system. Primary schools were upgraded, elite junior high schools created, and a comprehensive system of private universities introduced. The Ministry of Education and the National Science Council invested heavily in science and technology. Today, about 35 percent of Tai-

> **Reform Public Schools**
>
> For the past two decades, Taiwan has been overhauling its school system while investing heavily in science and technology.

wan's 500,000 university students are studying engineering—roughly four times as many per capita as in the United States. The government has also adopted various measures to lure highly trained émigrés back to the motherland: subsidized airfares, enhanced salary packages, generous research support, and other inducements. These initiatives, combined with the bursting of the high-tech bubble in the United States, helped stimulate the reverse brain drain.

Despite its visible hand in priming the country's economic engine, the government avoided developing elaborate central plans. Economic navigators such as Cabinet Minister Li insisted on free market competition. "In the precommercial phase, Taiwanese companies work together," explains TSMC's Chang. "After that, they are at each other's throats."

For those trained in the West, Darwinian survival offers the ultimate challenge. That's what drew Bobo Wang back to Taiwan—not once, but twice. Like thousands of Taiwanese students before him, the Shanghai-born engineer left his adopted country in the 1960s to attend graduate school in the United States. After ten years in America, he became a microprocessor specialist at Xerox's electronics division in El Segundo, California. "I had a midlife crisis," explains Wang, now fifty-nine. "So I decided to change my life." In 1980, he returned to Taiwan with four other repatriates to found Microtek International Inc. in Hsinchu Science Park.

Initially, the team developed obscure pieces of electronic equipment. Soon, however, they became interested in desktop image scanners, scoring a major coup with a device that fed both black-and-white and color photographs into a computer. Not only did they get their scanner to market ahead of the Japanese, but they sold it for less than half the price of a comparable Japanese product. The Taiwanese team then introduced a color slide scanner priced 30 percent below models being sold by competitors Nikon and Sharp.

During the decade, Microtek became the darling of the Taiwan Stock Exchange. When the company went public in 1988, the founders became multimillionaires. Wang, in fact, was featured on *Lifestyles of the Rich and Famous*. But in 1991, at age forty-five, he left the company, feeling it had become too conservative. Rather than pursue new technologies, his colleagues preferred a safer course, investing only in scanners. Wang decided he wanted to travel the world and spend more time with his family, who had remained in the United States to prepare the two children for high school and college.

Four years later, his children's schooling in place and his travel itch satisfied, Wang returned to Taiwan to start Aetas, a company focused on developing affordable color solutions for laser printers, copiers, and multifunction peripherals. Although officially headquartered in the United States, the

> **Encourage Dual Loyalties**
>
> Folk-hero Wang headquartered Aetas in the United States while keeping its engineering and manufacturing in Taiwan.

firm's engineering and manufacturing will be done in Taiwan and, to a lesser extent, China. After years of research and development, Aetas plans to introduce its first product line this year. Wang's folk-hero status, no doubt, has pacified any impatient investors, who have poured $80 million into the start-up.

"Focus is the key," says Wang. He credits much of his business success to his time in America. His only regret is that he can't convince daughter, Erin, twenty-nine, and son, Nicholas, twenty-seven, to relocate to Taipei. "They're both 'ABCs'—American Born Chinese," he laments. "And they just feel more comfortable in the States."

The tug of home hits many Taiwanese techies in midcareer. It was while walking through the offices of his Silicon Valley employer, microchip giant Intel, that Miin Wu realized his dreams could best be fulfilled in Taiwan. "I looked around and saw very few Chinese engineers above the director level," he recalls. "I don't want to call it racial discrimination, but it was not compatible with my ambitions." In the late 1980s, Wu sidestepped the glass ceiling and went home, where, with twenty-eight other returned engineers, he founded Macronix International Co., one of the world's top ten producers of flash memory chips and the first Taiwanese company listed on the NASDAQ.

For similar reasons, Chi-Chia Hsieh decided to trade in Silicon Valley for Silicon Island. In 1956, at age twenty-two, he had emigrated to America to earn a doctorate in electrical engineering at the University of Santa Clara. Then, it was on to nearby Harris Corporation to build a career as a microwave engineer. But by 1983, Hsieh and several of his transplanted Taiwanese colleagues had lost interest in their jobs, so they returned to Taiwan to set up Microelectronics Technology Inc. in Hsinchu Science Park. "We got together and agreed it was time to either start our own company or stay in the States and retire there," he explains. "We quickly decided it was time for us to pack up and go home."

Just a few decades ago, Taiwan business was dominated by rigidly hierarchical companies run by powerful titans—not a very attractive environment for eager-beaver returnees. But with the country's entry

into the Digital Age, the heroes of
the new Taiwan—Morris Chang,
Bobo Wang, Chi-Chia Hsieh, and
others—changed the character of
organizational life and made it
much more appealing to homegrown and imported talent. They
understood that, in the Innovation
Economy, intellectual property—
people—matters most. Success de-

> **Adapt—or Die**
>
> To attract homegrown and imported
> talent, many Taiwanese companies
> have replaced the command-and-
> control approach with a more
> partcipative style.

pends on having ample stores of fresh-faced knowledge workers who
are encouraged to alter the environment in new and exciting ways.
This new egalitarianism isn't just a matter of style; it's a matter of survival. Today, increasing numbers of Taiwanese companies are high-
paying meritocracies where power is shared, not hoarded, and where
genius can flourish.

Of course, money talks. From day one, the ROC's new generation
of corporate leaders has recognized that stock ownership is the currency of the times. Since stock options were illegal until recently,
Taiwanese firms instead offered generous stock grants and bonuses to
top off competitive local salaries. The robust Taiwan stock market, in
turn, has made many people wealthy. At Taiwan Semiconductor, for
example, engineers reportedly can earn up to $500,000 a year through
lucrative stock bonuses.

To some extent, these enticements have altered Taiwanese society.
"The biggest change is in the people," says Wen-Sen Chu, a former
University of Washington professor who is now a water resources entrepreneur. "Prosperity has made us more aggressive, selfish, and shortsighted." Eric Lean, a twenty-five-year veteran with IBM in America
and a leading force in Taiwan's optoelectronics industry, adds: "In the
1960s, we had a deep-rooted culture. Our traditional values were intact,
and people were good. Today, some of those values have been distorted
due to the greed brought on by a booming economy. But the spirit of our
hardworking, flexible, and aggressive people remains intact."

In any case, repatriates to Taipei, the heart of modern-day Taiwan, are rediscovering a vastly underrated city with a vibrant arts scene, exceptional restaurants, and mountain getaways just minutes from downtown. For years, the capital city was the ugly duckling of Asia, tarnished by rapid industrialization and population growth. Founded 120 years ago, Taipei grew from swampland and paddy fields into a hodgepodge of drab concrete office blocks, squatter housing, dusty streets, sluggish traffic, and horrific pollution. It had "all the glamour of an egg carton," wrote one disenchanted visitor.

In the late 1970s, however, city fathers began to remake the urban area—introducing stiff zoning and building restrictions, emission controls, and mass transit. So far, they appear to be winning. That said, Taipei is still a confusing sprawl of eclectic architecture that combines ornate Chinese design with Western high-rise glass and metal. The new Hsinyi District is fast becoming the city's most important business and shopping area. Its focal point is the World Trade Center, the epicenter of the country's three-decades-long export boom. Next door is the world's tallest building—the Taipei Financial Center, or Taipei 101—which, at 1,667 feet, dwarfs the urban skyline. Taken together, this massive complex reinforces the message that the business of Taiwan is business. "It symbolizes that Taiwan is in step with the world," boasts President Chen.

Although the capital looks increasingly like a westernized Asian city, it has not forgotten its heritage. Ages-old Chinese culture is preserved in all its glory at the magnificent National Palace Museum on the city's outskirts. The museum houses the world's greatest collection of Chinese arts and antiques, more than 700,000 priceless pieces dating as far back as the Sung Dynasty. Similarly, the CKS Memorial in east Taipei pays homage to the Generalissimo. The mammoth square with parade grounds is dominated by an enormous hall dedicated to Chiang that towers over the city. This is also the site of the National Concert Hall and National Theater. Contemporary art lovers flock to the I. P. Gallery, where a hip crowd often gathers in the upstairs bar. The smaller Shungi Taiwan Aboriginal Museum offers an impressive array of arts, crafts, and aboriginal clothing, while the Fine Arts Museum showcases leading local and foreign artists.

Taipei's 3 million-plus residents are especially passionate about shopping, dining, and entertaining. Fashionable Jenai Road contains a mélange of tony shops and alfresco cafés serving latté and cappuccino. The Hsimenting District, with its Japanese pop fashions, could easily be mistaken for Harajuku, Tokyo's trendy teenage stomping ground. By contrast, Tien Mu, where well-heeled expatriates live and play, is lined with international boutiques and chic restaurants. Then there are the city's famous night markets. The biggest, at Shih-Lin, contains a vast network of crowded alleys featuring everything from fake finery and snake soup to palm reading and sidewalk *pachinko*.

Taipei also offers a wide spectrum of dining options, ranging from Peking duck and Shanghainese dumplings to Japanese *teppanyaki* and Irish stew. Returnees often head to the noisy and garish Really Good Seafood Restaurant for steamed crab, grilled clams, and shark fin soup; others swear by Tainan Tan Tsu Mien noodle house. For snacking and schmoozing, nothing beats a local *pichiu wu,* or beer hall. The most famous is the three-story Indian Beer House on Pate Street, which can accommodate 1,000 customers.

Teeming with night life, Taipei's "Combat Zone," around Shaung Cheng Street, features rollicking Carnegie's, DV8, and 45. Blue Note on Roosevelt Road is a popular haunt of new-money moguls and jazz lovers. In the wee hours, many down $10 espresso martinis at the stately old Grand Hotel located atop a ridge at the northern end of the city.

To escape the downtown din, city dwellers can choose from a slew of new parks and shady hideaways. One of the most peaceful and serene urban oases is the perfectly manicured garden complex at Chiang Kai-shek's former official residence in Shih-Lin. What's more, lush mountain retreats and secluded sandy beaches are less than an hour's drive from the city's crowded streets. For the more adventurous, Taiwan's less-visited offshore islands make for ideal getaways. A current hot spot is the Penghu archipelago, west of the main island, world renowned for its windsurfing and sailing.

Small surprise, then, that returnees and newcomers are expressing appreciation of Taiwan's capital city. "Taipei's becoming a much better place to live," says Hong Kong–born T. C. Chan, who oversees Citigroup's Greater China operations, including branches in the PRC, ROC, and Hong Kong. "It's improved significantly in the past fifteen years. It's a very livable city and it's much more affordable than Hong Kong or Tokyo." Richard Vuylsteke, a nineteen-year resident, agrees. As executive director of the American Chamber of Commerce, he describes the country generally as "one of the easiest places in Asia for an expatriate to live. Between 85 and 90 percent of those posted here would like to extend their stay."

Despite the veneer of twenty-first-century sophistication, Taiwan suffers the familiar limitation of many island nations: provincialism. "It's on its way to becoming world-class," says Citigroup's Chan. "But it's not quite there yet. It's sometimes inward-looking and slightly uncomfortable in global affairs." Adds James Soong, political luminary and leader of the nation's second-largest opposition party, "Taiwan must develop a more international perspective. We must be more concerned about global issues."

Act Now

To achieve its global ambitions, Taiwan "must develop a more international perspective," says Soong. "We must be more concerned about global issues."

The country's cyberstars will need a more cosmopolitan outlook in confronting the challenges ahead. They must step carefully when it comes to their toughest competitors from both East and West. One of the world's fastest-growing economies—and one of the richest, with more than $239 billion in foreign reserves—is combating the prospects of an economic slowdown. Although GDP is projected to grow 3.6 percent this year, the ROC was stung in 2001 by its first contraction in half a century. No longer low-cost producers, Taiwanese companies today are faced with either raising prices or cutting profit margins. Add to that a preponderance of labor-intensive industries, an appreciating

Taiwan dollar, an aging infrastructure, and environmental concerns, and one wonders whether Silicon Island will become Fantasy Island.

For all the hand-wringing over the nation's economic future, business leaders aren't wasting time wondering what's ahead, and they aren't waiting for bad news. They are moving toward more advanced technology—biotech, nanotech, communications, and optoelectronics. "The only solution is to add value to our products," says Stan Shih, the recently retired chairman of Acer Group, Taiwan's leading computer maker.

> **Celebrate Science and Technology**
>
> "The only solution is to add value to our products," says Shih, founder of Taiwan's leading computer maker.

Hsieh's Microelectronics Technology, for instance, built its reputation making components for microwave-receiving equipment; now it makes complete systems for ships, including a portable unit that weighs just sixty-five pounds. TSMC, the foundry giant, is determined to avoid becoming a mere commodity producer. Last year, the company introduced an innovative "design service alliance" to allow its 250 active customers to track the progress of their orders over the Internet. "We're getting our customers involved in every stage of the process and giving them access to all the data," says chairman Chang. Taiwan's PC giants, Quanta Computer and Compal Electronics, which supply more than 60 percent of the world's notebooks, are also looking for new territory to stake out. Recently, they began producing mobile phone handsets because of their higher margins. Similarly, Acer, the world's number five PC maker, has started selling more desktop computers.

While moving up the value chain, clever Taiwanese tigers remain focused on what they do best. In local high-tech circles, finding a niche is the name of the game. "To succeed, you don't have to be big," says Wang of Aetas. "You just have to have vision and move fast." Lacking the economies of scale to take on the United States and Japan in a global free-for-all, the island's relatively small, nimble companies continue to concentrate on segments often overlooked by the big multinationals.

Taipei's technocrats are ensuring that island businesses stay ahead in their high-value niches. Government research and development spending has doubled in the past five years, and the Ministry of Economic Affairs has been encouraging—through technical and financial assistance—both foreign and domestic companies to establish cutting-edge R&D facilities in Taiwan. "Manufacturing is our safety net," says one government official. "But now we are moving toward research and development, where we can create more products and not compete with developing nations."

The government's approach is paying off. Today, sixty-six Taiwanese R&D centers are operating, far more than Taipei's initial goal of forty by 2006. These facilities employ more than 4,000 engineers, including 250 first-rate professionals recruited from abroad. In addition, twenty-two foreign companies, including Hewlett-Packard, Dell, IBM, Microsoft, NEC, and Sony, have or plan to have similar innovation hubs in place shortly. Projected employment is 550 highly trained scientists and engineers.

To further transform itself into a knowledge-oriented economy, Taiwan will need additional brainpower. The most important factor in ensuring the country's future competitiveness is human capital. And that's the rub here.

"We don't have enough people," laments Ho Mei-Yueh, the country's chief economics mandarin. In an interesting reversal of fortune, Taiwanese youth are no longer keen to go abroad to work or pursue graduate studies, particularly since the economy has improved and local universities have grown in stature. "The government is well aware of this trend," adds Ho. "So we are providing scholarships to postdoc Taiwanese students to enable them to have a couple of years' experience in foreign universities. When they come back, they will understand international developments and have a network of connections with foreign academics. We're also trying to attract more foreign students to Taiwan, providing them with scholarships."

Complementing these initiatives are a host of private- and public-sector alliances with leading overseas universities, including Stanford, UC Berkeley, Carnegie Mellon, and MIT. "In the past, Taiwan could only obtain technology from abroad by buying it," says government spokesperson Emily Hsu. "The fact that we are able to participate with other countries is proof of the R&D strength that Taiwan has now developed."

> **Nourish the Halls of Ivy**
>
> Taiwan universities are establishing partnerships with leading overseas universities, including Stanford and MIT.

The Republic of China will need all the strength it can muster to stay ahead of its cross-strait competitor. Since the late 1980s, when Taiwan lifted its ban on travel to China, tens of thousands of Taiwanese manufacturers have fled to the mainland in search of lower costs. In the early years, the government encouraged labor-intensive, low-tech factories to move offshore. By the late 1990s, however, high-tech firms had joined the exodus, including electronics and information technology companies—the pillars of the local economy. Although Taiwanese enterprises control 70 percent of the output of IT products in China, the fact that the PRC now produces more desktop PCs, optical devices, and liquid crystal than Taiwan has the ROC's business and government leaders worried.

For years, C. Y. Chang, president of National Chiao-Tung University, tried to convince his countrymen of the grave threat their gargantuan neighbor posed to the tiny island. He warned that China's growing economic and technological strength might eventually swallow Taiwan's best industries and talent, but no one believed him.

Even the highly respected Morris Chang was skeptical. Later, however, he had a change of heart. When Taiwanese entrepreneur Richard Chang established rival Semiconductor Manufacturing International in Shanghai four years ago and lured away fifty of Taiwan Semiconductor's best engineers, Chang acknowledged the PRC's emergence as a technological power. "I thought it would be very difficult for this venture to succeed," recalls Chang. "But when our engineers started going over to [the PRC], that changed my thinking. I wish these competitors would go away, but they're not going away." (Taiwan Semiconductor bolstered its defense by successfully suing its Chinese competitor for infringing on its intellectual property rights.)

> **Know Thy Competition**
>
> Morris Chang has changed his assessment of his cross-strait rival: "I wish these competitors would go away, but they're not."

To combat this industrial flight, President Chen has been appealing to Taiwanese businesses based in China to repatriate. Using a variety of incentives, Taipei is enticing more and more expatriates to redirect their investments back home. One scheme, for example, gives them preferential leases in five designated industrial districts around the country. To date, forty-four Taiwanese companies operating on the mainland have come back, representing roughly $750 million in reinvestment. "With our businesspeople in China returning to Taiwan," says Chen, "we can no longer have any hesitation or doubts about our country."

Several years ago, K. T. Li, the father of Taiwan's high-tech revolution, argued that what matters most is not whether local industry heads west (to invest in mainland China) or south (to invest in Southeast Asia), but whether it heads up. What Li had in mind was the critical importance of constantly upgrading the nation's creativity and innovation.

Taking a page out of Li's book, President Chen has been preaching the same message. "There is no so-called 'sunset industry,'" he recently warned his compatriots. "There is only a 'sunset product' or 'sunset management.' Only if we have the spirit of creation, speed, and ambition can our industries find a new vision ahead." His goal is to expand to fifteen the number of domestic products and technologies that are identified as "best in the world."

Chen's vision of a reengineered Taiwan is matched by pragmatic policies. Besides wooing back Taiwanese investors, he advocates increasing public funding of venture capital; providing additional training for workers in key industries (particularly biotech); lifting restrictions on foreign engineers and scientists and extending their work permits; and offering further inducements to native-born professionals working overseas.

None of these measures can guarantee Taiwan's long-term survival. Still, things could be worse. This vibrant democracy has enormous resources at its fingertips. With a cadre of highly skilled science and engineering graduates, lavish financial reserves for new ventures, and one of Asia's most entrepreneurial enclaves, the Republic of China appears better positioned to capitalize on the Chinese century than any other country.

mideast
miracle

Israel can win the battle for survival
only by developing expert knowledge
in technology.

—ALBERT EINSTEIN

Terrorism and regional strife. Double-digit unemployment and labor unrest. Fractious politics and religious conflict. Add to these woes the many uncertainties that have always plagued Israel, and it's no wonder potential returnees are uneasy. To most Americans, repatriation would seem the height of folly, given Israel's blood-soaked history. Yet, despite its manifold problems, there is something about this place that seeps into one's soul and beckons the Chosen People home.

To understand the Holy Land is to understand its profound religious significance. Located on the eastern shore of the Mediterranean, in the heart of the Middle East, Israel is the great land bridge connecting Europe, Asia, and Africa. It is the Promised Land to which Moses led the Children of Israel; the place where Jesus preached his sermons and Mohammed ascended to heaven. For Christians, there is the awe of retracing Jesus's footsteps in the Scripture's actual setting. For Muslims, there is the opportunity to pray at the third holiest shrine in Islam. For Jews, there is a spiritual reawakening, a feeling of coming home.

The country's rich biblical past carries special meaning for Jews. The Land of Israel, or *Eretz Yisrael* in Hebrew, was the kingdom of David and Solomon, as well as the home of Jesus and the Talmudic priests. Although the Jewish presence in the country has been unbroken for more than 3,000 years, several massive exiles created a diaspora throughout the world. Over the centuries, Jews have turned their gaze toward Jerusalem in daily prayer—faithful to the belief that someday they would return to their ancestral homeland, symbolized by Mount Zion.

Since its founding on May 14, 1948, tiny Israel (about the size of New Jersey) has been a nation of immigrants. The Law of Return, passed in 1950, granted all Jews the automatic right to Israeli citizenship. The Zionist goals of immigration and absorption became national priorities, with a dedicated government ministry complemented by a host of supporting agencies at home and abroad. As a result, Israel's Jewish population—650,000 at the time of its independence—tripled within ten years. During the 1990s, nearly 1 million *olim*, or immigrants, from the former Soviet Union—many of them highly educated and professionally qualified—poured into the country, increasing the head count by more than 10 percent. Today, half of the exceptionally young population of 6.7 million was born elsewhere. Nearly every cabinet member is an immigrant or the descendant of immigrants.

Dust Off the Welcome Mat

Repatriation to Israel is undertaken not for economic reasons but for a mixture of Zionist ideals, religious duty, and a desire to contribute to nation building.

Repatriation Israeli-style is strikingly different from the flight of human capital elsewhere, where native sons and daughters return home primarily for economic reasons. In Israel, many pilgrims immigrate based on a mixture of Zionist ideals, a sense of religious duty, and a passion to contribute to nation building.

Festering regional sores, primarily the Palestinian *intifada,* or uprising, and the mayhem in Iraq, have crimped Israel's human pipeline in the past five years. High-security alerts, roadblocks, and threats of suicide bombings make this one of the most conflict-ridden destinations on Earth. Every day innocent civilians pay the price for what is emphatically called the "fog of war." To worsen matters, the Bush administration's Middle East peace plan—known as the "road map"—appears stalled. All this has had a dampening effect on immigration. In 2004, new arrivals fell to 22,000, hitting a fifteen-year low. What to do? Israel has hired IBM to craft a marketing campaign.

Encouraged by the recent truce with Palestine, Israel is trying to shed its siege mentality. With the relative lull in terrorist attacks, spirits have begun to rise. Slowly, life is returning to normal, and Israel is regaining some of its swagger. The dangers haven't disappeared, of course. But not all of the Holy Land is a war zone. In cities such as Tel Aviv and Haifa, it is possible to forget about the conflict, at least for a time. Then, too, as 9/11 proved, there is some element of danger everywhere in the world.

Founded as a Jewish state, Israel is a mosaic of different religions, cultures, and social traditions—a cabinet of curiosities where extremes exist side by side. Jews make up 78 percent of the population; the balance is indigenous Arabs, mainly Muslims but also some Christians and Druze. In addition, some 3.5 million Palestinians live in the West Bank and Gaza Strip. In the combined areas of Israel, the West Bank, and Gaza, Jews outnumber Arabs by about 5.2 million to 4.9 million, according to figures from the Israeli government and the Palestinian Authority. But the Arab birthrate is substantially higher than that of the Jews; if current trends continue, Arabs will outnumber Jews within ten to twenty years.

Faced with this demographic time bomb, a string of Israeli leaders have sought to encourage massive immigration. In the early 1990s, the late Prime Minister Yitzhak Rabin encouraged the relocation of

millions of Russians to quiet fears of underpopulation. He also established a "directors-general committee," representing all relevant government ministries, to attract large
numbers of Israeli émigrés back
home. The focus was—and remains—the estimated 300,000 expatriates in North America, many
with much-needed scientific, technological, and managerial know-
how.

Target the Best Minds

In the mid-1990s, Prime Minister
Rabin encouraged massive Jewish
immigration, particularly of those
trained in science, technology, and
business.

Today, Prime Minister Ariel
Sharon, too, sees salvation in immi-
gration, or *aliyah* (literally "ascend"), to Israel. He wants to bring in 1
million would-be olim in the next fifteen years from the only other
country with 5 million-plus Jews—the United States. Although the
prospects seem unlikely, no one underestimates septuagenarian
Sharon's iron-willed resolve. "There is no single American figure to
compare with him," writes James Bennett, who served for three years
as the *New York Times* bureau chief in Jerusalem. "He is Andrew
Jackson, George Patton, Robert Moses."

Undaunted by worldwide detractors, Sharon constantly exhorts
his countrymen to make aliyah. Last July, in a ceremony that filled a
massive hangar at Ben-Gurion International Airport, the prime minister and two of his cabinet members welcomed nearly four hundred
immigrants from the United States and Canada. "We have to bring
hundreds of thousands of Jews from America to Israel," Sharon said.
"We need them here. It is important to you. It is important to us."

The newcomers were among the 1,500 new citizens from North
America who arrived last year under the sponsorship of a private
group, Nefesh B'Nefesh, meaning "soul to soul," in partnership with
the Jewish Agency, the quasi-governmental body responsible for settling immigrants. Created to spur Jewish immigration from North
America by removing logistical and economic obstacles, Nefesh
B'Nefesh is now "taking a more proactive role," according to co-

founder Rabbi Joshua Fass. "We're aggressively advertising—putting the word out to American Jews about the prospects of life in Israel. In addition, we're sending many of our successful U.S. olim back to the States to share their experiences, their inspiration."

Fass started Nefesh B'Nefesh after his cousin was killed in Israel in a terrorist attack. His partner Tony Gelbart, a prominent Florida businessman and the money man behind the organization, says Nefesh B'Nefesh provides assistance with finding employment and housing and comes with a built-in support system for aiding in social integration and navigating government processes upon arrival in Israel. The Israeli government, in turn, has enlisted U.S.-based groups such as Nefesh B'Nefesh to help spread the word that Israel needs their best and brightest. For the past two years, these organizations have vigorously encouraged rabbis of the 2,000 synagogues in North America to preach the value of Jews' relocating to their spiritual homeland.

North American immigrants have averaged a modest 3,000 to 5,000 annually for the past quarter-century, according to Israeli government figures. Nefesh B'Nefesh hopes to greatly increase that number. "In the next five years, we believe we can bring in 100,000 newcomers—mostly young professionals," says Fass (today, the average age is thirty-three). "The major issue is the country's ability to absorb them properly."

No one is more pleased with the renewed influx of potential settlers than Sharon: "As a Jew and as an Israeli, I commend the efforts of Nefesh B'Nefesh to increase aliyah from North America. It is through the realization of this dream of bringing the Jewish people back home to Zion that we can all unite to support the State of Israel."

During my most recent visit to Israel, government officials were also rolling out the red carpet to French Jews. France is home to 600,000 Jews, the largest Jewish population in Europe. In response to the Israeli prime minister's appeal to escape a climate of "wild anti-Semitism," hundreds of French Jews were climbing aboard specially chartered El Al flights in search of a new life in Israel. In the past three years, their numbers have doubled from 2,000 to 4,000, according to the Jewish Agency. In addition, 40,000 French Jews visited Israel last summer, many to buy apartments and to test the waters for a permanent aliyah.

Israel also has recently been bringing in thousands of Jews from India, Ethiopia, Peru, and elsewhere to preserve the demographic balance. Often, support comes from the most unlikely sources. For some time now, Christian Zionists have been growing in influence, and they are now a significant force in the surge of immigration to Israel.

Ray and Sharon Sanders, transplanted midwesterners, left their jobs in the United States and moved to Jerusalem in 1985. There, the couple helped found a biblical Zionist organization called Christian Friends of Israel (CFI). Their goal is to fulfill the biblical prophecy to defeat the Antichrists and support Jewish return to all the land between the Euphrates and Nile rivers. CFI literally believes in the words of the Hebrew prophet Amos: "I will restore the fortunes of my people Israel and they shall rebuild the ruined cities and restore them." Marshaling financial and moral support from evangelical Christians around the world, the organization has sponsored the migration of about 250,000 Jews from the United States, Russia, Ethiopia, and other countries.

Through a roller coaster ride that has included surviving several enemy attacks and resettling wayfarers speaking a hundred different languages from every corner of the world, Israelis have somehow managed to survive. To communicate, they resurrected Hebrew, the language of the Bible. To feed themselves, they formed *kibbutzim,* the iconic Israeli communities that took root during and before statehood. These socialist collectives, pillars of Jewish self-sufficiency, are no longer a dominant force; about 110,000 people live in them today, down from a peak of 125,000 in 1990. The ambitious younger generation has increasingly eschewed these agrarian communes for the bright lights of the big cities.

"Everything is going in the direction of the economy and materialism—and money, money, money," laments eighty-four-year-old Hanina Tadir, a self-professed patriot, socialist, and Zionist. Gone is the old socialist creed of working the land and toiling with one's hands, which was crucial to the early kibbutz movement. Today's buoyant, knowledge-oriented economy has given the country a Western look and living standard. Thanks to the Israeli ethos of *lehitgab'eer*—overcoming, or staying strong—deserts have bloomed, swamps have transformed into fertile agricultural valleys, and sand has given way to silicon.

Despite the financial burden of wars and mass immigration, Israel has enjoyed decades of relative prosperity. Periods of austerity, hyperinflation, and recession have been overcome; the country is expected to grow about 4 percent this year. In the past fifteen years, Israel has undergone a prolonged process of deregulation, privatization, and liberalization. The economy has evolved from one based largely on agriculture and low-technology industries such as textiles and clothing to a high-tech powerhouse. In 1992, diamonds and citrus were the country's leading exports; software accounted for just $125 million. Today, software exports exceed $3 billion, and more than half of Israel's exports are in high technology, a sector that encompasses approximately 4,000 companies.

> **Adapt—or Die**
>
> Over the years, the economy has grown from one based on agriculture and low-tech industries to one emphasizing state-of-the-art technology.

"Scientific research and its achievements are no longer merely an abstract intellectual pursuit, but a central factor in the life of every civilized people," proclaimed David Ben-Gurion, the country's first prime minister, in the early 1950s. At the time, the desire to transform the Holy Land, then a barren and disease-ridden region, into a modern state demanded a commitment to science and technology. Initially, the focus was on basic research, and on this foundation commercially oriented industries developed.

Israel is now at the forefront of computer hardware and software development, biotechnology and medical electronics, aeronautics and solar energy, agrotechnology and food processing. Seven universities, some world renowned, set exceptional standards. In the high-tech city of Haifa, for example, on the slopes of Mount Carmel sits Technion, Israel's first modern university, and its internationally acclaimed Institute of Technology. Since its inception in 1913, the institute's applied research program has paved the way for the rapid expansion of the country's leading-edge industries.

Nourish the Halls of Ivy

Several leading Israeli universities enjoy world-class status. The late King Hussein called Technion "a beacon of learning in our region."

Involved in everything from fiber optics to industrial robotics, Technion's 50,000-plus graduates represent the most substantial force propelling the nation forward. Almost three-fourths of Israel's high-tech founders and managers are alums, and two-thirds of its university research takes place here. Last year, Technion chemistry professors Aaron Ciechanover and Avram Hershko shared the first Nobel Prize awarded to Israeli scientists. Small wonder the late King Hussein of Jordan called Israel's version of MIT "a beacon of learning in our region."

In less than two decades, the land of milk and honey has become a land of tech and money. Except for northern California, Israel has arguably become the most important spawning ground for science- and technology-based companies. These two centers of innovation "have much in common," reports the *Economist*. "Both depend heavily on immigrants; are highly competitive in their business practices; respect learning and qualifications; and disdain those unprepared to take a risk." According to one Israeli CEO: "There are three fundamental traits in the Israeli psyche—wandering, insecurity, and the belief that anything is possible." Hence, venture capitalist Michael Moritz of Sequoia Capital calls this idea incubator "a second Silicon Valley," alternatively referred to as "Silicon Wadi" or "Holy Valley."

In patents per capita, Israel ranks third in the world after the United States and Japan. In patent royalties earned, Hebrew University and the highly acclaimed Weizmann Institute of Science are among the world's top five institutions, according to the *Israel High-Tech & Investment Report*. In engineers and scientists as a percentage of the workforce, the nation stands first, with 135 per 10,000 employees—roughly double the number in the United States and Japan. Nine out of every thousand workers are engaged in research and development, again about twice the rate in the United States and Japan. More than one hundred Israeli high-tech companies are listed on foreign stock exchanges, including seventy trading on the NAS-DAQ—the largest number of listings outside North America.

The innovation explosion of the past fifteen years was not born in a vacuum. "Thanks to quality education, Israel is one of the most advanced countries in the world," Bill Gates noted recently. Beyond its own well-educated workforce, Israel has also benefited greatly from the influx of highly trained Russian scientists and engineers. In addition, successive Israeli governments have poured money into innovative start-ups, assisting with funds for marketing and development.

> **Reform Public Schools**
>
> "Thanks to quality education, Israel is one of the most advanced countries in the world," says Bill Gates.

Another powerful propellant of the country's technological prowess is Israel's thriving military-industrial complex. As a pint-size Jewish nation in a vast, often hostile world, Israel has been an incubator for many high-tech companies—thanks to a rich lode of highly trained military veterans who honed their skills on classified army weapons systems funded, to a large extent, by the U.S. Defense Department and a host of foreign contractors. Most of the nation's technology enterprises have their origins in the Israeli defense industry, and corporate leaders disproportionately tend to be former high-ranking military officers.

The Israeli Defense Forces (IDF) is a people's army. With rare exceptions, conscription at age eighteen is universal, and almost every

Israeli serves a term. Most able-bodied youth are drafted after completing high school. Women serve slightly less than two years; men serve a minimum of three years on active duty, plus a reserve obligation until age forty-five, putting in twenty-four to thirty days per year. Foreign-born immigrants are not exempt from military service. Men under age forty-five can expect to be called, as can women under twenty-five.

"Putting on a uniform in this country is not only an obligation, it's a privilege," says Menachem Mautner, a professor and former law school dean at Tel Aviv University and a five-year military veteran. "Although opting out of military service is less stigmatizing today, it's still risky to avoid serving."

> **Reconsider National Service**
>
> "Putting on a uniform is not only an obligation, it's a privilege," says Mautner. "It's risky to opt out of military service."

Mandatory service in the IDF exposes the entire adult population to state-of-the-art equipment and advanced military technology. Much-coveted slots in the right military unit—the air force, army communications, or the intelligence corps—can mean as much on the résumés of Israelis as attending a prestigious university can mean in the United States. "What you get in the Ivy League, you get in our IDF technology units," says sixty-three-year-old Yossi Vardi, an air force vet and sage of Israeli high technology. "Kids are given multi-million-dollar projects and the leeway to make big decisions." Shabtai Adlersberg, a Technion grad and cofounder and CEO of AudioCodes Ltd., a highly regarded manufacturer of Internet telephony chips, agrees. "In the army, you're getting a profound education in technology," he says. "As in business, you're always working on a deadline and with a limited budget."

The military's approach seems to breed success in civilian life. Baptism under fire has spawned an army of no-nonsense business leaders. As an eighteen-year-old paratrooper, Amnon Landon hunted terrorists in southern Lebanon for the Israeli Defense Forces. After graduating from Technion in computer science, he eventually joined Mercury Interactive, a successful Web management company with roots in Israel but headquartered in Sunnyvale, California. Now forty-six and Mercury's CEO, Landon feels the company's rigorous culture and work ethic enable it to deal with the ever-present geopolitical risks. "You have to understand," he told the *New York Times,* "We were developing the early version of our products when Scud missiles were falling on Tel Aviv." Despite the barrage, Mercury managers brought the line out on time and under budget.

Thanks to universal military service and fifty-seven years of prodigious defense spending, Israel's well-trained technologists have given their country the fighting edge to outgun enemies. Here, homeland security is not only taken seriously but marketed globally. From document verification and remote sensing to Internet security and bomb detection systems, Israeli businesses are looking to expand beyond their borders. "We're still fighting for our survival," explains Roy Zisapel, a thirty-five-year-old former intelligence officer and chief of the $500 million RAD Group, which develops, manufactures, and markets solutions for the networking and telecommunications industries. "Because we're a small country, we think globally from day one. It's not enough to have a local presence, so we open subsidiaries overseas. But we keep R&D here because of the availability of strong talent."

The peace initiatives of the 1993 Oslo Accords also expanded international opportunities for Israeli business. But given the small size of the domestic market, like fledglings, young companies have always felt that they had to leave the nest to thrive. And access to customers, capital, and managerial know-how usually meant emigrating to America.

There is no better illustration of the pioneering spirit in Israel's globalizing economy than Mirabilis Ltd. The small software company, which developed a unique program notifying Internet users when their friends were online, was started by four ex-army buddies. After completing their military service, they toured California's Silicon Valley, saw what was going on, and brought that knowledge back to Israel. On an initial investment of $2 million, the founders sold the firm to America Online for $407 million in 1998.

"Israelis are culturally very open to U.S. business," says Martha Bennett, an analyst at Giga Information Group, regarding the recent rash of cross-national deals. Microsoft, Eastman Kodak, Lucent, Cisco Systems, and General Electric are just a few of the American heavyweights sifting the sands for Israeli high-tech companies. They represent a welcome source of funding and a means of exploiting one of Israel's greatest weaknesses: global marketing and strategy.

"We bring an American base to the company," says Isabel Maxwell, president emeritus of Commtouch Software Ltd., an Israeli-conceived but California-based provider of consumer e-mail applications. "Israelis have the prescience to choose the U.S. market and the lack of ego to allow someone else to help [them] achieve [their goal]." Maxwell concedes, however, that much of the company's scientific creativity comes from its software lab in Netanya, on the outskirts of Tel Aviv.

Today, more than two hundred Israeli high-tech enterprises have operations in the United States, although research and development typically is retained back home, where scientific and engineering talent costs a third less. At Silicon Valley–based Mercury Interactive, for instance, one-fourth of the 1,600-person workforce, including most of the R&D staff, lives in Israel.

The biotechnology industry also aspires to the global reach of Israel's defense-ignited companies. Until the late 1990s, the country's life scientists remained cloistered in their labs, relying heavily on government grants. Few had any idea how to raise money or commercialize their ideas. However, with the recent development of the local venture capital industry, numbering more than a hundred firms, the integration of life sciences and business is taking off.

"There's huge talent out there," says Yoam Millet, head of AG-Tech, an Israeli venture capital fund dedicated to biotechnology. "About 40 percent of the nation's scientists are involved in life sciences." In addition, Israel has more physicians per capita than most other countries and boasts more than fifteen specialized research institutes with leading-edge laboratories in its hospitals. Here, too, one finds firms with a foothold in both the United States and Israel.

> **Target the Best Minds**
>
> "There's huge talent out there," says AG-Tech's Millet, referring to the number of scientists involved in biotech.

For example, Pharmos Corp., which develops and commercializes novel therapeutics to resolve neurological disorders, is based in New Jersey. However, its R&D staff works in the glitzy Kiryat Weizmann Science Park in Rehovot, a forty-minute drive south of Tel Aviv. Conversely, D-Pharma, Ltd., which focuses on innovative lipid-based drugs for the treatment of central nervous system problems and autoimmune diseases, calls the same park home while maintaining its business development unit in Princeton.

Four years ago, U.S.-based Monitor Co. critiqued Israel's prospects as a major player in life sciences. The consultants, while generally positive, concluded that the industry's major challenge was to shift from a loose network of relatively small firms to larger, more broadly based businesses, supported by an infrastructure designed to produce long-term growth. The best-known success story is $4.5 billion Teva Pharmaceutical Industries, the world's largest maker of generic drugs as well as an innovator of drugs for neurological and autoimmune diseases. Roughly 90 percent of its sales come from abroad.

Today, the Israeli government is targeting healthcare—broadly defined—as a key strategic sector. In the so-called medical tourism business, for instance, the focus is on big-ticket surgical procedures, from face-lifts to liver transplants. Arriving patients are greeted warmly at Ben-Gurion Airport and whisked off to one of five designated hospitals. They are treated and housed in classy facilities alongside local patients. When fit to travel, patients and their families are encouraged to visit the country's sun-soaked seaside resorts as part of their rehabilitation package.

"The globalization of healthcare is changing rapidly," says Ofer Carmel, senior assistant to the director general of Maccabi Health Services, a top Israeli healthcare provider in Tel Aviv. His organization and others are attempting to replicate some of the winning strategies of Asian market leaders in Singapore, Thailand, and India.

Israel's mix of close ties to the United States, highly educated workforce, entrepreneurial spirit, and extensive R&D infrastructure has also attracted numerous multinationals, including IBM, Intel, Microsoft, Cisco, and Johnson & Johnson. Many of them have set up major research hubs in the country. In 1974, Intel chose the Holy Land as the location for its first design and development center outside the United States. Thirty years later, the world's largest chip maker employs 5,300 Israelis in eight locations, including 3,700 at its $1.8 billion state-of-the-art plant in Kiryat Gat, a town of 52,000 in the central part of the country. Few know that Intel's new centrino chip was developed at its Haifa design center.

Since half of Israel is desert, the lion's share of business activity takes place in the populous northern part of the country. Eventually, all economic roads lead to Tel Aviv. Age-old Jerusalem may be the heart and soul of the country and, of course, its government center, but Tel Aviv, Israel's hippest city, is where the action is. And these days the action, particularly in business, is hot.

Since Jerusalem was divided in 1948, Tel Aviv, the new city that grew as a northern extension of the ancient Mediterranean trading port of Jaffa, has established itself as the commercial hub of Israel. After independence, the city mushroomed—first, with refugee camps housing the hundreds of thousands of Holocaust survivors who poured into the country; later, with vast, ugly housing projects. Then, in the past three decades, what was an ungainly and uninteresting heap of concrete underwent a slow, carefully crafted revolution.

Today, Tel Aviv is proudly secular and downright sexy—everything the holy city of Jerusalem is not. Described as the city that never sleeps, it is at the heart of Israel's most densely populated region. Two out of every four Israelis live within its metropolitan area, which reaches to the exclusive resort of Herzliyya in the north, Rishon le-Ziyyon in the east, and Bat Yam in the south.

Tel Aviv is riding the wave of the country's economic success, and it shows everywhere. Its stock exchange and hotels buzz with the energy of global business deals. Glass-and-steel skyscrapers are juxtaposed with gentrified old neighborhoods that delineate the city's eighty-seven-year history. There you'll find the art scene in Florentine, Tel Aviv's Soho; wealthy repatriates in the quaintly restored pastel homes of trendy Neve Tzedek; chichi cafés and boutiques in Shenkin; and exotic aromas and tastes in Kerem Ha-Temanim, the Yemenite Quarter. To the west are the sea and some of the finest, most accessible urban beaches in the world. On the Tayelet, the promenade along the Mediterranean, are bustling pubs and oyster bars, nightclubs and samba lessons. For the ultra-Orthodox bearded, black-suited Hasid, the mere mention of thriving Tel Aviv conjures up an image of Gomorrah in its worst depravity.

Come nighttime, Tel Avivians love to eat and play. The growing popularity of dining out has given rise to a host of chic restaurants—from Indian to Tex-Mex, from *falafel* and *hummus* to French *haute cuisine*. The city's most fashionable foodie favorite is the Golden Apple, which serves serious French fare in a Bauhaus-style townhouse. In sister city Jaffa, locals head for Dr. Shakshuka, a North African eatery that offers everything from freshly caught sea bass to stuffed beef intestines. Coconut milk casseroles and fried bananas in mango sauce can be had at Thai House, just off Ben-Yehuda Street, while Mandy's Singing Bamboo on Ha-Yarqon Street presents a vast array of dim sum.

Pub crawlers trek to Elimelech on Wolfson Street, an old-fashioned blue-collar watering hole. There's Bonanza for the older crowd, Ego Trip for younger people. Athletic types prefer M.A.S.H. on Dizengoff Street for its legendary burgers and big-screen TV sports nights.

Culture enthusiasts needn't feel neglected. Performing groups, ranging from the Israeli Philharmonic to the New Israel Opera, have put Tel Aviv on the musical map. Reportedly, Israel has more

museums per capita than any other country on earth. The largest is the
Tel Aviv Museum of Art, which features a comprehensive collection of
Israeli and Jewish art, along with the works of Renoir, Monet, Van
Gogh, and Picasso. The Diaspora Museum, on the Tel Aviv University
campus in Ramat Aviv, is a fascinating attraction that offers a sweep-
ing look at nearly two millennia of Jewish migration.

Speaking of migration, the country's primary challenge is to woo
back Israelis living in the United States, many with extensive managerial savvy and hands-on experience in the American market.

> **Expand the Workforce**
>
> The country's primary challenge is to poach Israelis living in the United States, many with extensive experience in the large American market.

The United States has been a magnet for Jews for centuries. Com- ing to America carried special meaning for Luis de Torres. In 1492, Christopher Columbus's interpreter was the first member of the expedi- tion—and its only Jew—to set foot in the New World. Earlier that year, Ferdinand and Isabella had signed the infamous Expulsion Decree, directing all Jews to leave Spain. Four days later, Columbus set sail for America with the hurriedly baptized de Torres. Five centuries and more than 3 million immigrants later, American Jewry—5.8 million strong—represents the largest, most prosperous, and most power- ful such community in the world. In the New World, Jews found not only a haven but unparalleled opportunity in economics, politics, and culture. Today, they are thoroughly interwoven into the American fabric.

"Over the years, the majority of American Jews have evolved a balanced attitude towards their own identity," writes Joan Comay, author of *The Diaspora Story*. "They have come to accept that as Jews they belong to a historical community that is held together by pro- found ties of faith, emotion, and mutual responsibility that cut across national frontiers and that have their center in Israel. On the other hand, the United States is their country; they feel firmly rooted in it."

In contemporary Israel, a clearer national identity has emerged that is diverging from the interests of Jews in the United States. "We're moving away from being brothers to being cousins," one of Sharon's close advisers told the *New York Times,* when speaking about Americans. Whether brothers or cousins, young, upwardly mobile Israelis continue to view America as the land of opportunity.

In the 1980s, when the local economy was going through an especially rough patch, many Israelis—engineers, in particular—emigrated to the United States. "Anyone working for an American company here had to go back to the States to grow their career," recalls AudioCodes CEO Adlersberg. "But for most Israelis, U.S. management culture has always had tremendous appeal." Those departing the country, however, frequently were stigmatized as turncoats or, worse yet, wimps—and pejoratively referred to as *yordim,* meaning to descend, decline, or deteriorate, the opposite of *aliyah.* At the time, Prime Minister Rabin was one of their most vocal critics. However, in the early nineties, when it became clear that his already talent-shy country was losing its best and brightest, he decided that the time had come to bring Israeli brains home.

It didn't take much prodding to convince Eli Barkat. "I never intended *not* to return," the computer scientist and former paratrooper told me. "I never applied for U.S. citizenship or wanted a green card. But what I thought would be a two-year sojourn lasted eight years."

The thirty-something Barkat has been called an Internet visionary in local circles. In 1988, he and his brother Nir founded (and are the *B* in) BRM Technologies, one of the country's first venture capital houses. One of their early home runs was Check Point Software Technologies, a leading provider of Internet security systems. This venture and others that followed made the BRM boys wealthy, but Barkat wanted more: the challenge of building his own high-tech company.

In 1996, the Jerusalem native moved his family to Silicon Valley where, as CEO, he launched BackWeb Technologies, a NASDAQ-listed Internet communications infrastructure provider. But in 2004, the Barkats became homing pigeons. "Our friends were shocked. They asked, 'How can you trade in Palo Alto for Tel Aviv?' People were always searching for some mysterious reason for our decision," confides Barkat. "But it simply came down to home, sweet home. You can't replicate your family and friends in a foreign country."

The northern California lifestyle, he admits, was far superior to that in Israel, and Eli, his wife, and their three children "cherished" their stay there. "But our soul was here," he says. "And you can't live without soul." The recent returnee, now home just a year, serves as managing director of BRM Capital, which has more than $250 million under management, focusing exclusively on local software and communications companies. "Israelis have come a long way in closing the technology gap," he beams proudly. "Roughly 10 percent of the world's start-ups are based here. We definitely have critical mass today."

But what typically has been missing from homegrown enterprises is scale. Israelis make great entrepreneurs but lousy managers. That's the word from many of the country's corporate and government advisers. "We're great at improvising," one high-tech leader told me, "but when it comes to building a substantial, global business, we're a disaster." Yoram Yahav, CEO of the Technion Institute of Management (TIM), set out to change all that.

Nourish the Halls of Ivy

Technion recruited well-traveled Yoram Yahav to put its new business school on the map.

"We were concerned that foreign companies were buying our brainpower because we didn't have the proper expertise," TIM's cofounder says. "We had to create the proper learning environment for our firms to grow and become global forces. We also felt that, unless we did something very significant in management education, the whole high-technology boom was going to be a temporary phenomenon."

The challenge of eliminating the Achilles' heel of Israeli business is largely what lured home this former intelligence officer, Fortune 500 executive, and world diplomat. After twelve years of living in the

United States, the UCLA and USC grad and his American wife decided to return. "Israelis always dream of coming back," he explains. "But the real turning point came over drinks one evening in Jaffa, while taking in a beautiful Mediterranean sunset. My wife told me unequivocally, 'I'm not going back!'"

Reentry wasn't easy. "The first year was horrible," Yahav confesses. "I left the country thirty-five times on business trips, in many cases for silly reasons. But I didn't want to close the door on my overseas, mostly American, contacts. And I was afraid that a new door might never open."

That door did open, in 1998, when friends of the American Technion Society convinced Yahav to spearhead a new program for the renowned technology institute. The idea was to transform Israeli entrepreneurs and techies into disciplined, globally oriented managers. Today, TIM sits in Atidim Industrial Park near Tel Aviv, amid some of the country's best-known high-tech companies. It boasts an international faculty from the world's leading business institutions, including MIT, Harvard, Northwestern, and Insead. Lester Thurow, the MIT economist and former Sloan School dean, serves as TIM's chairman.

Recognized as Israel's preeminent business school, Technion draws five or six executives from a half-dozen companies to work on case studies drawn from their own experiences. They set goals for a six-month period, are coached by industry professionals, and report to their bosses at the end of the semester. As part of the training, classes take to the road, looking at best practices in successful spots such as Ireland, Finland, and Singapore. "We're trying to benchmark Israel against countries that are roughly our size but, for some reason, seem to outperform us," says Yahav. "For our country, it's not just an academic exercise—learning from others is a matter of survival."

> **Know Thy Competition**
>
> "We're trying to benchmark Israel against countries that are roughly our size but outperform us," says Yahav. "It's a matter of survival."

Besides nation building, family concerns pull Israelis back to Zion. In 1956, the Gutfeld family emigrated to America in search of a better life. Their defiant fifteen-year-old son Arnon went "kicking and screaming all the way and without a word of English." Like many earlier Jewish immigrants, the bewildered newcomers settled in Manhattan's West Side, where life, at first, was difficult. Eventually, the family prospered. Arnon graduated with honors from George Washington High School and attended Montana Tech and, later, the University of Montana. To make ends meet, he worked the graveyard shift in Anaconda's infamous Butte mines, toiling 4,500 feet below the earth's surface in temperatures occasionally reaching 130 degrees. "I was a mucker, the guy who cleans the trolley tracks and sharpens equipment," he recalls, "the lousiest job in the mines. But eventually, I progressed to become a real hard-rock miner."

The combination of hard work and a growing affection for the American West nurtured a deep interest in his adopted country. Gutfeld graduated from Montana with a degree in U.S. history; then it was on to UCLA for a doctorate in the same field. At age thirty, the freshly minted academic was weighing a variety of teaching offers, "with no interest in ever returning home." However, duty called. His father had recently died, and his ailing mother, who had returned to Israel, needed him. So, in 1971, the son schlepped home, with no prospects of employment.

"You can imagine how many Israeli universities were interested in a specialist in American history," he says. "Zero." Only by offering to teach for free, while assisting international students, did Gutfeld land a faculty appointment at Tel Aviv University. Today, the popular professor, with a dozen books to his credit, is a frequent visitor to overseas universities that, invariably, ask him to stay. "But our family ties are just too strong," Gutfeld says. "Families here are much closer than in America. Plus, my wife's parents are Holocaust survivors, so togetherness carries special meaning, special responsibility."

Friends are another important component of the homing pigeon phenomenon. "In the U.S., people are much more mobile. So it's tougher to preserve friendships," says Menny Mautner, the former law school dean at Tel Aviv University. "But in Israel, it's quite common to include your classmates from as far back as elementary school in Shabbat gatherings. That could never happen in America."

How difficult, then, is it for foreign-born olim to assimilate into Israeli society? "I'm afraid it's extremely difficult, maybe even impossible," Mautner answers. "Our culture is unique. If émigrés haven't had the same set of shared experiences—schooling, military service, and the like—it's very hard for them to feel truly comfortable."

Take the case of Stanley Fischer, the Zambian-born former number two at the International Monetary Fund and one of the world's best-known economists. Despite a severe pay cut and the threat of losing his U.S. citizenship, Fischer recently accepted an appointment as governor of the Bank of Israel. But not everyone in the country wanted him. Avraham Poraz, a former cabinet minister, questioned Fischer's Zionist credentials: "If he has not been in the wars, and his heart did not palpitate, and he did not go through our anxieties in terror attacks, he is cut off from the Israeli experience."

No question, the transition to Israel can be a jarring experience. Many arrive knowing only one word of Hebrew—*shalom*—or wondering whether they'll ever be able to work in their profession again. By most estimates, roughly one in three U.S. emigrants leaves Israel after only three years. "American spouses of Israelis have the toughest time adjusting," contends TIM's Yahav. "My guess is only one in 10,000 is successful." Reasons abound—from difficulty mastering Hebrew to the constant threat of terrorism. Some settlers are spooked to discover that Israeli homes are required by law to have bomb shelters and/or safe rooms, and that gas masks are standard attire.

More often than not, though, it's the locals' brusque, in-your-face behavior that has outsiders heading for the exits. The Hebrew word

> **Adapt—or Die**
>
> Immigration to Israel can be a jarring experience—from the difficulty of mastering Hebrew to the constant threat of terrorism.

for a native-born Israeli is *sabra,* which literally refers to a prickly cactus with sweet and juicy fruit inside. Unfortunately, many neophytes never get to experience the soft side of the home team. "I was a Zionist before I went to Israel," Rachel Gold told *Tachlis,* a chat room for those making aliyah. "Unfortunately, all that changed. I have never experienced such rude, ignorant, arrogant people. Everyone is trying to do everyone in. Every day is a battle, whether you're going to the bank or the post office. My kids were so unhappy. My youngest cried solid for over a year."

Such charges expose a perpetually raw nerve in Israel: Is the country truly open to newcomers and new ideas or is it a biblical backwater hobbled by parochialism? "For the cosmopolitan, well-educated, secular person, there are definite drawbacks," says Mautner. "Over 60 percent of our population are either Arabs or Jews whose families originated in Arab countries. Generally speaking, they're impoverished, poorly educated, and extremely conservative. Unfortunately, they carry tremendous influence in local attitudes and politics. This can make things rough."

Despite its heritage and location, reborn Israel was as European as it was Levantine. But that may be changing. "Many fear the country is becoming less European, less Western," Mautner senses. Another legal scholar, Oren Gross, agrees: "We were definitely tilting toward the West, but in the past few years we're behaving much more like a Middle Eastern country—with all the corruption, cronyism, and insularity that goes with it."

These undercurrents profoundly affect Gross and his wife, Fionnuala, as they ponder Israel's place in their future. After graduating first in his law school class at Tel Aviv University, Gross went on to Harvard Law for his master's and doctoral degrees. There, he met an equally talented Irish-Catholic girl, who later would become his wife. The Grosses' odyssey took them to New York (Columbia Law School for her; the venerable Sullivan & Cromwell for him), Tel Aviv (teaching assignments at Hebrew and Tel Aviv universities, respectively), Princeton (as visiting scholars), and Minneapolis (where they each hold professorships at the University of Minnesota Law School). She also has a chair in law at the University of Ulster in Northern Ireland and serves as a member of the Republic of Ireland's Human Rights Commission. In academic circles, the high-powered couple—still in their thirties—are leading authorities in human rights law. Hence, they could live and work anywhere.

For now, Minnesota suits them. "Minneapolis offers a great family environment," says Gross. "There are good schools, sports, lots of culture, and a substantial Jewish community. As important, given our travels, it's a hub city, so we can fly anywhere in the world from here." But the Grosses are constantly reevaluating their options. Their two young children are trilingual, speaking English, Hebrew, and Gaelic. For family reasons, the most likely long-term locations are the United States and the United Kingdom.

Returning to Israel is not in the cards. "Life isn't easy here," Gross confides over coffee during a recent visit to Tel Aviv. "Israelis are constantly living on the edge. And, despite the high cost of living, faculty salaries are roughly a third less than those in Europe or the States. Taxes, too, are insane. Full-loaded, they can reach 70 percent."

Nevertheless, the prospect of permanent separation from his ancestral homeland weighs heavily on Gross: "It's mentally hard. I feel very conflicted. How do I tell my children that Israel is our home, but we live in the United States?"

Like Albert Einstein, who purportedly had trouble finding his way home, Jews continue to

> **Encourage Dual Loyalties**
>
> Many Israelis living in America feel conflicted. "How do I tell my children that Israel is our home, but we live in the United States?" asks Gross.

wander the world. "If it weren't for Zionist feelings, many of us would be living in America," one business leader confided to me. Unlike most other people, Israelis are defined by their religion, a faith they have clung to over centuries of exile and persecution. In the final analysis, the modern reincarnation of this ancient Jewish state and the implacable hostility of its neighbors summon them home. "For all their shortcomings, people here are prepared to sacrifice their lives for each other," says Technion's Yahav, in explaining his heartfelt love of country. "Tell me, where else does that happen?"

Perhaps the late Prime Minister Rabin was right when he quoted the biblical passage defining Israel as a nation that stands alone. The long-standing odd man out in the Middle East remains isolated diplomatically. Israel has not been invited to join NATO, the European Union, or the United Nations Security Council. At the 2004 Athens Games, the International Olympic Committee failed to sanction Iran when one of its athletes boycotted a "judoka from the Zionist regime."

Fortunately, an Israeli windsurfer reversed the snub a week later, winning his nation's first-ever gold medal. As his country's flag flapped above all others, Gal Fridman triggered a wave of national pride, reminding the world that Israel is impossible to ignore. Hundreds of Israeli fans, many cloaked in blue-and-white flags, celebrated this rare Olympic triumph. The victory had special meaning for them because of the massacre of eleven Israeli athletes by Palestinian terrorists at the 1972 Olympic Games in Munich.

Back home, thousands of others rejoiced as the flag-raising was carried live on public television and state-run radio. For those in this perpetually threatened nation, Athens Olympic gold eased Munich's thirty-two-year-old wound and reaffirmed Israeli courage and resourcefulness. "This is the best answer to suicide bombings," Tel Aviv resident Moshe Arieli said in a *Christian Science Monitor* interview. "Showing the whole world by winning in athletics, without violence and without aggressiveness."

Exhausted by regional conflict, battle-weary Israelis realize that growth and prosperity will come up short unless the country resolves its main foreign-policy issue and achieves peace with the Palestinians and their neighbors. Until then, the nation remains hamstrung. "You can't isolate economics and security from the politics of war and peace," warned the swashbuckling former president Ezer Weizman, who created Israel's air force.

Clearly, there have been missteps on both sides, and much depends on how Israeli and new-generation Palestinian leaders respond. If and when peace finally comes, this remarkable nation could emerge as the Middle East's economic engine. In so doing, the Holy Land could deal a devastating blow to global terrorism.

bienvenidos,
amigos

In Mexico, nothing happens
until it happens.

—PRESIDENT PORFIRIO DÍAZ

In April 2003, Jose Antonio Gutierrez received in death something that had eluded him in life: United States citizenship. The twenty-two-year-old U.S. Marine Corps lance corporal was one of the first soldiers to die in Iraq. He was killed in a tank battle trying to secure Umm Qasr, a post vital for humanitarian aid. Moved by his death, Congress and President George W. Bush hastily approved legislation to expedite citizenship for the thousands of so-called "green card soldiers" who volunteered to fight for their adopted homeland. At last count, 37,000 noncitizen troops, including 7,331 Marines, were among the 1.4 million service members on active duty. Hispanics made up by far the largest group, composing almost half of the total.

Near his home in Torrance, California, Cpl. Gutierrez was given a funeral befitting a military hero: a flag-draped casket, a contingent of

high-ranking Marines, and a twenty-one-gun salute. But this ceremony included an extra formality: an immigration official came to present a citizenship certificate. For the young Marine, the posthumous
award was the culmination of his American dream.

Orphaned as a boy in Guatemala, Gutierrez left school at age
eight to work a series of odd jobs to support himself and his sister. He
learned about the United States from an American aid worker at a
homeless shelter. With *muchas ganas*—a great desire to get ahead—
the youngster began his hellish journey north. Crossing Guatemala's
lawless border into Mexico, Gutierrez's tortuous, 3,000-mile trek
included walking through deserts, enduring sweltering bus trips, and
stowing away on freight trains. He got waylaid in Mexico for a couple
of years, but eventually the fifteen-year-old made his way into the
United States—illegally.

"I came from far away where angels live in misery, dress themselves in filth, and eat dreams," Gutierrez later wrote of his trail of
tears. His pilgrimage next took him to Los Angeles and a string of foster homes. Finally, in 2000, he came to live with Nora and Marcelo
Mosquera—themselves immigrants from Costa Rica and Ecuador.
They not only took him in, they loved him and called him their son.
Buoyed by his new family and his strong Catholic faith, Gutierrez mastered English, completed high school, and began studying architecture
at nearby Harbor College.

It was September 11 that convinced him to give something back to
his adopted country. All of America felt the pain of that dreadful day,
but something else filled Gutierrez's soul: a need to act, a responsibility to serve. Weeks later, without telling his foster parents, Gutierrez
joined the Marines. "It's my job," he later explained. "It's also my
duty." Upon graduating from Parris Island in March 2002, the Marine
Corps became his second family.

Gutierrez knew the danger that awaited him in the Gulf. Before
leaving, he told the Mosqueras: "I can't stand having a regime do to
women and children what this regime is doing in Iraq. Saddam has to
be confronted. I'll give my life if I have to."

No death of any Marine goes unmourned. But the death of this young man who died for a country that was not his had special meaning to Latinos at home and abroad. The U.S. Embassy in Mexico City was swamped with requests to enlist in the U.S. military. Even as American casualties were coming home, would-be Americans demonstrated their willingness to join the fight against terrorism if it meant having a chance to live a better life in the United States, or *Gringolandia,* as Latinos from Guatemala to Mexico like to call their northern neighbor.

Just days before September 11, President Bush declared that the United States had "no closer relationship" than the one with Mexico, a nation one-fourth its size. Nearly two-thirds of the 41.3 million Hispanics who live in the United States are of Mexican origin or, like Gutierrez, spent time in the country, and most of them have a vote that counts. During the 2004 U.S. elections, Bush cozied up to this constituency with his guest-worker proposal for immigrants, while the Democrats later aired the first-ever Spanish-translated rebuttal to the State of the Union address. Both sides spent record sums on Spanish-language advertising.

For centuries, Mexicans seldom moved from their place of birth. Emigration was negligible until the 1870s, when U.S. companies recruited Mexican workers to build railroads and toil on the farms in the Southwest. A trickle of émigrés became a stream between 1910 and 1920, when 713,000 fled north during the violent Mexican Revolution. In the 1940s, an increasing number of guest workers called *braceros,* or strong arms, were temporarily imported to work on farms in California, Texas, and other states. Despite the abolition of the Bracero Program in 1964, Mexicans continued to leave the country in search of opportunities across the border.

Over the past two decades, migration has accelerated dramatically. The number of Mexicans living in the United States today is almost five times that of twenty years ago, according to the International Office for Migration. These new immigrants include middle-class, educated workers, as well as the poor. This brain drain, in turn,

has fueled anxieties that Mexico is losing some of its most productive
citizens.

Yet, despite Mexico's vital and growing importance to the United
States, most Americans know next to nothing about their country's
southern neighbor, second-biggest
trading partner, and single most
important source of immigrants.
"Probably nowhere [else] in the
world do two countries as different
as Mexico and the United States
live side by side," writes Alan Riding in *Distant Neighbors*. "Probably nowhere in the world do two
neighbors understand each other
so little."

> **Know Thy Competitor**
>
> "Probably nowhere else in the world
> do countries as different as Mexico
> and the United States live side by
> side and understand each other so
> little," writes Alan Riding.

Over the past 150 years, Mexico has felt the reach of American
power. In the nineteenth century, it lost half its territory to its northern
neighbor; in the twentieth century, it became economically dependent
on the United States. Yet, truth be told, Mexico has had a more subtle
influence on America.

"Many people talk about the great influence of the United States
on Mexico," says Carlos Fuentes, the prominent Mexican author and
former ambassador to France. "But the influence of Mexico on the
U.S. is much deeper. It's in the young and in the family, and in a million things that are far deeper." As large numbers of Mexican immigrants are absorbed into America's melting pot, they also change the
contents of the pot. That's what concerns some Americans, notably
professors Samuel Huntington of Harvard and Victor Davis Hanson
of Stanford's Hoover Institution. Huntington's chief worry is "Mex-
america," which he sees undermining America's English-speaking,
Anglo-Protestant culture. In Hanson's view, "Mexifornia," if
unchecked, will produce a "hybrid civilization," where the Spanish
language enjoys equal standing with English, and Americanization
hardly stands a chance. Mexican immigration, both men believe, will
turn the United States into a bilingual, and hence divided, nation.

In an era when Mexican newcomers are counseled by some to hang onto their culture and celebrate their diversity, the "American" in "Mexican American" could be in some danger. Immigrants from across the Rio Grande traditionally have been difficult to assimilate because their homeland is so close that they often zip back and forth over the border. They also tend to be much less likely than other immigrant groups to take up U.S. citizenship: 34 percent become citizens, versus 67 percent among Asians and European. Nonetheless, most available evidence suggests that Mexican immigrants follow the same path as, say, immigrants from Ireland into middle-class American life. They are purchasing homes and setting up their own businesses. Their purchasing power, now approaching $1 trillion, is on the rise, and corporations are rushing to embrace this burgeoning market.

As for balkanization, forget it. Gregory Rodriguez, an Irvine senior fellow at the New America Foundation, points out that Mexicans have made absolutely no attempt at political separation; nor have they tried to set up Spanish-language schools to teach their children their mother tongue as, for instance, Japanese immigrants have done. By the third generation, two-thirds of Mexican families speak only English at home. The United States, Rodriguez reminds us, is a language graveyard.

Therefore, it is flat-out wrong to assume that Spanish-speaking newcomers represent an assault on American ideals. Cpl. Gutierrez is a case in point. "Are you more likely these days to find a photo of a young Marine holding a place of pride on the family mantle in a Latino or a Harvard household?" asks William McGurn of the *Wall Street Journal.*

No matter how much Mexico's economy grows in the short run, the United States remains a magnet. "Mexicans go north seeking the American dream, and those who reach it return south looking for the Mexican dream," explains Primitivo Rodriguez, coordinator of the Mexicans' Abroad Right to Vote Coalition. "They live a life torn between two dreams."

In 2000, Mexican president Vincente Fox charmed his countrymen living in America by courting them aggressively and calling them "national heroes." Mindful that his nation was losing some of its most productive citizens and potential leaders, he began to pave the way for Mexican expatriates to return home for careers in business, government, and academia. In the 2003 midterm elections, at least six returning immigrants ran for political office. Andrés Bermúdez, who runs a prosperous farming business near his residence in Sacramento, California, was elected mayor of his hometown, Jerez, in Zacatecas. He is one of the first migrant candidates to win elected office in Mexico, but many more are pondering future campaigns. "My victory opens the door for a lot of migrants," Bermúdez told the Associated Press. "Just like we left in droves, a wave of us will come back in droves and help our towns out of poverty."

Dust Off the Welcome Mat

When President Fox called his countrymen living in America "national heroes," he began a steady campaign to recruit potential repatriates.

That's Jose Lopez's agenda. For years, he watched his birthplace of La Erre suffer an exodus of hundreds of young people heading to the United States—for jobs in Texas construction companies, California wineries, and Pennsylvania mushroom farms. Five years ago, Lopez decided to reverse the outflow, convincing Taylor Fresh Foods, based in Salinas, California, to establish a farming operation in La Erre, a fertile town in the central state of Guanajuato. To date, some three hundred locals have signed on to work for Taylor. "It may not sound like much," says Lopez. "But this is just the beginning. We're pioneering something new here."

From milk farms in Oaxaca and coffee plantations in Chiapas to the high-tech corridor along the U.S.-Mexican border, Mexico's government is developing a series of economic programs that are resulting in more jobs, wooing people home. Besides the Fox initiatives, Mexican states such as Michoacán, Zacatecas, and Jalisco are intensifying courtship of their prosperous expatriates in America. In addition to opening migrant affairs offices, they are reaching out to an estimated six-hundred-odd "hometown associations" registered in thirty U.S. cities. As well as seeking political support and funds for public works, officials are urging potential repatriates to make their mark in their states.

Returnees are "agents of prosperity," says Miguel Moctezuma, an immigration expert specializing in binational trends at the Autonomous University of Zacatecas. "They're keenly interested in slowing emigration and improving the quality of life back home." Carlos Gonzalez Gutierrez, director of the Institute for Mexicans Abroad, the Fox administration's vehicle for bridging the gap between Mexico and its expatriates, agrees: "These immigrants have carved a transnational niche. They're part of a phenomenon that will grow rapidly in time."

Mexico is also reaching out to another long-neglected audience: Mexican Americans. For years, Mexicans viewed those who left—and their descendants—as sellouts or, worse, cowards. Conversely, Mexican Americans tended to look down on Mexicans, considering them backward and poorly educated. It's no surprise, then, that in American films, Mexican characters were usually maids, prostitutes, or drug dealers; in the news, when Mexicans were mentioned, it was usually in connection with illegal immigration or gangs. Recently, however, it's become hip to be Hispanic. Consequently, a small but growing number of Mexican Americans with little or no direct link to Mexico are reconnecting with their roots.

Encourage Dual Loyalties

Binational pioneer Salazar is one of many Mexican Americans attracted to their ancestral homeland.

Ana Maria Salazar is one of the most prominent repatriates. Born in Tucson, Arizona, but reared in Hermosillo in northern Mexico until her teens, she was among her country's elite. She was a member of Mexico's national swim team, and her father was a famous heart surgeon. After high school, she attended the University of California at Berkeley and Harvard Law School, then entered the U.S. Foreign Service, including a five-year posting as judicial attaché at the U.S.

Embassy in Bogotá, Colombia. Then, it was on to various assignments in the State and Defense departments. As deputy assistant secretary of defense for drug enforcement policy and defense, Salazar was recognized as one of the one hundred most influential Hispanic Americans in the United States.

But she never lost her passion to return to Mexico. "In truth, I had never been completely cut off from the country because my parents live here," she says. Blood binds Mexico, where *la familia* is the nucleus of society. The combination of family, culture, and economic opportunity drew Salazar home. Five years ago, at forty-one, she returned to work for a prestigious Mexico City think tank and, before long, began hosting *Living in Mexico,* an in-depth television news program designed to inform outsiders of the country's cultural, economic, and political life. Salazar, a binational pioneer of sorts, believes that Americans and Mexicans are "more intertwined than ever." She credits the Fox administration with making Mexican Americans feel they are part of the country. "You have millions of Mexicans who have ties on both sides of the border," she told the *Dallas Morning News.* "Mexican leaders used to feel ambivalent about such people. Now they welcome them."

Nevertheless, plopping down in one of the world's most populous and most polluted cities poses challenges for any transplant. The Districto Federal, or "el D.F." (as Mexicans call Mexico City), is a bit like Los Angeles: a seething metropolis set against an often smog-obstructed backdrop of spectacular mountains, crisscrossed by traffic-choked arteries and expressways. The city itself is a low, swarming mass of gray and brown buildings anchored along a rectangular pattern of narrow streets. The pattern is broken by several broad boulevards lined with modern high-rise apartments and commercial offices, large open plazas, and numerous forested parks.

The 677-year-old megacity, once the center of Aztec civilization, recently completed a much-needed $400 million face-lift. Exhilarating yet overpowering, Mexico City is a place to love and loathe. It blends great wealth and poverty, colonial palaces and sprawling slums, earsplitting traffic and peaceful enclaves. It is the center of economic, political, and cultural life—and home to nearly half the country's people.

Yet in this grand and troubled old city, *chilangos,* as residents of the D.F. are called, find enjoyment in many attractive *colonias,* or neighborhoods. From the Almed, a leafy center of activity since Aztec times, and Zona Rosa, a chic shopping neighborhood, to polished Polanco, the city's most exclusive address, and the marvelous Bosque de Chapultepec, with its many museums, gardens, and walking paths, Mexico City offers endless options for newcomers and returnees.

Non-Latinos, too, have found life south of the border attractive. An estimated 1.04 million Americans reside in the country. That's by far the largest number of U.S. expatriates living in any foreign locale. The principal allure is not hard to fathom: *la vida cheapo.* Inexpensive land, labor, and living are big draws. Those with fat pensions or golden parachutes can live lavishly in Mexico, while the more frugal claim they can do nicely on their Social Security checks.

American transplants are also keen on Mexican healthcare. Though U.S. citizens living in Mexico are not covered by Medicare for doctors' visits and medical services (unless they travel back to the United States), the national insurance program is available to foreigners and costs only $300 a year. Relatively inexpensive, private Mexican or international medical coverage is also available.

Other attractions include American-style shopping in a country where Wal-Mart, Sam's Club, Costco, and Blockbuster reign supreme. As for familiar amenities, you'll find ATMs, American cable TV, cybercafés, and direct-dial, long-distance phone service in towns featuring small plazas, quaint churches, and solemn donkeys pulling carts. "The foreignness of Mexico isn't so foreign anymore," says Don Bradley, a sociologist at East Carolina University, who is studying the movement of Americans south of the border.

Mexico's diverse geography lends itself to a variety of lifestyle options. Many sun-seeking expats prefer the pristine beaches of the Baja peninsula or the party capital of Cancún; others, the high country and cosmopolitan charm of San Miguel de Allende. Whether it's watching the sunset drizzle liquid gold over the waves or enjoying the sunny weather and laid-back culture, Americans are finding Mexico a sublime place to live.

Increasingly, a new breed of intrepid retirees is eschewing the rocking chair for a second career. Former Silicon Valley fast-trackers Bill Kirkwood and Barbara Hart-Kirkwood moved to the Pacific coast town of San Francisco, known to locals as San Pancho, to set up a bed-and-breakfast. Karen Blue "chucked corporate life" in the San Francisco Bay Area to settle in Ajijic, a charming town on Lake Chapala, a short drive from Guadalajara, where she conducts seminars and offers a subscription Web site for people thinking of moving to Mexico. In the tiny beach community of Sayulita, you'll find a retired school principal and teacher—Rollie and Jeanne Dick—formerly of Salinas, California, running Rollie's, the area's leading restaurant.

In the past, most of those moving south were retirees and aging baby boomers. But recently, American migrants have become younger. "Families are coming because they want a different kind of lifestyle, especially for their children," says one transplant, noting the sharp increase after the September 11 terrorist attacks. More and more newcomers are high fliers in their thirties and forties, seeking a better life. This reflects both advances in communications and, more important, the country's improved economic prospects.

Tim and Sandee Cottrell were looking for a lifestyle change when they moved to Monterrey, Mexico's northeastern industrial hub, six years ago. "We wanted a new cultural experience," said Tim. "Our previous life in Dallas was quite restricted and U.S.-centric. Few people were interested in what was happening outside the United States." So the accomplished CPA leaped at the opportunity to become director of tax planning—

Target the Best Minds

Looking for a new cultural experience, financial guru Cottrell found happiness with Cemex, Mexico's second-largest company.

and the highest-ranking American—at world-class Cemex, Mexico's number two company, with almost $8 billion in revenues.

However, the biggest plus may be raising their five children in their adopted country. "It's a wonderful family environment," says Sandee. "The American School is fabulous. We believe our kids are getting a better education here than they would in the States." The Mormon couple, now in their late thirties, claims to have never hooked up the TV. "It's like America in the fifties," they beam. "We consider ourselves Mexicans—we're here to stay."

When Chad Barton told his colleagues he was quitting to get an MBA, they congratulated him. But when he told them he was heading off to Mexico, they questioned his sanity. "I had the credentials to get into some fairly decent graduate business programs in the States," the thirty-four-year-old says. "But they didn't offer the kind of experience you can get here."

Barton is in his final year at Instituto Technólogio y de Estudios Superiores de Mexico, or ITESM, in Monterrey. Looking back, his choice makes perfectly good sense. In a recent *Wall Street Journal/ Harris Interactive* survey of B-schools, ITESM ranked tops in Latin America and seventh in the regional category, coming in ahead of the University of Southern California, Notre Dame, Emory, and many other excellent programs. Housed in a brick-red, Mexican-minimalist rotunda designed by famed architect Ricardo Legorreta, the school prides itself on its diverse student body. Roughly 85 percent of its MBAs are non-Mexican; in fact, there are more Peruvians in the program than Mexicans. Another major attraction is the exchange opportunities with leading institutions in the United States and Europe, including the McCombs School of Business at the University of Texas at Austin.

"It's the best of both cultures," says Barton, who left a small Princeton, New Jersey, software company to enroll in ITESM. As for regrets, he only misses "pretty trivial stuff," namely America's smooth roads and drinking fountains. "Actually, when I go back to the States,

> **Nourish the Halls of Ivy**
>
> American Barton discovered "the best of both cultures" at ITESM, one of Mexico's growing number of up-and-coming business schools.

I feel more like a foreigner than I do here in Mexico." (As fate would have it, Barton was born on September 16—Mexico's Independence Day.)

No doubt, Monterrey's proximity to the United States and its increasingly bilingual, bicultural character make the adjustment process relatively easy for Americans. Prosperous, conservative, and decidedly pro-American, this sprawling and spacious metropolis is an oasis of U.S.-style malls and office buildings, leafy suburbs, trendy restaurants and shops, and some of the nation's best schools and universities. It is the cradle of entrepreneurship, where captains of Mexican industry hold sway. There are more millionaires there than anywhere else in the country. Monterrey's 230-foot, orange *El Faro de Comercio* (Lighthouse of Commerce) reminds all that industry shaped this city—and industry will carry it forward.

Whether it's in Monterrey or Mexico City, what we are seeing is a nascent trend in which successful Mexican, Mexican American, and North American trailblazers are trying to make a difference. Of course, the government's recruitment efforts will not halt the northward flow of poor migrant workers. Mexicans can earn far more in the United States than they can at home, and crossing the Rio Grande remains an escape from poverty. More than 450,000 illegals pour across the porous 1,951-mile border each year. They send so much money home that it amounts to Mexico's third-largest source of revenue, trailing only oil and manufacturing. That figure is expected to reach a record $15 billion this year.

Given the importance of this income from the north, migration is likely to continue, perhaps for decades. "As long as our economy falters," predicts one business leader, "Mexicans will keep on coming." But this stampede for the exits masks the fact that Mexico is undergoing enormous change. In July 2000, this vast and enigmatic country officially became a democracy, finally booting out the party that had lorded over Mexican politics for seventy-one years.

The Mexican people have survived centuries of stifling oppression. The Spaniards ruled for three hundred years. After their reign, the nineteenth century brought a war of independence, war with the United States, civil war, a conflict with France, then three decades of dictatorship. The latter passed with the revolution of 1910, leading to a new constitution in 1917. This, in turn, gave way to what Peruvian novelist Mario Vargas Llosa has called the "perfect dictatorship."

> **Spur Immigration Reform**
>
> As long as Mexico's economy sputters, thousands of illegals will pour across the border into the United States.

The PRI, whose initials stand for the Spanish words meaning Institutional Revolutionary Party, operated one of the most durable and, during the era of one-party rule, authoritarian regimes. Emerging from the chaos and bloodshed of the Mexican Revolution, the PRI concentrated virtually all power in a president who ruled uncontested for six years. Freedoms of speech and press were curtailed, and elections were controlled by a combination of machine politics, corruption, and fraud. With full control of the state treasury, the party bought off intellectuals and union organizers; those who couldn't be bought off were dealt with by other means. Successive governments erected trade barriers, confiscated foreign oil holdings, distributed farmland to landless peasants, and encouraged nationalistic and anti-American feelings.

Mexico's version of the welfare state was clumsy, brutal, and rigid, but for two generations it worked fairly well. The country developed, U.S. influence was kept at arm's length, and the power elite was able to avoid the anarchy and civil war that had scarred Mexican history until the revolution.

But by the late 1960s, support for the PRI's power monopoly was waning. The perfect dictatorship's dark side was exposed in the massacre of some three hundred students a few months before Mexico hosted the 1968 Olympic Games. Then, in 1985, when an earthquake killed 10,000 people in Mexico City, the government's response was slow and inefficient. The bottom fell out with the economic meltdown of 1994–95, which spelled the end for any lingering claims the party might have had to economic competence. Since then, opposition parties have grown in power and legitimacy. Five years ago, Mexican voters—fed up with official corruption and economic hardship—dethroned the PRI and overwhelmingly elected Fox, a former chief executive of Coca-Cola de Mexico.

At the time, Mexico's 105 million people seemed poised for momentous change. Rich in natural resources, blessed with strong family ties and a hardworking populace, the country appeared ready to graduate from the ranks of emerging nations to become a modern player on the world stage. But almost from day one, Fox and his center-right National Action Party (PAN) were a disappointment. By now, most Mexicans have given up on the president's ability to transform their country. Hindered by the global economic slowdown that began early in his term, Fox has been unable to deliver on the promises of job creation and income growth that many voters were counting on when they rejected the PRI. In the choppy waters of coalition politics, the likable but ineffective leader has failed to win legislative backing on a series of structural measures to overhaul Mexico's energy regulations, tax system, and labor laws. However, in a country where presidential reelection is banned, Fox's biggest faux pas occurred two years ago when First Lady Marta Fox flirted with the idea of succeeding her husband when he leaves office in 2006. Shortly thereafter, the president's private secretary and chief spokesman, Alfonso Durazo, resigned in a huff.

> **Adapt—or Die**
>
> After years of corruption and economic hardship, Mexicans voted Fox into office. To date, his efforts have been disappointing.

Now in the final year of his presidency, Fox is incapable of implementing change. "He's not just a lame duck, he's a dead duck," commented George Grayson, an expert in Mexican politics at the College of William and Mary. Given this leadership vacuum, the PRI's hard-line "dinosaurs" appear to be staging a comeback. At the time of this writing, the most likely scenario is that Fox's followers and the PAN team will be spectators in the 2006 elections.

Could Mexicans weary of this chaotic new democracy turn to a Vladimir Putin–like figure to restore growth and stability? Probably not. Although cynics in the country believe democracies benefit only a privileged few, they don't want a return to dictatorship. According to Latinobarómetro, a Chilean polling organization, only 14 percent of Mexicans prefer an authoritarian government to a democratic one.

Despite the problems, there are reasons to be optimistic. Mexican politics today are far more competitive and much cleaner than they were a decade ago. The country's recent move to free markets, open elections, and a more transparent government tends to buffer the occasional political ripple. Thanks to the 1994 North American Free Trade Agreement (NAFTA), Mexico's links to the United States are so strong that they help it override serious turmoil. "Mexican politicians are powerless to mess up their economy—at least while the U.S. economy stays healthy," contends the *Financial Times*.

All things considered, Mexico's evolution toward First World status appears to be taking hold. While the process is neither linear nor certain, conditions are improving. After a three-year slump, the economic tide began to turn in 2003. The stronger U.S. economy and cheaper peso brought Mexico's export factories back to life. For a while, the country's role as chief low-wage producer for the North American market appeared to be in jeopardy. Between 2000 and 2003, Mexico lost an estimated 400,000 jobs to China, which replaced it as the number two exporter to the United States, after Canada. However, improvements in workplace training and manufacturing productivity—plus proximity to North America—helped spur the nation's export revival. "Mexico has two things China doesn't," a U.S. government official observed. "The United States right next door, and a democracy."

This claim might sound jingoistic, but in a world of just-in-time production, living next to the world's biggest marketplace counts. Mexico's greatest advantage over China and other Asian competitors is its location. Approximately 90 percent of its exports are destined for nearby United States and Canada.

Credit NAFTA with transforming this former economic light-weight into a Latin heavyweight. *Business Week* has called the compact "one of the most radical free trade experiments in history," adding that it "ranks on par with Europe's creation of the euro and China's casting off Marxism for capitalism." These are bold words, but the facts speak for themselves. An estimated 1 million to 2 million jobs have been created below the Rio Grande—not only new jobs, but better jobs, with higher salaries and better benefits than the Mexican average. Mexico today has the world's ninth-largest economy, up from number fifteen in the pre-NAFTA days. What's more, foreign direct investment in the country jumped 46 percent last year.

Also, the anticipated mass migration of jobs from the developed north never fully materialized. It is significant that the first dozen years of NAFTA coincided with the lowest unemployment figures in the United States and Canada since the 1960s. Besides, Mexican companies—directly or indirectly—have created 150,000 jobs in the United States, about one-fourth of them in manufacturing. Since 1994, Mexico has climbed to sixth from number thirty-three on the list of foreign investors in the United States, ranking just behind France and Japan, reports the Organization for International Investment, a Washington-based trade association of foreign companies with American subsidiaries. "This is the second wave of NAFTA kicking in," says Todd Malan, the group's director. The accord has "enabled Mexico to invest abroad, and that investment is creating thousands of jobs for U.S. workers."

Shielded by decades of tariff protection and an insular corporate mentality, Mexican companies traditionally focused on the country's large internal market. Yet, with the opening of the economy by NAFTA and subsequent trade deals with the European Union and Japan, Mexico has been going multinational in a variety of industries.

Corporate Mexico now employs thousands of workers in more than two dozen countries, generating close to $10 billion in annual revenue. To illustrate: Steel and petrochemical conglomerate Groupo Alfa maintains operations in Venezuela, Russia, and parts of Asia. KoSa, the world's top polyester maker, operates in Canada, the Middle East, and Asia. Cemex, Latin America's leading multinational and the number three global cement producer, has its flag in the United States, Colombia, Spain, the Philippines, Egypt, and Eastern Europe. Groupo Mabe, Mexico's leading appliance company, is a dominant force throughout Latin America, from Argentina to Ecuador. Food giant Groupo Industrial Bimbo churns out bread in Chile, confectioneries in Germany, and gummi candies in the Czech Republic.

"We're seeing a new kind of *conquistador,* a reversal of roles where now Mexicans are conquering new markets by producing goods and services that satisfy international demand," says Jaime Alonzo Gomez, dean of the ITESM graduate business school. In the post-NAFTA world, the United States' southern neighbor has been mining opportunities far beyond North America. "Free trade unleashed Mexico as a serious global force," adds Alfredo Coutino, a Latin America specialist at the Ciemex-WEFA econometrics group in Philadelphia.

Whether Mexico is on the brink of becoming the next development success story is debatable. *"Estamos en peñales"*—meaning "We're in diapers"—is how one executive describes his country's progress. Yet most business leaders are delighted at playing the role of David in a world of foreign Goliaths. "Mexicans love to say, 'We are not superior, but we can learn,'" says Celso Garrido, an Argentine economist teaching at Mexico City's Autonomous Metropolitan University. "They use their inferiority complex to their advantage."

Looking enviously at Asian tigers such as China, Taiwan, and Singapore, Mexico dreams of becoming a Latin jaguar. However, the country's frustration at being outmaneuvered in low-wage manufacturing generated some serious soul-searching. "It's forced us to do more value-added, better-educated work," says Deputy Economic Secretary

> **Know Thy Competition**
>
> Looking enviously at the Asian tigers, Mexico dreams of becoming a Latin jaguar.

Angel Vallalobos. Recently, the country has been moving up the industrial food chain, focusing on more sophisticated products. Mexico's formidable labor force has swiftly climbed the value ladder, from sorting supermarket coupons and sewing blue jeans to assembling auto engines and manufacturing aircraft components.

Take, for example, U.S.-based auto-parts maker Delphi Corp. It's now Mexico's largest employer, with 70,000 people in more than sixty plants. The company recently opened product design and development centers, employing more than 2,000 engineers and technicians—many of them returnees from the north. In addition, the U.S. aerospace industry is turning south to keep costs down and stay competitive with global rivals. Like the automakers that turned the cities of Toluca, Hermosillo, and Saltillio into Little Detroits a decade ago, aerospace giants Boeing, General Dynamics, Honeywell International, and General Electric's Aircraft Engines Division have made Mexico a base for both parts manufacturing and assembly.

Mexico is also going gung-ho on high technology. In the mid-1980s, Guadalajara, the country's second-largest city with 5 million people, earned the nickname "Silicon Valley South." Lured by tax breaks and a government mandate that only companies manufacturing nationally could sell into Mexico's potentially lucrative market, a range of offshore companies—from IBM and Dell to Motorola and Hewlett-Packard—established a strong and growing presence. Over time, they have upgraded their operations to include state-of-the-art factories and technical centers.

Perhaps more impressive is Mexico's proposed "Silicon Border" project. That's the name of a futuristic, 10,000-acre high-tech park that a group of American tech entrepreneurs, working with Mexican officials, plan to build in Mexicali. "It's designed to be a science-based industrial park, similar to what you see in Taiwan and cropping up in China," says Stanley Myers, president of the Semiconductor Equipment & Materials International trade group, which has been working on the $400 million venture. "On a global basis, it will be very positive," he adds, noting that Mexicali, the state capital of Baja

> **Celebrate Science and Technology**
>
> With its proposed "Silicon Border" project, Mexico aims to create a science-based industrial park that will catapult it into the high-tech big leagues.

California, is only 150 miles from San Diego and 500 miles from Silicon Valley. Abundant water and power, three nearby universities, and an ample supply of technical talent are among the area's other attractions.

The Mexican government, for its part, has put together a package of incentives to lure companies to the park. "We're aiming for industry that is at the higher end of the value chain," says Eduardo Solis, chief of Mexico's Office for International Trade and Investment Promotion, who is in charge of wooing high-tech businesses to the country. Besides the Silicon Border initiative, government officials have opened thirty-six research and development centers and claim to have 4,000 Ph.D.s undertaking technical research in Mexico.

Of course, Silicon Border and Mexico's high-tech ambitions are not sure things. Unfortunately, there's no quick fix for the country's skills deficit, a result of decades of inadequate funding for science and education. Mexico spends a paltry $70 million annually on scientific research and fields scientists at a level closer to Angola than Israel. It is certainly paying the price, having to rely on outside science and technology. "The country has to import all this," says Nobel Prize–winning scientist Mario Molina, a Mexico City native, who is now a professor at MIT. "Living in the shadow of the U.S. technology dynamo has bred complacency among Mexicans," he claims. "Mexican students are not educated to be innovators or to create their own science or inventions."

As if that were not enough, Mexico's education system rests at the bottom of quality rankings among developed nations. Roughly 1 million Mexicans enter the workforce yearly, but most lack the skills needed for increasingly sophisticated value-added jobs. Although the number of science and engineering college grads has nearly doubled over the past decade, to 73,300, this still pales next to India and China, which graduate 314,000 and 363,000 students in these fields, respectively. As a result of this shortage of human capital, the International Monetary Fund recently rated Mexico forty-fourth among 102 nations in technological competitiveness.

Reform Public Education

"Mexican students are not educated to be innovators," says MIT's Molina, a Nobel Prize–winning scientist. The country's public schools rank at the bottom of developed nations.

The Fox government has responded, elevating to cabinet level a federal commission that monitors and plans to award $400 million in annual research and development grants. But many pundits hold out little hope for results, based on the administration's lame-duck record. "Mexico needs to start right now on the path that led India to be an information technology powerhouse," says Miguel de Icaza, one of the country's brightest techies. "It took India about fifteen years and a major investment in education. But look at them now!" He argues that if Mexico can achieve an Indian-style economy, it will vastly reduce its disparity with the United States and substantially slow the brain drain.

Homing pigeon de Icaza sold his Massachusetts-based software company to Novell to launch Gnome, an icon-based interface for computers running the Linux operating system. He sees great promise in Mexico's technological potential but is concerned about the lack of risk capital for budding entrepreneurs. "Who is there in Mexico that would fund a high-tech start-up?" he asks. "Today, the money has to come from your own pockets or the wallet of a family friend. The billionaires in Mexico only put their money on sure bets, but that's not how this country will grow."

"In Mexico, we don't lack innovation, but rather the ability to execute." That's the opinion of Jorge Zavala, one of the nation's information technology leaders, the founder of six start-ups and a seasoned veteran of North America. The forty-nine-year-old entrepreneur has been working with the federal government to achieve its dreams of building a global IT industry. The major shortcoming, he laments, is "a general lack of investment in technology, computers, and telecommunications infrastructure."

Consider, for instance, IT funding and Internet access. The country spends 3.2 percent of its GDP on information technology, placing it a dismal fiftieth in the world. Internet usage, too, remains abysmally low, with a meager 6 percent penetration rate in 2004. In fairness, the government, under its five-year National Development Plan, aims to raise IT spending to the OECD average of 4.3 percent by 2014 and, through its heralded e-Mexico program, boost Internet access to 10 percent by year-end 2005.

Encouraged by these initiatives, repatriates such as de Icaza and Zavala see an upside in their motherland. "Here," de Icaza says, "we can make a difference in the way Mexican society and the government regard high technology."

Not every new arrival or returnee adjusts smoothly, though. Most Americans experience some measure of culture shock. "Our two cultures have opposing attitudes toward wealth, death, time, and taxes," explains Ruth Ross-Merrimer, a former Californian who has lived in Mexico for twenty-one years. "Americans tend to flaunt their wealth; Mexicans shield it, sometimes behind walls of spiked glass. Americans consider death the end of life; Mexicans consider it part of life. Americans obsess about time; Mexicans are casual about it. Americans pay their taxes without protest; Mexicans put them off or ignore them."

Then there's the ongoing fear of lawlessness in their adopted country. Expatriates generally feel safe, but increased street crime, drug dealing, and guerrillas worry most residents. Although violence may be no worse than in many big U.S. cities, poor policing and weak courts make it seem that way.

Returning Mexicans also experience bumps in the road. They come armed with new, progressive ideas on everything from how to globalize business to how to move the country forward. For many, it's a frustrating experience, dealing with what they refer to as the go-it-slow approach of a paternalistic, autocratic society.

"I missed the order, efficiency, and punctuality of the United States," confesses a nostalgic Jorge Santistevan. "There's also not a lot of social mobility here. So I had some adjustment issues." The fifty-one-year-old attorney studied law at the University of Illinois and went on to do a three-year hitch at prestigious Baker & McKenzie, serving international clients in Spain and Latin America. Santistevan credits his time up north with making him "more pragmatic and a better legal consultant."

> **Dust Off the Welcome Mat**
>
> Although he misses America's order and efficiency, Santistevan prefers Mexico's more balanced, easygoing lifestyle.

In 1992 he returned to Mexico City to launch Santistevan Abogados, a law firm representing a variety of blue-chip multinationals, including Oracle, Beatrice Foods, and Mitsubishi Heavy Industries. Looking back on his decision to repatriate, Santistevan says he prefers Mexico's more balanced, easygoing lifestyle. "There was enormous stress and competition in the United States," he remembers, calling it a "never-ending, uphill climb that often left everyone behind." Santistevan returned home to recharge his batteries and find peace of mind. "Here, there's less stress," he says, "plus a wonderful opportunity to serve Mexico as an interface between our two countries."

For patriots like Santistevan who are trying to put Mexico back on its feet, it is vexing to reconcile this nation so bright with promise but deeply tangled in the past. That frustration, like so much that impedes Mexico, is a legacy of failed public policies. Growth and decline, hope and disappointment, all play out across the centuries. Hope remains elusive, at least for the moment, because of the widening gap between rich and poor, overpopulation, pollution, crime, corruption—and government malfeasance. Just as a society cannot fulfill its potential without engaging all its people, the Fox administration's efforts to broaden the benefits of the NAFTA-fueled boom have made little headway.

It is not surprising, given this tumultuous backdrop, that even the most optimistic returnees are troubled by the lack of progress. "What is most impressive is the enormous potential for greatness," says Ana Maria Salazar, the transplanted U.S. diplomat. "But what is frustrating is why this potential hasn't been realized."

Mexico struggles with progress like a Latin dance: two steps forward, one back. The truth is that our southern neighbor, like its Latin counterparts, is full of contradictions. When the Spanish conqueror Hernán Cortés reached the Gulf Coast of Mexico in 1519, he burned his ships to prevent crews from returning home. Now, almost five hundred years later, there is no turning back. In an era of globalization, Mexico can prosper only with links to the outside world, and repatriates from the north provide the oxygen the country so desperately needs. Today, this proud but misunderstood nation is caught in yet another contradiction—somewhere between its turbulent past and its promising future.

10

confronting
the future

Americans always try to do the right thing—
after they've tried everything else.

—WINSTON CHURCHILL

Whither America? In normal times, this question might seem presumptuous. But these are not normal times. As the twenty-first century proceeds, the United States is realizing the limits of its superpower status. The nation that performed so brilliantly in times of economic growth, abundant natural resources, and essentially domestic markets now suffers under a softening economy, shrinking resources, and globalizing markets.

Technology is leveling the playing field. Players once excluded from the world economy are now fully engaged in the game. As we have seen, no nation today need be written off as an economic backwater provided it has access to high-caliber talent.

From Iceland to India, a wide range of countries are pursuing bold initiatives to poach America's best and brightest and bring home their own. Until recently, this reverse brain drain went largely unnoticed. But the mounting loss of exceptional minds can no longer be dismissed. U.S. brainpower, once thought to be untouchable, is very much up for grabs. "Worldwide, ominous, and growing" is how Yale historian Paul Kennedy, author of *The Rise and Fall of Great Powers,* describes the prevailing headwind.

This change represents not so much the decline of the United States as the revival of the rest of the world. "For the first time in American history," says Henry Kissinger, "we can neither dominate the world nor escape it." Understandably, many Americans are unnerved by the new competitive challenges—especially the growing threat posed by emigrating foreigners educated and trained in the United States. As the stories in this volume suggest, these skilled professionals—lured in part by government enticements—are rushing home to start their own ventures. Global mobility has become more a curse than a cause for celebration.

So what can the United States do to halt, or at least slow, the reverse brain drain? The issue, at its core, is whether to play offense or defense. Is the country best served by an offensive strategy of attracting and retaining more newcomers, or a defensive one that focuses on replenishing its homegrown talent? To date, our response has been uneven, with no clear-cut guidelines for resolution. Clearly, parochialism is straining America's pride in being a nation of immigrants. Popular angst about outsourcing and homeland security has triggered an anti-immigrant backlash. More and more people want to pull up the drawbridge, triggering a number of contentious and ill-conceived proposals to shut the door on highly qualified foreigners.

To safeguard and build up its talent base, the United States needs a call to action. When the engine breaks down, you don't call into question the principle of internal combustion. You repair the engine. That repair, in this case, involves a dramatic overhaul. It means reenergizing America's appeal to the best and brightest immigrants, while building the bench strength of its native-born sons and daughters.

"Dress me slowly, I'm in a hurry!" Napoleon once remarked. This describes the double bind confronting the country: the challenge of reengaging its cache of top-flight newcomers and restoring its home-grown competencies. But how? Here are a dozen strategies for winning the talent war.

1 • KNOW THY COMPETITION

The fulcrum of international wealth and power is shifting away from the United States. As more countries realize that attracting human capital is the key to economic growth and prosperity, U.S. preeminence inevitably will diminish.

Every American leader should buy a plane ticket to China, India, or any of a number of other nations to see firsthand the economic supernovas rising in once-isolated locales. These include not only the highly publicized tiger economies but also nanonations such as Iceland (genetic engineering), Dubai (cargo and financial services), Bermuda (reinsurance), and Macao (gambling).

"The nation-state has become too small for the big problems in life, and too big for the small problems," sociologist Daniel Bell once observed. Robert Kaplan, senior fellow of the New America Foundation, predicts that by 2100 the city-state will be "the organizing principle of the world," emulating vibrant enclaves such as Singapore and Hong Kong. Even in fast-growing China and India, progress has been confined largely to a handful of big cities where policymakers can more easily construct the incentives needed to secure top talent. The United States—like Gulliver tied down by Lilliputians—must counter the remarkable rise of these upstart competitors.

2 • ADAPT—OR DIE

"This is an unfair world," says Singapore's Lee Kuan Yew. "But the world has never been fair. If it were, other empires would have stopped the Romans, or the Moguls, or the Ming or Qing, or the Czars. There are cycles in human history." U.S. hegemony need not end soon, but the country needs a comprehensive public policy that builds on its inherent strengths of flexibility and entrepreneurship, while maintaining a haven for skilled immigrants.

"All truths are easy to understand once they are discovered," wrote astronomer Galileo Galilei. "The point is to discover them." Rather than resist the realities of outsourcing, the United States should exploit them. "Outsourcing is a phenomenon that's not going to stop," says Arjuna Mahenchan, chief economist at Credit Suisse private bank in Singapore. No company can afford to deprive itself of low-cost, high-skilled workers. Tactically, it is like fighting a war of attrition. If the United States opts to prohibit outsourcing, business will migrate elsewhere. That's how a global economy works. So what to do?

The answer lies in adaptation. Ravi Aron, who worked for Citicorp in his native India and now teaches at Wharton, says the United States should improve the safety net—through retraining, lifelong learning, and wage and healthcare insurance—for those who lose their jobs to lower-paid workers abroad. But eventually, he says, "Every American should ask, 'Where in the value chain can I position myself?'"

On the bright side, the money saved by outsourcing can be reinvested to build new industries, create new jobs, and develop new capabilities at home. More quality work, in turn, means more quality jobs. Already there is evidence that increasing numbers of U.S. companies are upgrading their capabilities in core processes such as higher-value manufacturing and product development. Smart repositioning, combined with intelligent policies from Washington, could set the stage for a new round of economic growth.

Dynamic, competitive economies such as America's are always evolving—with the greatest rewards going to those who have the most advanced skills and thus can create higher-value products and services. The key is to focus on new jobs—in new industries. As knowledge workers search for the Next Best Thing, the United States must continue to woo the best and brightest from around the world. In the end, a flexible, open economy and a commitment to innovation are critical to America's success.

3 • SPUR IMMIGRATION REFORM

The 9/11 attacks in New York and Washington altered the course of history. In their aftermath, the United States has struggled to find the right balance between openness and caution. Today, four years after September 11, tens of thousands of highly skilled foreigners trying to get into America to work and study find themselves entangled in new rules and regulations. The *Chicago Tribune* has described our stringent immigration system as a "Tower of Babel—a cacophony of contradictory laws, strategies, and messages that ill serve the interest of the U.S. or the immigrants."

The influx of scientists, engineers, and academics is dropping off precipitously. The number of foreigners with advanced degrees or exceptional skills allowed into the United States plummeted 65 percent in 2004, while international student enrollments fell for the first time since the early 1970s. An important reason for this is the time it can take to get a visa—sometimes six months or more. This is deterring untold numbers of would-be U.S. knowledge workers. One wonders, could the next Einstein be among them?

As a promising young business professor in Hong Kong, Dilip Soman, originally from India, was actively recruited by several leading U.S. business schools, including Harvard, Duke, and the University of Chicago. Yet, even with job offers in hand, Soman found the process of getting a visa so tortuous that he gave up the idea of teaching in the United States and went instead to the University of Toronto. In my travels, I heard countless other stories of how a visa system tangled in red tape and misconceived security rules is hurting the country.

"Osama bin Laden and other terrorists are on the brink of achieving an unanticipated victory, one that could have long-term consequences for the United States," says Robert Gates, a former director of the CIA and now president of Texas A&M University, writing in the *New York Times* about the roadblocks foreign students encounter trying to obtain U.S. student visas. Twenty-five leading academic and scientific societies, including the Association of American Universities and the American Association for the Advancement of Science, called on the Department of Homeland Security—which oversees U.S. Citizenship and Immigration Services—to liberalize visa rules and reduce the logjams. They labeled the present situation a "crisis" that could leave the country isolated as top scholars seek training elsewhere.

"Competition is out there, and that's not just a phenomenon that's part of the post 9/11 period; it started well before, and I think we were a little bit asleep at the wheel because the U.S. had been so dominant as a destination for international students," says Ursula Oaks, a spokeswoman for NAFSA: Association of International Educators in Washington. Another consideration: foreign students bring approximately $13 billion into the U.S. economy annually.

The impact of turning talent away is felt far beyond the academic world. In American industry, visa delays are sapping the bottom line. Up to 40 percent of U.S. companies report serious delays in bringing skilled employees and customers to the country. Many say their businesses are in jeopardy—and so are the jobs of many Americans. "Six hundred to seven hundred American jobs are at stake if I can't get the six foreign technicians I need," says Larry Nelson, the president of Great Northern Sea Products. The company employs Japanese specialists during the summer at processing plants in Alaska to grade and sort salmon roe for sale in Japan.

"The changes since September 11 have had a huge impact on our clients," laments Elizabeth Stern, who heads the business immigration practice at Shaw Pittman, a law firm in Washington. "There has always been tension between business needs and security policies. But that has now become a very significant gap." (In 2005, legislation passed to ease the hiring restrictions on seasonal workers from abroad.)

No one can deny the importance of effective border controls, but America's chances of remaining top dog in the Innovation Economy are being compromised by shortsighted visa and immigration policies. Reportedly, things seem to be improving—delays in visa processing are shorter than a year ago, according to both the U.S. State Department and outside observers. Washington is hoping that, at least in the short run, technology (transmitting security clearances electronically coupled with a new Web interface, for instance) will allow it to find the elusive balance between security and openness. But the government should expedite the visa and security clearance process by hiring more bilingual consular officers and facilitating multiple-entry, long-term privileges for anyone not deemed a security risk. Also, a more targeted immigration policy that increases the number of H-1B visas and provides more entry slots to skilled workers and professionals would attract the kind of brainpower America needs.

4 ● DUST OFF THE WELCOME MAT

Reversing the brain drain won't be easy. "It's very difficult to make people come back," says Jean-Christophe Dumont of the Organization for Economic Cooperation and Development, the Paris-based economic monitoring agency. Therefore, retention of knowledge-oriented workers should be the first line of defense. U.S. leaders in business, government, and academia need to consider ways to make it more attractive to stay put.

Hospitality in Greek is *filoxenia,* or "love for the foreigner." That ancient virtue has been under strain lately. The flip side of filoxenia is *xenophobia,* so much in evidence in the current anti-immigrant movement. Just as other nations cling to terms such as *étranger, auslander,* and *gaijin* to heap second-class status on their immigrants, the United States maintains an equally frosty moniker: "resident alien."

"[The word] *alien* has always given me the chills," says Hungarian-born Zsofia Varadi, a ten-year resident of the United States. "It implies that I am a stranger on this planet, a little green creature with one eye and antennae on my egg-shaped head. But if you were to see or talk to me, you wouldn't know that I wasn't born here. I fit in quite seamlessly." Rebranding Fortress America is essential if the country is to reestablish itself as the Promised Land. Varadi's new term of choice would be *honorary citizen*.

While we are at it, we should change the law forbidding foreign-born citizens to seek the nation's highest office. Does that mean Arnold Schwarzenegger would become president? Perhaps. More to the point, loosening the restrictions would expand the talent pool of candidates for the Oval Office. Senator Orrin Hatch and Representative Barney Frank have proposed a constitutional amendment that would allow immigrants to run for president after twenty years of citizenship. Let's choose our presidents based on merit, not bloodline.

"Life is really simple," said Confucius, "but we insist on making it more complicated." New laws and new technology can, no doubt, help sweeten the bad taste in the mouths of many immigrants. But how about a warm welcome to the Land of Opportunity? "Smile more!" suggests Israeli entrepreneur Eli Barkat. "A simple smile would go a long way toward making newcomers feel more at home. Unfortunately, your surly immigration and customs officials love to display a traffic-cop mentality. Basically, they're saying: 'You're not welcome. We don't want or need you.'"

First impressions count. The United States should provide hospitality training to its immigration and customs personnel. Teach them to extend a simple welcome to foreign visitors. Not every newcomer is a potential Mohammad Atta.

Our ability to absorb the foreign-born and weave them into the fabric of American society is historically one of our greatest strengths. "The country owes more to Ellis Island than the Mayflower," the *Wall Street Journal*'s William McGurn reminds us. Each wave of tired, hungry, huddled masses has taught the nation something new, making it more flexible, innovative, and creative. From Peter Drucker and Enrico Fermi to I. M. Pei and Andrew Grove, new Americans have been influential drivers of our collective well-being. They should be cherished, not cowed.

5 ● TARGET THE BEST MINDS

"Give us your geeks!" should be our national rallying cry. In the race for gifted minds, other countries are scoring great gains. Canada and Australia pioneered "points" schemes to select would-be immigrants with special skills; Germany and Britain quickly followed suit. The United States, however, has responded unevenly in extending temporary visas for gifted workers. Recently, it has given out fewer than 100,000 H-1B visas a year, which is less than 0.0004 percent of the 294 million total population. What's more, U.S. immigration policy is heavily skewed toward reuniting families. More than 70 percent of annual visas go to family reunification, while only 20 percent are given to professionals and skilled workers.

Adam Smith concluded more than two hundred years ago that economic self-interest was the catalyst of the capitalist engine: "It is not from the benevolence of the butcher, the brewer, or baker that we expect our dinner." U.S. economic and military might owes a great deal to émigré brainpower. Therefore, Americans would find it in their nation's interest to boost the number of visas reserved for skilled immigrants to 50 percent.

The United States benefits enormously from being a magnet for international students and workers, particularly in science and engineering. Without these immigrants, this country would be hard pressed to maintain its worldwide advantage in the global economy. Almost 30 percent of our graduate students are foreigners, and the percentage is rising. Traditionally, many of them, particularly at the doctoral level, have chosen to stay here after receiving their degrees—a wonderful talent pool for academia and private industry. But, as we have seen, the homing pigeon phenomenon is taking hold.

"Economies are doing well elsewhere," says Mohammad Karim, originally from Bangladesh, now dean of engineering at the City

University of New York. "When I came here, a lot more students stayed. These days, a substantial number go back to wherever they came from—or to some third country." With scientists and engineers crucial to America's future prosperity, the United States must beef up its efforts to secure these imported stars.

We must aggressively attract foreign students at the university and postgraduate levels by making visas and financial aid easier to obtain. Overseas scholars now make up only 4 percent of America's students; by contrast, they represent more than 17 percent of those enrolled in Australian and Swiss universities. The United States should also reach out to high school–age individuals eager to get an education in the West. Although the United States is potentially the most popular destination for international students, it has shunned the teenage market. The number of such individuals attending our high schools has plummeted in the last decade—partly because of security concerns, partly because schools and families are less willing to play host. Australia, New Zealand, Canada, and Great Britain have been far more accommodating. Yet, foreigners understand that going to high school here makes it easier to get into an American university—which, in turn, clears the way to getting residency, a passport, and a job. Let's make attracting those with productive potential a national priority.

6 • ENCOURAGE DUAL LOYALTIES

"What you cannot avoid, welcome," recommends an old Chinese proverb. The flow of brainpower is no longer one way, and leaks in America's talent pool are inevitable as its rivals close in. Rather than lament the fallout, the United States should forge alliances with those departed migrants eager to straddle two worlds.

Returnees often take with them a strong appreciation of American culture and an eagerness to collaborate with U.S. businesses and universities. Many of them, though optimistic about the prospects in their native land, want to maintain close ties with their friends and former institutions. These so-called "astronauts," who shuttle across the planet, are a fertile source of valuable technological and scientific know-how. We should harness their skills by fostering loyalties on both sides of the pond. Our leaders should develop special incentives—from dual citizenship to adjunct professorships—aimed at sharing these mobile superstars. After all, half a loaf is better than none at all.

7 • REFORM—REALLY REFORM—PUBLIC EDUCATION

Americans are no longer shocked to learn that their schools perform poorly and have been losing ground compared to those in other industrialized nations. Despite U.S. taxpayers' pouring billions into K–12 education, our achievement continues to lag. Not even one in three American eighth graders meets U.S. proficiency standards in reading and math. Nationwide, 21 percent of teachers in public schools have children enrolled in private schools, reports the Thomas B. Fordham Institute, an education reform group. In many urban areas, that number approaches 40 percent. Why? Private and parochial schools impose greater discipline and achieve higher academic standards, the teachers told researchers.

Yet, we know that nothing affects the quality of human capital more than education. It is crucial to our future prosperity. In the years ahead, the United States must create a public education system whose students can compete with their counterparts in India, China, and a host of other nations. "The only way to ensure we remain a world economic power is by elevating our public schools," says Carlyle Group chairman Louis V. Gerstner Jr.

Over the past two decades, we have seen wave after wave of education reforms. Each has been squashed by teachers' unions and administrative bureaucrats who fear change and reject accountability. "If we could capture 1 percent of the hot air that has gone out of this topic [education reform] and turn it into results, it would be wonderful," says Intel chairman Craig Barrett, calling the current crisis a "ticking time bomb."

The bipartisan No Child Left Behind Act, even if wanting in its implementation, points the nation in the right direction. It requires states to meet national standards for school performance and increases spending on teaching basic skills. The *New York Times* has called this legislation "potentially the most important education reform since the nation embraced mandatory schooling."

In the meantime, it is clear that too many of America's public schools are failing and that the federal role in education is limited. Moreover, I agree with Senator John Kerry's conclusion that a top-down, one-size-fits-all formula leaves much to be desired. There are many arrows in the education quiver—from vouchers and charter schools to school choice and merit pay—and local communities are in the best position to choose the right ones.

In the final analysis, simple solutions—lengthening school days or years and demanding more homework—may be the best medicine for the ills of public education. But these ridiculously straightforward suggestions require sacrifice by America's students, spoiled by the 2:30 p.m. school bell, abbreviated school year, and light homework load. Changing adolescent and teenage behavior is never easy, particularly when it comes to hard work.

The country is soft when it comes to running its schools but hard when it comes to making a living, contends Michael Barone, celebrated columnist and author of *Hard America, Soft America*. Basically, the United States got it wrong—coddling its youngsters, while demanding the most from its adults.

"Americans like to view their children as passive recipients of education—as products of their schools," says Jonathan Rauch in the *Atlantic Monthly*. "If the product is defective, fix the factory. You will know that Americans are finally serious about education reform when they begin to talk not just about how the schools are failing our children but also about how our children are failing their schools." Amen.

8 ● NOURISH THE HALLS OF IVY

Conversely, Americans can find many reasons to be complacent about higher education. Citing a study mentioned earlier, eight of the world's top ten universities are American, with Harvard and Stanford occupying the number one and two slots. But there is no guarantee that the U.S. university system will remain the world's best, especially under the cost-cutting pressures now facing cash-strapped state governments.

Our public institutions have played a fundamental role in American society, from spurring technology to allowing students to experience overseas living. What's more, they educate some 80 percent of the nation's 14 million undergraduate students. Yet, increasingly, flagship universities such as the University of Virginia and the University of Colorado have seen their state's contribution shrink to less than 10 percent of their annual operating budget. "We have a system of public financing of higher education that is probably dysfunctional, both nationally and in most states," says Patrick M. Callan, president of the National Center for Public Policy and Higher Education, which produced a scathing report on America's colleges.

The United States must reverse its long decline in academic spending. Besides boosting support for its public and private universities, the country must provide additional funding for graduate science and engineering. Since 1997, the number of science and engineering doctorates going to U.S. citizens or permanent residents has dropped by 16 percent. That includes a 25 percent decline in math and computer science Ph.D.s. "A quiet crisis," is how Shirley Ann Jackson, president of Rensselaer Polytechnic Institute and chair of the American Association for the Advancement of Science, describes the present malaise. "If we don't increase support for basic research, science, and engineering, and if we don't develop our own talent, where will we be?"

Policymakers must continue to explore why our native-born students aren't competing in these critical areas. Counting on the continuing flow of foreigners because the professions can't attract homegrown talent is a risky strategy. "The time to redouble America's efforts is now," urges Charlene Barshefsky, U.S. trade representative under President Clinton. "We must strengthen our talent pool . . . or we will lose our competitive edge within a generation."

That's why putting more financial muscle behind America's universities is essential. "Technology is central to what's shaping our world today," says Harvard business-savy president, Lawrence H. Summers. As part of his grand plan to reshape America's oldest university, Summers wants to create a school of engineering with the same status as Harvard's prestigious business and law schools. That's the kind of ante needed to protect scholastic eminence. Rather than try to be all-encompassing, the new school will focus on information technology, bioengineering, and nanotechnology.

9 ● CELEBRATE SCIENCE AND TECHNOLOGY

Clearly, many of America's smartest students have lost their enthusiasm for science and engineering—the underpinnings of the Innovation Economy. As a result, we are paying the piper. Technologically, Asians and Europeans are ahead of us in several areas, such as broadband usage, digital displays, synthetic-language software, and cell phone networks. The only solution is for the United States to reverse this trend. "We must reinspire the nation of the value of people who work in science and engineering," says MIT president Susan Hockfield. Eventually, the country's ability to develop its young people in these fields will determine whether the United States will grow or stagnate.

Money isn't the problem. For various reasons, science and engineering are not perceived as exciting or encouraging. The stereotypes of the mad scientist and the computer geek suggest that these fields are "not a people culture," says Judith Ramaley of the National Science Foundation. By contrast, "in Ireland, computers are cool and geeks are good," claims Michael Ryan of Dublin City University.

Here, the image is far less flattering. "Students think, 'Why am I working this hard to become a nerd?'" says William Wulf, president of the National Association of Engineering. He blames our university curricula—overloaded with math, physics, chemistry, and very few exciting electives. "We follow a boot camp model. We throw really hard math and science at students for two years and only then let them do some of the fun stuff. No wonder we're losing them."

No doubt, the infamous boom-and-bust cycles and waves of layoffs also have contributed to the no-confidence vote in science and engineering. "I wouldn't recommend the profession," says Andy Moore, fifty, who got his bachelor of science degree in mechanical engineering. "Companies view engineers as labor to be discarded when things are tough." In search of more rewarding careers, America's young people are not about to repeat the sins of their fathers. "Engineering is a profession where a son often follows a father into the field and learns from the work and knowledge the father has done," says Thomas M. Hout of Boston Consulting Group and a lecturer at Harvard Business School. "If the father isn't getting involved in some of these technologies anymore, the son isn't going to follow either."

Engineering and many scientific disciplines remain classic bastions of male domination. For decades, universities have lamented the fact that some of their brightest female students shun these fields. However, things may be improving. Women now make up half the student body of the nation's medical schools. Partly as a result of universities' recent move to interdisciplinary programs, the number of female graduates in science and engineering is rising. In computer science, for instance, women represent roughly 28 percent of those receiving undergraduate degrees and 23 percent of new doctorates. What's more, they also earn more than one-third of all science and engineering Ph.D.s versus 10 percent three decades ago.

"We're trying to get younger people, earlier in their lives, excited about technology," say Samuel J. Palmisano, CEO of IBM, and G. Wayne Clough, president of Georgia Institute of Technology. They serve as co-chairs of the Council on Competitiveness—an organization of business, labor, and academic leaders committed to creating a more hospitable climate for scientists and techies. No one has been a more effective cheerleader than Microsoft chairman Bill Gates. But he admits "there doesn't seem to be the sense of buzz, excitement, and understanding to work and study in science and technology." To reverse this sentiment, the world's wealthiest man has been touring U.S. campuses, reassuring students that lucrative careers can be had in the high-tech world.

These efforts—highly respected leaders taking the initiative to speak out for science and technology—could not have come at a better time. By all accounts, the world is on the threshold of an innovation revolution in biotechnology, nanotechnology, energy, space commercialization, and several other vanguard areas. Whether the United States will lag behind or lead the innovation renaissance depends largely on the combined abilities of Washington and corporate America to stimulate research and development.

Government, for its part, must foster the institutional and attitudinal framework to plant fresh green shoots of discovery. Among other things, this means continuing efforts to rationalize regulation, increase tax incentives, protect intellectual property, and, most important, increase funding for basic and early-stage research. In the post–World War II and Sputnik eras, the U.S. government became the principal supporter of basic research of all kinds—so much so that Americans came to see their federal grants as a birthright.

But in the post-9/11 world, the United States has lost much of its adventurous spirit. Government support for research and development has wavered, with the majority of funding going to defense and health. Even the National Institutes of Health, the main benefactor of university research, saw its grants grow by less than 3 percent last year. Starved for funds, young scientists and engineers are quitting academia, which in turn is creating a wave of anxiety in the scientific and technology community. Often it is these young bright minds that come up with the most original ideas. Recall that Albert Einstein produced his four seminal physics papers when he was only twenty-six.

Thomas G. Donlan of *Barron's* proposes postdoctoral grants of $100,000 a year for ten years to every one of the 27,000 or so who earn their doctorates in science and engineering each year. This annual $27 billion investment would "send them into the world with the means to work as they wish until the money runs out. After they prove themselves, they will have to support themselves by winning jobs in industry, academia, foundations, or the government." Others suggest that these grants should have some matching component of hard money, not contributions in kind, from U.S. industry.

The government should also unshackle research in sensitive areas such as stem-cell research and defense-related activities. Emerging technologies can be exploited only in a world of scientific freedom. In 2004, California got it right with its ten-year, $3 billion fund to support stem-cell research—a field dominated by the United Kingdom, Singapore, Israel, and South Korea. This biotech booster could make the Golden State the epicenter of human embryo research in the future—and help reverse the brain drain.

"My sense is that a lot of people are going to move to California—a lot of students and postdocs," predicts Harvey Lodish, a professor of biology at MIT and a researcher at its Whitehead Institute for Biomedical Research. "There are a lot of future leaders who would find it attractive."

Corporate America, for its part, seems well positioned to participate in an innovation rebirth. When it comes to providing the economic incentives for sustained creativity, the country's well-developed capital markets and huge venture capital industry are unmatched. From northern California to Boston's Route 128, the nation is blessed with a system of innovation habitats composed of die-hard entrepreneurs, knowledge-oriented workers, university researchers, venture capitalists, and business consultants. In global terms, no other locale has the critical mass and sheer significance of these crucibles of the Innovation Economy.

Yet, even *BusinessWeek,* hardly a journal to foment revolution, huffed about the hubris of America's Silicon Valleys. "It pays to remember that ecosystems can become unstable. Even today, Silicon Valley is no Eden."

America's spirits needn't sag. These valleys are not about to become the Venices of the Information Age. Yet, as other nations are closing the innovation gap and, in some cases, surpassing the United States, Americans should continue to ask: Who will take us into the future? My advice: Nurture the nerds!

10 • EXPAND THE WORKFORCE

As the talent war heats up, the United States faces a wrenching manpower and skills shortage. In nations both rich and poor, families are having fewer children. According to the United Nations population division, global fertility rates are now only half what they were in the 1970s. Meanwhile, our average age will increase dramatically. An aging population, in turn, means less productivity because older people, rightly or wrongly, are considered to be less entrepreneurial.

A growing population, on the other hand, spurs innovation. "Economic expansion depends entirely on pushing more people into the workforce and getting more out of them," says Phillip Longman, a senior fellow at the Washington-based New American Foundation and author of *The Empty Cradle*. "In the future, shrinking labor pools will mean higher taxes, longer work hours, and less leisure than would otherwise be possible, as fewer and fewer working-age people have to support an ever-growing number of dependent elders."

America's traditional antidote to this demographic time bomb has been attracting immigrants—who, on average, are younger and have higher fertility rates than the general population. But, in a world of flight capital, immigration is not a panacea. Trying to raise birthrates is also impractical because people's fertility, particularly in wealthy nations, does not respond to financial incentives.

The best way forward is to broaden workforce participation among working-age people and to defer retirement. At present, the overall employment rate is almost 70 percent in the United States—relatively high among industrialized nations. Hence, policymakers in business and government are attempting to extend the retirement age, while hiring back their former employees, especially those with scientific and technological know-how.

To help the country cope, I support the multiple solutions proposed by MIT's David W. DeLong, author of *Lost Knowledge: Confronting the Threat of an Aging Workforce.* Solutions include phased retirements, debriefing sessions for prospective retirees, and nurturing ties with corporate alumni. Ford, General Motors, IBM, Monsanto, and General Electric are pacesetters in these techniques.

America's future retirees, in turn, are less inclined to walk out the door. Sensing their increasing leverage in the job market, many are rejecting the rocking-chair image of old age and pushing back their departure dates. In a recent Gallup survey, *Rethinking Retirement,* 57 percent of respondents said they planned to defer retirement. According to the American Association of Retired Persons, fully 80 percent of the nation's 79 million baby boomers—people between forty and sixty years old—plan to work into their seventies. In addition, roughly 15 percent of the population sixty-five and older are heading back to work—either because they wish to stay active or because of economic pressures. In today's talent-tight world, America's seniors are holding many of the cards.

11 • RECONSIDER NATIONAL SERVICE

"Ever distant frontiers and ever brighter tomorrows," wrote *Time* editor George M. Taber, "created a nation of optimists, who believed that a rising tide lifts all boats." That ethos is the embodiment of the American Dream. However, in recent years, we have been reminded of the imperfections of contemporary capitalism. The country, at times, seems unable to maintain, let alone build, the bridges needed to synthesize a diverse population.

The glib solution to a society increasingly viewed as cold and uncaring is to withdraw from it—a topic of countless magazine articles, talk-show discussions, and self-help books. If America is to regain the hearts and minds of all its people, it must reestablish values of trust and sharing. What I propose is a Re-United States of America, with some form of compulsory national service as its centerpiece.

Government could begin the process by drawing on the immense untapped reservoir of energy, enthusiasm, and ability of America's youth. More specifically, the country could introduce a system of national service with the following features: (1) an entry age ranging from eighteen to twenty-three years; (2) a minimum of two years' active duty, including three months of rigorous basic training; (3) a four-year reserve requirement; and (4) a wide range of assignments in military and nonmilitary units—the Marine Corps or the Peace Corps, it makes no difference. Senators Evan Bayh and John McCain have proposed a similar plan. Any such scheme must be applied uniformly and equitably in all areas: registration, selection, and assignment policies. Experience has shown that Americans will not accept conscription unless they perceive it as fair.

The mood is right for inciting national esprit. As Israel, Singapore, and Taiwan have shown, a strong commitment to public service can bring all segments of society together in an energizing way. At the very least, a program of effective conscription might give new meaning to "duty, honor, and country" and reinvigorate the communitarian values and institutions needed to survive future decades.

12 • ACT NOW

We live in interesting times. In this Brave New World, one of leadership's most important challenges is to safeguard any country's most important resource—its talent. Regrettably, the United States has lost some of its glow as the spread of democratic capitalism has created opportunities elsewhere. In a world in which economic growth and competitiveness depend above all on human capital, policymakers cannot dillydally. Restocking our talent base could take years, even decades. "Even if action were taken today," says the National Science Board, "the reversal is ten to twenty years away."

America's leaders cannot afford to equivocate. That taking serious steps is not only appropriate but critical in reversing the brain drain is itself a shocking admission. A mere decade ago nothing could have seemed farther from the truth. But in this young century, powerful centrifugal forces are weakening America's hold on its best minds.

• • •

Having reviewed this list, I am struck by two things: first, the urgent need to meet this daunting challenge; second, the enormous financial demands on a nation already beset by debt. Squaring these recommendations with today's fiscal realities will surely test the country's will. However, long after the defeat of terrorism and the return of global harmony, the talent war will remain.

America is in a state of transition, at the beginning of an economic and attitudinal revolution. Inevitably, this revolution means restoring the American Dream. For this to happen, all segments of society will have to pool their talents. Henry Ford said it best: "Coming together is a beginning; keeping together is progress; working together is success."

The principle of indivisibility—coming together, keeping together, and working together—is deeply ingrained in the American character. We should follow our roots to pursue the modern-day equivalent of "one nation indivisible." As in any philosophical search, the risks are great, and the outcome is uncertain. Is there any alternative? I, like most Americans, think not.

notes

Unless otherwise indicated, quotations are from interviews with the author or his associates. The following references, in chapter sequence, complement those interviews.

PREFACE

xi   President Bush's remarks are cited in Elisabeth Bumiller, "Bush Woos Hispanics and Moderates," *New York Times Digest,* January 8, 2004, p. 1. See also Vincent J. Cannuto, "The Making of Americans," *Wall Street Journal,* January 29, 2004, p. D5.

xii   Craig Barrett is quoted in "Intel CEO: Let's End Political Games and Compete," *USA Today,* April 28, 2004, p. 13A.

xii   The Herman Melville quote may be found in Melville's *Moby Dick* (New York: Harper & Row, 1851), p. 104.

CHAPTER 1. HEADING HOME

1   For additional background on the talent war, see Bruce Tulgan, *Winning the Talent Wars* (New York: W. W. Norton, 2001); Ed Michaels, Helen Handfield-Jones, and Beth Axelrod, *The War for Talent* (Boston: Harvard Business School Press, 2001); Roger E. Herman, Thomas G. Olivo, and Joyce L. Gioia, *Impending Crisis* (Winchester, Va.: Oakhill Press, 2003); Edward E. Gordon, *Skills War* (Woburn, Mass: Butterworth-Heinemann, 2000); Neil Howe and William Strauss, *Millennials Rising* (New York:

Vintage Books, 2000); and Richard Florida, *The Flight of the Creative Class* (New York: HarperBusiness, 2005). See also Alan M. Webber, "Reverse Brain Drain Threatens U.S. Economy," *USA Today,* February 24, 2004, p. 13A; "Outward Bound," *Economist,* September 28, 2002; Doreen Carvajal, "Calling Scientists Back Home," *International Herald Tribune,* July 7, 2004, p. 11; Pete Engardio, Aanon Bernstein, and Manjeet Kripalani, "The New Global Job Shift," *BusinessWeek Online,* February 3, 2003; Stephen Baker, "The Coming Battle for Immigrants," *BusinessWeek,* August 26, 2002, pp. 138–140; Emily Bazar, "Immigrants Return to Greener Pastures," *Honolulu Star-Bulletin,* March 27, 2005, p. D6; "High-Tech Brain Drain," *Wall Street Journal,* May 4, 2005, p. A14; and David Heenan, "The Job Wars," *Journal of Business Strategy,* November–December 1994.

2   Edward Tian's quote is from Dexter Roberts, "Bring It All Back Home," *BusinessWeek,* June 22, 1998, p. 58. See also Alejandro Reyes, "Networking for a New China," *Asiaweek.com,* March 30, 2001, p. 1; and David Sheff, "China's Change Merchants," *Chief Executive,* March 2002, pp. 50–55.

4   Pete Engardio introduced "brainiacs" in his "Scouring the Planet for Brainiacs," *BusinessWeek,* October 11, 2004, p. 100.

6   MiinWu is quoted in Thomas Crampton, "Taiwan's Industrial Ambition," *International Herald Tribune,* March 18, 1999, p. 15.

6   Edison Liu's quotes are from Trish Saywell, "Ambition in a Test Tube," *Far Eastern Economic Review,* January 9, 2003, pp. 34, 36.

7   James Gao's remarks are in Alysha Webb, "Back to the Motherland," *Far Eastern Economic Review,* August 29, 2002, p. 60. See also David W. Chen, "For Many Chinese, America's Allure Is Fading," *New York Times,* September 7, 2003, p. A4; and John Markoff, "Have Supercomputer, Will Travel," *New York Times,* November 11, 2004, p. C1.

7   Gao Weining's quote is from Janet Ong, "High-Tech Luring Laid-off Expatriates Back to China," *Honolulu Advertiser,* January 2, 2003, p. D3. See also Louise Kehoe, "The Trans-Pacific Valley," *Financial Times,* May 15, 2002, p. 9.

7   The Vajpayre quote is from Amy Waldman, "India Harvests Fruits of a Diaspora," *New York Times,* January 12, 2003, p. 4; and "India Taps Émigrés to Boost Its Economy," *Honolulu Star-Bulletin,* January 12, 2003, p. A4.

7   Rama Velpuri's story is reported in Eryn Brown and David Kirpatrick, "The Reverse Brain Drain," *Fortune,* November 11, 2002, pp. 39–40. See also Manjeet Kripalani and Pete Engardio, "The Rise of India," *BusinessWeek,* December 8, 2003, pp. 66–73.

8   Kalosh Josli's quote is from Edward Luce, "India Lures the High-Tech Expat Dollar," *Financial Times,* February 28, 2001, p. 12. See also Amy Waldman, "Economy Drawing Indians Back Home," *Honolulu Star-Bulletin,* July 24, 2004, p. A9; and Robert D. Hof with Manjeet Kripalani, "India and Silicon Valley: Now the R&D Flows Both Ways," *BusinessWeek,* December 8, 2003, p. 7.

8   David Thai's repatriation is discussed in David Lamb, *Vietnam Now* (New York: Public Affairs, 2002), pp. 214–215. See also Keith Bradsher, "Outsourcing Finds Vietnam," *New York Times,* September 30, 2004, p. W1; Margot Cohen, "New Taste for the Good Life," *Far Eastern Economic Review,* October 28, 2004, pp. 44–46; Cohen, "Foreign Companies Turn to Web to Recruit Vietnamese Managers," *Wall Street Journal,* February 5, 2003, p. B7A; and Sheridan Prasso, "Hello, Vietnam," *Chief Executive,* March 2005, pp. 34–36.

8   For more on Silicon Valley South, see Jack Epstein, "Brazil Strives to Tempt Settlers to a 'Silicon Valley,'" *Christian Science Monitor,* April 12, 1995, p. 8.

9   Kwume Bostu is discussed in Michael M. Phillips, "On Ghana's Tech Frontier," *Wall Street Journal,* May 22, 2002, p. B1. See also G. Pascal Zachary, "Searching for a Dial Tone in Africa," *New York Times,* July 5, 2003, p. B5; Joseph Berger, "American Dream Is Ghana Home," *New York Times,* August 21, 2002, p. A17; Lynette Clemetson, "For Schooling, a Reverse Emigration to Africa," *New York Times,* September 4, 2003, p. A1;

and Marc Lacey, "Accents of Africa: A New Outsourcing Frontier," *New York Times,* February 2, 2005, p. C1.

10 Kári Stefánnson's repatriation is variously reported. See, for example, Joel Baglole, "Iceland Transforms Itself into a Hotbed of New Industries," *Wall Street Journal,* March 13, 2001, p. A21.

10 Daddi Gudbergsson is quoted in Marco R. della Cava, "Iceland Warms to the Net," *USA Today,* March 27, 2000, p. 1B.

10 For more on the Farrens, see David L. Lynch, "Flourishing Ireland Calls Its Children Home," *USA Today*, March 16, 1999, p. 13A.

11 See Stuart Anderson, "The Multiplier Effect," *International Educator,* Summer 2004, pp. 14–21. See also "Give Us Your Nerds," *Wall Street Journal,* July 16, 2004, p. A12; Amanda Paulson, "Immigrants' Children Ace Sciences," *Christian Science Monitor,* August 31, 2004, p. 13; Patrick Welsh, "Motivation, Focus Send Foreign-Born Students Soaring," *USA Today,* August 25, 2003, p. 11A; Otis Port with John Carey, "Meet the Best and Brightest," *BusinessWeek,* March 28, 2005, pp. 88–91; and Michael Winerip, "For Immigrants, Math Is a Way to Success," *New York Times,* May 18, 2005, p. A19.

11 Arjun Suri is quoted in Tracey Wong Briggs, "Parents Plant Encouraging Seeds to Learn," *USA Today,* May 12, 2004, p. 2D.

11 Anderson, "The Multiplier Effect," p. 18.

12 The Cigna/WorldatWork study is reported in Gretchen Lang, "Going Home Isn't Always Best Option," *International Herald Tribune,* June 26–27, 2004, p. 18. See also Taylor Brule, "'Get Me Outta Here,'" *Financial Times,* November 7, 2004, p. W20; Jay Solomon, "India Woos More Western Executives," *Globe and Mail,* February 22, 2005, p. B16; and Jerry Schwartz, "Americans Steadily Choosing to Move Out," *Honolulu Star-Bulletin,* April 24, 2005, p. A3.

12 The Association of Executive Search Consultants' findings are reported in Anne Fisher, "Joining the March of Jobs Overseas," *Fortune,* May 17, 2004, p. 54, and her "Offshoring Could Boost Your Career," *Fortune,* January 24, 2005, p. 36.

13 Norman Prouty's remarks are from Megan Rutherford, "Dark-Horse Jockey," *TIME,* April 10, 2000, p. 21.

13 Ms. Gershenfield is quoted in "To New Zealand, and a Quieter Life," *Christian Science Monitor,* September 16, 2002, p. 15. See also Corie Brown, "It Reminds Them of California," *Los Angeles Times,* October 2, 2003, p. 6.

13 The Denman quote is from Sharon Reier, "'Silicon Valleys' Take Root in Europe," *International Herald Tribune,* March 18, 1999, p. 12. See also "An International and Creative Character," *International Herald Tribune,* December 10, 1998, p. 7.

14 Keith Ross is quoted in "A New Dimension for Web Forums," *International Herald Tribune,* December 14, 2000, p. 15. See also "Côte d' Azur: IT's Creative Coast," *International Herald Tribune,* December 2, 2002, p. 9; "Côte'd' Azur: Doing IT Right," *International Herald Tribune,* June 28, 2001, p. 7; "Côte d' Azur: Where IT Flourishes," *International Herald Tribune,* November 27, 2000, p. 7; and Raphael Minder, "Sophia Antipolis: "A Haven from the Downturn," *Financial Times,* September 26, 2001, p. 14.

14 Mark Davies' story is from Phillips, "On Ghana's Tech Frontier," p. B4.

14 The Zacca quote is from Regan Morris, "Eastern Europe Draws More U.S. Companies," *International Herald Tribune,* June 25, 2004, p. 13.

14 Dan Carroll's remarks and the mayor's response are found in Simon Romero, "U.S. Farmers Put Down Roots in Brazilian Soil," *New York Times,* December 1, 2002, p. 3. See also Andrea McDaniels, "New Age Followers Head for Brasilia," *Financial Times,* August 7–8, 1999, p. xxiv; Larry Rohter, "South America: World's New Breadbasket," *International Herald Tribune,* December 13, 2004, p. 1; and Alex Beattie, "Top of the Crops: Brazil's Huge Heartland Is Yielding Farms That Can Feed the World," *Financial Times,* June 23, 2005, p. 13.

15 See Andy Grove: "'We Can't Even Glimpse the Potential,'" *BusinessWeek,* August 25, 2003, p. 88.

15 Dean Simon's quote is from William J. Broad, "U.S. Is Losing Its Dominance in the Sciences," *New York Times,* May 3, 2004, p. A18.

16 Coach Harris is cited in "They Said It," *Sports Illustrated,* March 14, 2003, p. 30.

16 Charles Barkley's remarks are from "End Quote," *Honolulu Advertiser,* January 12, 2004, p. C10.

16 NBA Commissioner Stern is cited in L. Jon Wertheim, "The Whole World Is Watching," *Sports Illustrated,* June 14, 2004, p. 86.

17 The Japanese baseball quote is from Ned Barnett, "Japan's National Pastime," *Honolulu Star-Bulletin,* July 9, 2003, p. B2.

17 The McKinsey study is variously reported. See, for example, "A World of Work: A Survey of Outsourcing," *Economist,* November 13, 2004, p. 18; and Diana Farrell, "Beyond Offshoring: Assess Your Company's Global Potential," *Harvard Business Review,* December 2004, pp. 82–90, and her "Offshoring Is the Way to Go," *International Herald Tribune,* February 7–8, 2004, p. 6.

17 Professor Thurow's remarks are from "'The Pluses Exceed the Minuses,'" *International Herald Tribune,* December 13–14, 2003, p. A19.

18 "Gates Slow to Criticize Outsourcing of U.S. Jobs," *Honolulu Advertiser,* October 2, 2004, p. C1.

18 The Grove quote is from Mark Landler, "China's High-Tech Role Worries Some U.S. Firms," *International Herald Tribune,* May 30, 2001, p. 13.

18 For more on "brain circulation," see "Keeping Out the Wrong People," *BusinessWeek,* October 4, 2004, p. 9; and Kehoe, "The Trans-Pacific Valley," p. 9.

19 Charles McMillion's quote is found in David R. Francis, "U.S. Runs a High-Tech Trade Gap," *Christian Science Monitor,* June 2, 2004, pp. 1, 4. See also Floyd Norris, "U.S. Tech Exports Slide, but Trash Sales Are Up," *New York Times,* January 14, 2005, p. C1; and Thomas L. Friedman, "American Ingenuity Lags on Global Playing Field," *Honolulu Star-Bulletin,* May 13, 2005, p. A13.

19 The Diploma Project is cited in Nicholas D. Kristof, "The Lesson of Outsourcing," *International Herald Tribune,* February 12, 2004, p. 6.

19 See Louis Gertsner Jr., "Bad Schools + Shackled Principals = Outsourcing," *Wall Street Journal,* October 7, 2004, p. 22A.

19 The ACT study is reported in Karen W. Arenson, "Study of College Readiness Finds No Progress in Decade," *New York Times,* October 14, 2004, p. A25. See also Alvin P. Sanoff, "Survey: High School Fails to Engage Students," *USA Today,* May 9, 2005, p. 50.

20 The third Trends Study is reported in Greg Toppo, "U.S. 8th-Graders Gain in Math, Science; 4th-Graders Weak," *USA Today,* December 15, 2004, p. 8D.

20 The OECD Survey is cited in Floyd Norris, "U.S. Students Fare Badly in International Survey of Math Skills," *New York Times,* December 7, 2004, p. A17. See also Ben Feller, "Science Education Lags in U.S. Schools," *Honolulu Advertiser,* July 4, 2004, p. A22.

20 Cornell's Robert Richardson is quoted in Claudia Dreifus, "The Chilling of American Science," *New York Times,* July 6, 2004, p. 2. See also William J. Broad, "National Science Panel Warns of Far Too Few Scientists," *New York Times,* May 5, 2004, p. A18.

20 MIT president Susan Hockfield's remarks are from "A Breakthrough for MIT—and Science," *BusinessWeek,* October 4, 2004, p. 100.

21 See "Europe's Brain Drain," *Wall Street Journal Europe,* August 18, 2004, p. A6; Ann Mettler, "Europe Is Steadily Losing Its Scientific Elite," *Financial Times,* July 15, 2004, p. 15; and Isabelle De Pommereau, "To Halt Brain Drain, Germany Adopts 'Competition' Mantra," *Christian Science Monitor,* February 1, 2005, p. 7.

22 The Huggins ranking is cited in Anna Fifield, "U.S. Ranks Highest in Knowledge Economies' Index," *Financial Times,* April 13, 2004, p. 6.

22 The best-universities ranking is found in Graham Bowley, "How Harvard Got Ahead," *Financial Times,* October 16–17, 2004, p. W2.

22 See Webber, "Reverse Brain Drain," p. 13A.

CHAPTER 2. IRISH UPRISING

25   For more on Gerard Denneny, see David J. Lynch, "Flourishing Ireland Calls Its
      Children Home," *USA Today,* March 16, 1999, p. 13A.

26   John FitzGerald's "homing pigeons" is from his "Ireland on the World Stage," unpub-
      lished working paper, Dublin, 2003, p. 2.

26   Mary Corcoran's quote is from John Burgess, "Brain (and Muscle) Drain Over, Irish
      Head Home," *International Herald Tribune,* March 18, 1998, p. 1. See also Mary
      Corcoran, "The Process of Migration and the Reinvention of Self: The Experiences of
      Returning Irish Emigrants," *Éire-Ireland,* 2002, pp. 175–191.

27   Tim Pat Coogan is quoted in Richard Rapaport, "When Irish IT Is Smiling," *Forbes
      ASAP,* May 31, 1999, p. 114.

27   For more on the Celtic Tiger, see Ray Mac Sharry and Padraic White, The *Making of the
      Celtic Tiger* (Cork: Mercier Press, 2000); Jan Morris, "Ireland: Shiny, Brash and
      Confident," *New York Times Magazine,* November 31, 2004, pp. 73–109; Richard
      Conniff, "Ireland on Fast Forward," *National Geographic,* September 1994, pp. 4–29;
      Thomas Moore, "In the Eye of the Tyger," *Irish Times,* July 29, 2001; James B.
      Burnham, "Why Ireland Boomed," *Independent Review,* Spring 2003; Rapaport, "When
      Irish IT Is Smiling," pp. 114–124; Eugene P. Trani, *Dublin Diaries: A Study of High
      Technology Development in Ireland* (Richmond: Virginia Commonwealth University;
      and Dublin: Keough-Notre Dame Centre), November 2002.

27   Ireland's upbeat assessments appeared in "The Luck of the Irish," *Economist,* October
      16, 2004, pp. 1–12; Rick Smith, "EU's Poorest Newcomers Look to Ireland at End of
      Rainbow," *International Herald Tribune,* February 12, 2004, p. 20; Brian Lavery, "U.S.
      Technology Firms Flash to Ireland Again," *International Herald Tribune,* June 18, 2004,
      p. 13; Shelly Emling, "Ireland Works to Stay in the Outsourcing Game," *International
      Herald Tribune,*June 5, 2004, p. 19; Bob Dye, "Ireland Has the Solution for What Ails
      Us," *Honolulu Advertiser,* March 17, 1999, p. A14; Doreen Carvajal, "In Ireland,
      'Tigresses' Burn Bright," *International Herald Tribune,* March 17, 2004, p. 11; Debra
      Marks, "Ireland Seeks Fresh Angle on Economy," *Wall Street Journal,* November 13,
      2002, p. B5C; John Murray Brown, "Booming Ireland Goes Looking for Labour,"
      Financial Times, June 24–25, 2000, p. 4, and his "How Ireland Fixed Its Economy,"
      Financial Times, May 27, 2005, p.11; Joseph A. Harris, "Ireland Unleashed,"
      Smithsonian, March 2005, pp. 80–87; Barbara Wall, "In Ireland, Signs of Renewed
      Vigor," *International Herald Tribune,* March 15, 2005, p. 14; and Thomas L. Friedman,
      "Ireland Earns Gold at End of the Rainbow," *Honolulu Star-Bulletin,* July 1, 2005, p.
      A15.

28   For more on the Great Famine and Irish emigration, see Cecil Woodham-Smith, *The
      Great Hunger: Ireland, 1845–1849* (New York: Harper & Row, 1962); Christine Kinealy,
      The Great Calamity: The Irish Famine, 1845–52 (Dublin: Gill & MacMillan, 1994);
      Cormac Ó Gráda, *The Great Irish Famine* (New York: Macmillan, 1989); and Mary Daly,
      The Famine in Ireland (Dublin: Dublin Historical Association, 1986).

28   See Joseph O'Connor, *Star of the Sea* (New York: Harcourt, 2002), p. 123. See also Jo
      Kerrigan, "Dunbrody: Rebirth of an Emigrant Ship," *Ireland of the Welcomes,* March–
      April 2003, pp. 40–47.

28   Historian Mitchell's quote is cited in Tom Kelley, "The Great Famine and Its Legacy in
      Poverty, Emigration and Death," in Ciaran Brady (ed.), *The Encyclopedia of Ireland*
      (New York: Oxford University Press, 2000), p. 138.

28   Mary Robinson's quote is from her address at the opening of The Famine Conference,
      New York University, May 19, 1995. See also "The View from Afar," *Economist,* No-
      vember 2, 2002, p. 11.

29   Kevin Whelan is cited in Kerrigan, "Dunbrody," p. 44.

29   Irish immigration to the U.S. is reported in Kerby Miller's seminal *Emigrants and Exiles:
      Ireland and the Irish Exodus to North America* (New York: Oxford University Press,

1985); Timothy Meagher, *Inventing Irish America: Generation, Class and Ethnic Identity in a New England City, 1880–1928* (South Bend, Ind.: University of Notre Dame Press, 2001); Linda Dowling Almeida, *Irish Immigrants in New York City, 1945–1995* (Bloomington: Indiana University Press, 2001); Kerby Miller and Paul Wagner, *Out of Ireland: The Story of Irish Emigration to North America* (Washington, D.C.: Elliott & Clark, 1994); Kathleen Sullivan, "Digging into Roots of Irish in America," *San Francisco Chronicle,* March 10, 2004, p. E1; and Michael Barone, *The New Americans* (Washington, D.C.: Regnery, 2001), especially pp. 15–64.

30   See Geraldine O'Connell, *The Children of the Far-Flung* (Dublin: Liffey Press, 2003), p. 22.

30   From Linda Dowling Almeida, "Irish American: What Does It Mean and Who Defines It in the Late 20th Century," speech delivered to The Scattering Conference, New York, September 1997, p. 2.

31   From John O'Brien, *The Vanishing Irish: The Enigma of the Modern World* (London: W. H. Allen, 1954).

31   The reversal of Irish emigration is variously reported. See, for example, Nina Bernstein, "Greener Pastures (on the Emerald Isle)," *New York Times,* November 10, 2004, p. A21; Michael Judge, "The Long Journey from Ireland Leads Back to It," *Wall Street Journal,* March 16, 2001, p. W17; Mary Corcoran, "Global Cosmopolites: Issues of Self-Identity Among the Transnational Irish Elite," *Etudes Irlandaises,* Fall 2003, pp. 3–5; Burnham, "Why Ireland Boomed"; Lynch, "Flourishing Ireland," p. 13A; Burgess, "Brain (and Muscle) Drain Over," p. 1.; John D. FitzGerald and Ide Kearney, "Migration and the Irish Labor Market," Economic and Social Research Institute, Dublin, June 26, 1998; Mike Allen, "Ireland, New Promised Land," *New York Times,* May 31, 1998, section 4, p. 1; and Stephen Coronella, "An Accidental Irishman," *Christian Science Monitor,* August 19, 2003, p. 11. See also Beth Lordan, *But Come Ye Back* (New York: Morrow, 2004); David Monagan, *Jaywalking with the Irish* (Oakland Calif.: Lonely Planet, 2004); Wayne King Livingston, *A Sojourn with Ireland* (Bloomington, Ind.: lst Books Library, 2002); Kevin Myers, *Banks of Green Willow* (Dublin: TownHouse, 2001); and Nina Bernstein, "N.Y.'s Irish Tide Is Flowing Home," *International Herald Tribune,* November 10, 2004, p. 1.

32   See Mary Corcoran, "Global Cosmopolites," pp. 3–5.

32   John FitzGerald's quote is from his "Ireland on the World Stage," p. 16.

32   See Alan Barrett and Philip O'Connell, "Is There a Wage Premium for Returning Irish Migrants?," *Economic and Social Review,* January 2001, pp. 1–21. See also Barrett and Fergal Trace, "Who Is Coming Back? The Educational Profile of Returning Migrants in the 1990s," *Irish Banking Review,* Summer 1998, pp. 38–51.

33   Marlborough's Jason Kennedy is quoted in Alan Cowell, "From Backwater to Boom Town," *New York Times,* October 31, 2000, p. C8. See also Lynch, "Flourishing Ireland," p. 13A.

33   John Ardagh's prediction is from his *Ireland and the Irish: Portrait of a Changing Society* (London: Hamish Hamilton, 1994), pp. 311 and 318.

33   The De Valera transition and beyond are reported in Kevin Whelan, "The Celtic Tiger," unpublished working paper, Trinity University, Dublin, 2003, pp. 2–4. See also Peadar Kirby, Luke Gibbons, and Michael Cronin (eds.), *Reinventing Ireland: Culture, Society and the Global Economy* (London: Pluto Press, 2002); and Ardagh, *Ireland and the Irish,* pp. 69–73.

35   The rankings of Irish education are from *Education at a Glance* (Paris: OECD, 2003). See also Burnham, "Why Ireland Boomed," pp. 15–16; and "Achieve European Competitive Advantage in Ireland," *IDA Ireland,* 2003, p. 2.

34   The *Financial Times* survey is from John Murray Brown, "Why Irish Eyes Are Still Smiling over Nation's Technology Sector," May 7, 2001, p. 3.

36   The attraction of U.S. multinationals is discussed in Burnham, "Why Ireland Boomed"; Rapaport, "When Irish IT Is Smiling"; Trani, *Dublin Diaries,* pp. 6–10 and 17; Ardagh, *Ireland and the Irish,* pp. 73–81; and David J. Lynch, "Grants, Tax Breaks Help Economy Boom," *USA Today,* August 19, 1997, p. B1.

36 PM Ahern's quotes are from Rapaport, "When Irish IT Is Smiling," pp. 114 and 124.

37 Eoin O'Neill's remarks are from Rapaport, p. 116.

36 Ed Ryan's quote may be found in Niall McKay, "Ireland, the Silicon Isle," wired.com.news, October 29, 1998.

37 Professor Ryan's sentiments are from Rapaport, p. 120.

38 Deputy PM Harney's discussion of leapfrogging is reported in Rapaport, p. 155.

38 IDA's Colm Donlon is quoted in Lavery, "U.S. Technology Firms Flash," p. 13.

39 The role of Dublin as a financial center is described in Shawn Pogatchnik, "Dublin Is Doing Business," *Honolulu Star-Bulletin,* February 11, 1997, p. C1; John Murray Brown, "Ireland's 'Fair City'—an Attractive Place to Do Business," Financial Times, November 24, 2003, p. 5; Burnham, "Why Ireland Boomed," pp. 18–19; Whelan "The Celtic Tiger," p. 12; "Achieve European Competitive Advantage," p. 2; "Europe's Back Office," *Economist,* November 16, 1996, pp. 82–83; and Brian Lavery and Timothy L. O'Brien, "Insurers' Trails Lead to Dublin," *New York Times,* April 1, 2005, p. C1.

38 For more on the Digital Media District, see Daintry Duffy, "Éireheads," www.darwin-mag.com, July 2001, pp. 78–86 and Eoin Lichen, "Now It's Ireland.com," *International Herald Tribune,* June 24, 1999, p. 23.

39 Quoted from Burnham, "Why Ireland Boomed," pp. 3 and 29.

39 See Robert Kuttner, "Ireland's Miracle: The Market Didn't Do It Alone," *Business-Week,* July 10, 2000, p. 33.

40 Ms. Harney's preference for Boston is from Trani, *Dublin Diaries,* p. 24. See also J. J. Lee, "Spiritually Closer to Boston than Berlin?" in Michael Boss and Eamon Maher (eds.), *Engaging Modernity: Readings of Irish Politics, Culture* (Dublin: O'Brien Press, 2003), pp. 31–42.

40 Eamon Delaney's assessment is reported in his "Nineties," *Dubliner,* October 2003, p. 75.

40 The "BioLink USA-Ireland" conference occurred in New York City, October 9–10, 2003. Various quotes are attributed to session presenters. A second BioLink session was held in San Francisco, June 4–5, 2004; a third was held in Boston, June 16–17, 2005. See also John Murray Brown, "Ireland Extends Its Hospitality to Top Scientists," *Financial Times,* November 28, 2003, p. 12; and "Ireland: A National Commitment to Biotechnology," naturejobs.com, February 24, 2000.

41 Mr. Weddle's comments on biotechnology are from Jim Hopkins "States Flock to Biotech Like Gamblers to Lottery Tickets," *USA Today,* November 3, 2003, p. B1.

44 William Harris's comments on "Sputnik time" and SFI funding may be found in Trani, *Dublin Diaries,* p. 11. See also William Harris, "When Knowledge Wins: Building an Irish Science Strategy for the 21st Century," speech to the Irish Management Institute's National Management Conference, Dublin, April 26, 2002.

44 Dr. O'Neill is cited in "The Scientists and Engineers of Science Foundation Ireland," SFI, 2003, p. 18.

46 Evelyn Combat's quote is from Sabine Lovët, "Ireland Trying to Attract Biotech Brains," Bioenterpisenews.com, July 31, 2003, p. 2 (originally published in *Nature Biotechnology*). See also John Murray Brown, "Galway Gets to the Heart of the Matter," *Financial Times,* February 11, 2005, p. 8.

46 For more on Cormac Kilty and Biotrin International, see "Bridging the Chasm. . .," published by Biotrin, Dublin, 2003; "High Visibility for Irish Companies at BioVision," Irish Biotech News, Summer 2003, p. 3; "Trinity Interest in Biotrin," p. 8; and Lynch, "Flourishing Ireland Calls Its Children Home," p. 13A.

48 Dr. Kilty's positive comments about Sec. Thompson are from Susan Aldridge, "Ireland States Its Claims as a Future Biotech Leader," *Genetic Engineering News,* January 1, 2003, p. 7.

49 The Farrens are also introduced in Lynch, "Flourishing Ireland Calls Its Children Home," p. 13A.

50 For more on Dublin, see Alan Cowell, "From Backwater to Boom Town," *New York Times,* October 31, 2000, p. C1; Kitty Bean Yancey, "Stars over Dublin," *USA Today,*

May 30, 2003, p. D2; Daniel Franklin, "Dublin Calling," *TIME,* September 2002, pp. A32–33; "The Creative Side of the Emerald Isle," *Christian Science Monitor,* February 26, 2003, pp. 12–21; Catherine Reynolds, "Dublin," *New York Times' Sophisticated Traveler,* March 3, 2002, pp. 6–14; Robert O'Byrne, "In Dublin Lots to Talk About," *New York Times,* February 29, 2004, pp. 9–14; Brian Lavery, "Dublin: A Stylish Stay Along the Liffey," *International Herald Tribune,* February 11, 2004, p. 22; and Kieran Cooke, "Blessed with the 'X' Factor," *Financial Times,* October 4, 1999, p. III.

51 James Joyce is cited in Franklin, "Dublin Calling," p. A33.

52 John FitzGerald's quote is from Cooke, "Blessed with the 'X' Factor," p. III.

51 Kevin Courtney's descriptions are discussed in Alan Cowell, "Ireland, Once a Celtic Tiger, Slackens Its Stride," *New York Times,* February 19, 2003, p. C1.

53 Seamus Heaney's "mythologically grounded" comments are from his "Correspondences: Emigrants and Inner Exiles," in Richard Kearney (ed.), *The Irish at Home and Abroad* (Dublin: Wolfhound Press, 1990), p. 23.

53 Mary Corcoran's quote is from Corcoran, "The Process of Migration," p. 190.

54 PM Ahern's quote is from Quentin Peel, "Toughing It Out in Europe," *Financial Times,* March 27–28, 2004, p. W3. See also "Scale of Immigration," *Irish Times,* October 15, 2003, p. 19.

54 Eugenie Houston's remarks are from Sathnam Sanghera, "Skills Crisis Looms as Irish Workers Head Back Home," *Financial Times,* May 28, 1999, p. 9. See also Burgess, "Brain (and Muscle) Drain Over," p. 7; and Lizette Alvarez, "Suddenly Rich, Poor Old Ireland Seems Bewildered," *New York Times,* February 2, 2005, p. A1.

55 Professor Corcoran's quote may be found in her "Global Cosmopolites," p. 14.

55 Provost Hegarty's quote is from Vincent Browne, "A Man Unburdened by Pretension with a Happy Lifelong Passion for Knowledge," *Irish Times,* March 17, 2001, p. 3. See also "New Trinity Provost Back Home Among His Own in Claremorris," *Western People,* March 28, 2001, p. 1. For more on Hegarty's reentry, see Austin Garvin, "Claremorris Man Is Appointed Provost of Trinity College, Dublin," *Mayo News,* March 14, 2001, p. 1; "Claremorris Native Is New Provost of Trinity College," *Connaught Telegraph,* March 14, 2001, p. 1; Michael Commins, "Claremorris Man Is New Trinity Provost," *Western People,* March 14, 2001, p. 1; and Emmett Oliver, "A Man of Science Not Prone to Waxing Lyrical About Tradition," *Irish Times,* March 12, 2001, p. 5.

55 See Laza Kekic, "The World's Best Country," *Economist,* 2005, p. 66.

56 Eugene Trani's "wake-up call" is from his *Dublin Diaries,* p. 24.

56 Kevin Whelan's warning is from his "The Celtic Tiger," pp. 8 and 13; and Trani, *Dublin Diaries,* p. 8.

56 PM Ahern's vision is reported in "Ahern Pledges to Build a Better Ireland," *Irish Times,* October 13, 2002, p. 6.

56 The Shaw quote is reported in "Thoughts on the Business of Life," *Forbes,* March 17, 2003, p. 196.

CHAPTER 3. MIRACLE ON ICE

57 For more on Iceland, see David Roberts and Jon Krakauer, *Iceland: Land of the Sagas* (New York: Villard, 1990); Pamela Sanders, *Iceland* (Salem, N.H.: Salem House, 1995); Terry G. Lacy, *Ring of Seasons* (Reykjavík: University of Iceland Press, 1998); Gunnar Karlsson, *The History of Iceland* (Minneapolis: University of Minnesota Press, 2000); Jesse L. Byock, *Medieval Iceland: Society, Sagas and Power* (Berkeley: University of California Press, 1988); Jóhannes Nordal and Valdimar Kristinsson (eds.), *Iceland: The Republic* (Reykjavík: Central Bank of Iceland, 1996); "Cod's Own Country," *Economist,* May 17, 2003, p. 45; "Dancing to a New Tune: A Survey of the Nordic Region," *Economist,* June 14, 2003, pp. 1–15; and Richard F. Tomasson, *Iceland: The New Society* (Minneapolis: University of Minnesota Press, 1980).

58   For a discussion of the Icelandic economic miracle, see Christopher Brown-Humes, "A Country Which Defies the Elements," *Financial Times,* September 19, 2000, pp. I–II, and his "Promised Land of Ice and Plastic," *Financial Times,* May 3, 2000, p. 7; Anna Margrét Björnsson, "Riding the New Wave," *Iceland Business,* Vol. 41, March 2003, pp. 72–73; Joe Baglole, "Iceland Transforms Itself into a Hotbed of New Industries," *Wall Street Journal,* March 13, 2001, p. A21; Michael J. Kissane, "Isolation Breeds Innovation for Small Island Economy," *Barron's,* May 31, 1999, p. MW9; Marco R. della Cava, "Iceland Warms to the Net," *USA Today,* March 27, 2000, p. 6D; and *The Economy of Iceland* (Reykjavík: Central Bank of Iceland, 2002).

60   Ms. Sanders' quote is from her *Iceland,* p. 20.

61   Icelandic emigration is discussed in Karlsson, *The History of Iceland,* pp. 228–230, 234–238, and 334; Nordal and Kristinsson, *Iceland,* chapter 2; and Lacy, *Ring of Seasons,* pp. 213–214. See also Byron J. Nordstrom, *Scandanavia Science 1500* (Minneapolis: University of Minnesota Press, 2000), pp. 158–162 and 230–236; Thorstina Walters, *Modern Sagas: The Story of Icelanders in North America* (Fargo, N.D.: North Dakota Institute for Regional Studies, 1953); Wilhelm Krisjansson, *The Icelandic People in Manitoba* (Winnipeg: Wallingford Press, 1965); and Anne Brydon, *Celebrating Ethnicity: The Icelanders in Manitoba* (Hamilton, Ont.: McMaster University Press, 1987).

62   Gunner Karlsson's quote is from *The History of Iceland,* p. 237.

62   Andur Hanksdóttir is quoted in "Dancing to a New Tune," p. 9.

63   Difficulties assimilating to Iceland are discussed in Sanders, Iceland, p. 44; and Lacy, *Ring of Seasons,* pp. 246–249. See also Jonathan Wilcox, *Iceland* (New York: Times Books, 1996), pp. 48–49.

63   Iceland's global reach is described in Edward Weiman, "Boom Town," *Iceland Review,* April 2004, pp. 38–43; Nicholas George, "Reykjavík Raiders Spring a Surprise," *Financial Times,* June 18, 2004, p. 166; and Jane Wardell, "Icelanders in an Expansion Mode," *Honolulu Star-Bulletin,* May 15, 2005, p. D3.

64   Recent repatriation statistics are from Karlsson, *The History of Iceland; and Statistics Iceland,* December 20, 2002, pp. 5–6.

64   For more on deCODE and Kári Stefánsson, see Edward Weinman, "The Language of Life," *Iceland Review,* Vol. 41, April 2003, pp. 18–21; Nicholas Wade, "Icelandic Company Says It Has Found Osteoporosis Gene," *New York Times,* November 3, 2003, p. A4, and his "Scientists in Iceland Discover First Gene Tied to Stroke Risk," *New York Times,* September 22, 2003, p. A1; Christopher Brown-Humes, "Isolation Is the Key to Success," *Financial Times,* September 19, 2000, p. IV; Michael Specter, "Decoding Iceland," *New Yorker,* February 18, 1999, pp. 40–51; Paul Billings, "Iceland, Blood & Science," *American Scientist,* May–June 1999, pp. 192–204; Robert Langreth, "Attacking Heart Attacks," *Forbes,* June 21, 2004, pp. 152–165; John Dodge and Mark Uehling, "The Icelandic Man Cometh," *Bio-IT World,* January 13, 2003, pp 1–5; Steve Sternberg, "Drug May Block Deadly Gene," *USA Today,* February 9, 2004, p. A1, and his "Why Heart Attacks Run in Families: Genetics," *USA Today,* December 22, 2004, p. A1; Nicholas Wade, "Scientists Find DNA Region That Affects Europeans' Fertility," *New York Times,* January 17, 2005, p. A12; David Ewing Duncan, "Tracking Genes in Iceland," *San Francisco Chronicle,* October 6, 2003; and "Drug May Lower Chemicals Linked to Heart Attacks," *Wall Street Journal,* May 11, 2005, p. D4.

65   Stefánnson's "failed writer" comments are from Specter, "Decoding Iceland," p. 50.

65   "Medicine is so anachronistic" is from Robert Langreth, "The E-Gang: Medical Marvels," Forbes.com, September 2, 2002, p. 2.

65   "I am first and foremost a physician" is from "Ask the Scientists," *Scientific American Frontiers Archives,* Fall 1990 to Spring 2000, p. 2.

67   Stefánnson's comments on Milton Friedman's university are also reported in Specter, "Decoding Iceland," p. 57.

67   His disparaging comments about the government are from James Meek, "'Decode was Meant to Save Lives . . . Now It's Destroying Them,'" *Guardian,* October 31, 2002, p. 5.

67 Stefánnson's "besieged" remarks are from Specter, "Decoding Iceland," p. 47.

70 "There's no genetic operation . . ." quote is from Langreth, "The E-Gang," p. 1.

71 Jonathan Rosand's comments are from Wade, "Scientists in Iceland," p. A1.

71 Lawrence Raisz's views are cited in Wade, "Icelandic Company," p. A14. See also Weinman, "The Language of Life," p. 20.

72 Jonathan Knowles is quoted in Wade, "Scientists in Iceland," p. A17.

72 The Orwellian quote is from Mary Carmichael, "Genes: Boning Up Treatment Options," *Newsweek,* November 10, 2003, p. 8.

74 "Professor Hydrogen" is described in "H2—Powering the Future," CBS News, March 2, 2003, pp. 1–3 of transcript; Richard Middleton, "First Hydrogen Service Station Opens in Iceland," *Honolulu Star-Bulletin,* April 28, 2003, p. C4; and "Iceland Powers Up," *Economist,* May 17, 2003, p. 71. See also Bragi Árnason and Thorsteinn I. Sigfússon, "Iceland—a Pilot Country to Demonstrate the Road to the Hydrogen Economy," lecture delivered to the National Research Council–Canada, April 2003.

76 David Oddsson's quote is from Dan Roberts, "Hydrogen: Clean, Safer than in the Past and Popular with the Politicians," *Financial Times,* May 13, 2003, p. 13.

76 President Grímmson's quote is found in "H2—Powering the Future," p. 2.

77 Shell's de Koning is quoted in Roberts, "Hydrogen," p. 13.

77 Dr. Árnason's assessment is variously reported. See Middleton, "First Hydrogen Service Station, p. C4.

78 See Richard Sale, *The Xenophobe's Guide to the Icelanders* (London: Oval Books, revised 2001), p. 24.

78 Daddi Gudbergsson is cited in della Cava, "Iceland Warms to the Net," p. 6D.

79 Dr. Hvannberg's quote is from della Cava, p. 6D.

79 OECD information on Internet usage may be found in "Iceland: A Secure and Cost Competitive Location for Data Centers," Invest in Iceland Agency, February 2003.

79 Iceland's various ratings are reported in "Ranking Most Tech-ready Countries," *Christian Science Monitor,* February 21, 2003, p. 24; "Iceland Ranks Fifth in Information Technology Use," *Iceland Update,* March 7, 2003, p. 1; Naomi Koppel, "U.N. Finds Poor Nations Poorer," *Honolulu Advertiser,* July 9, 2003, p. A7; and Francis Williams and John Burton, "Singapore Overtakes U.S. to Lead World in New IT," *Financial Times,* March 10, 2005, p. 6.

81 The KPMG study "Business Costs in Iceland" is found in *Iceland: The Cost-Competitive Edge* (Reykjavík: Invest in Iceland Agency, 2002).

81 For more on Iceland's global reach and diversification, see "Small Country, Big Ambitions," *Economist,* February 19, 2005, p. 61.

84 For more on swinging Reykjavík, see Hallgrímur Helgason, 101 Reykjavík (New York: Scribner, 2003); "A Clean, Green Capital," *Iceland Review,* March 2003, Vol. 41, pp. 62–65; "Fire and Ice," *BusinessWeek,* February 24, 2005, pp. 136–137; Rachael Jolly, "Bubbling Under," *Business Traveler,* January 2004, pp. 48–50; Paul Gould, "Why Should Hotter Spots Be More Fun?," *Financial Times,* May 29–30, 2004, p. W20; and Steve Dougherty, "In a Cold Country, the Nights Are Hot," *New York Times,* December 19, 2004, Section 5, p. 1.

85 Egill Olafsson's remarks are from "What's the Best Thing About Living in Reykjavík?" *Iceland Review,* March 2003, p. 58. For a view of contemporary Iceland by the country's best-selling novelist, see Olaf Olafsson, *The Journey Home* (New York: Anchor Books, 2000).

86 Ms. Sverrisdóttir's comments are from della Cava, "Iceland Warms to the Net," p. 6D.

86 Hallgrímur Helgason's quote is from his *101 Reykjavík,* p. 28.

87 Margaret Mead's "islands" quote is from "Remarkable Columbians," www.c250.columbia.edu, p. 9.

87 For more on Iceland's various ratings, see Frances Williams, "Diversity 'Must Be Embraced' to Ensure Stability in Globalizing World," *Financial Times,* July 16, 2004, p. 5; and "No Banana Republic," *Iceland Review,* April 2003, p. 6.

87 The "idyllic circumstances" quote is from "Dancing to a New Tune," p. 4.

CHAPTER 4. INDIA RISING

89   The Narayanans' quote may be found in Justin Fox, "Where Your Job Is Going," *Fortune,* November 24, 2003, p. 92. See also Thomas L. Friedman, "The Secret of Our Sauce," *New York Times,* March 7, 2004, p. A13.

90   For a discussion of India's return-home phenomenon, see Amy Waldman, "Economy Drawing Indians Back Home," *Honolulu Star-Bulletin,* July 24, 2004, p. A9; Lindsey Tanner, "U.S. Radiology Scans Head Overseas," *Honolulu Star-Bulletin,* December 6, 2004, p. A7; Eryn Brown and David Kirkpatrick, "The Reverse Brain Drain," *Fortune,* November 11, 2002, pp. 39–40; Manjeet Kripalani and Pete Engardio, "The Rise of India," *BusinessWeek,* December 8, 2003, pp. 66–73; Khozem Merchant, "India's Next B2B Means Back to Bangalore," *Financial Times,* May 19, 2004, p. 8; Manjeet Kripalani, "For India's Tech Grads, There's No Place Like Home," *BusinessWeek,* February 3, 2003; Amy Waldman, "India Harvests Fruits of a Diaspora," *New York Times,* January 12, 2003, p. 4; Scott Thurm, "Indian Immigrants Return Home Where Software Jobs Await Them; Giving Up a Pool for Maid Service," *Wall Street Journal,* December 16, 2003, p. B1; Raj Jayadev, "Reverse Brain-Drain: U.S.-Based Indian Tech Workers Go Home," *Pacific News Service,* July 30, 2003, p. 1; and Oliver Ryan, "India's Top Expert: Headed Back Home?" *Fortune,* June 13, 2005, p. 30.

90   The NASSCOM estimates on repatriation are from Saritha Rai, "From India, Genius on the Cheap," *International Herald Tribune,* December 15, 2003, p. 12. See also Kris Maher, "Next on the Outsourcing List," *Wall Street Journal,* March 23, 2004, p. B1. For more on Indian immigration to the United States, see S. Mitra Kalta, *Suburban Sahibs* (New Brunswick, N.J.: Rutgers University Press, 2003).

90   Vishal Bali's observations are reported in Ray Marcelo, "India Hopes to Foster Growing Business in 'Medical Tourism,'" *Financial Times,* July 2, 2003, p. 5.

90   See "A Skeptic's View of India," *Business Standard,* February 11, 2004, p. 13.

91   Sumant Anand's remarks are from James Cox, "As Economy Expands, India Is 'On the Verge of Something Big,'" *USA Today,* February 9, 2004, pp. A1–A2. See also Tom Forenski, "Entrepreneurs Who Are Shining in Silicon Valley," *Financial Times,* May 19, 2004, p. 8.

91   Despa Paranjpe's quote is from Stephen Baker and Manjeet Kripalani, "Software: Will Outsourcing Hurt America's Supremacy?" *BusinessWeek,* March 1, 2004, p. 92. See also Nachammai Raman, "Indians Ride Tech Wave by Staying Close to Home," *Christian Science Monitor,* February 25, 2005, p. 7.

92   The Nehru quotes are from Bill Allen, "India: Fifty Years of Independence," *National Geographic,* May 1997, p. 2. See also Shashi Tharoor, *Nehru: The Invention of India* (New York: Arcade Publishing, 2003). For a closer look at India, see Gurcharan Das, *India Unbound* (New York: Viking, 2000); and Stephen Cohen, *India: Emerging Power* (Washington, D.C.: Brookings Institution Press, 2001).

93   Gartner's Partha Iyengar's comments may be found in Saritha Rai, "Indian Companies Prepare to Fight Backlash," *International Herald Tribune,* February 9, 2004, p. 8.

93   Monsanto's Ranjana Smetacek's quote is found in Cox, "As Economy Expands . . .," p. 2B.

93   The A. T. Kearney study is cited in Joe Leahey and Justine Lau, "Frontier of a New Global Contest," *Financial Times,* June 1, 2004, p. 3.

93   Aon economist Leonard's remarks are from Marilyn Alva, "India Is Becoming Powerhouse; Growth Expanding Middle Class," *Investor's Business Daily,* February 13, 2004, p. A5. See also Eric Bellman, "Venture Capitalists Book a Passage to India," *Wall Street Journal,* October 14, 2004, p. C1; and Krishna Guha, "India's Appeal for Foreign Investors Grows," *Financial Times,* October 13, 2004, p. 6.

93   Arvind Panagariya's comments are found in Cox, p. 2B.

94   V. S. Naipaul's "wounded civilization" description is cited in Jonathan Power, "Slowly But Steadily, India Will Overtake China," *International Herald Tribune,* May 17, 2004, p. 6.

94   The U.N. findings on Indian poverty are reported in Manjeet Kripalani with Pete Engardio, "India: Will a Shocking Election Upset End the Economic Boom?" *BusinessWeek*, May 31, 2004, p. 44.

95   The predictions on India's economic progress are from Jeffrey D. Sachs, "Welcome to the Asian Century," *Fortune*, December 29, 2003, p. 53. See also Power, "Slowly But Steadily," p. 6; Michael Morgan, "India Could Outpace Growth in China," *Financial Times*, April 16, 2004, p. 28; James Mehring, "India: Growth Goes Way Back," *Business Week*, April 26, 2004, p. 30; and Yasheng Huang and Tarun Khanna, "Can India Overtake China?" *Foreign Policy*, July/August 2003, pp. 74–81.

95   For an excellent discussion of India's economic and political modernization, see John Stemlau, "Dateline Bangalore: Third World Technopolis," *Foreign Policy*, Spring 1996, pp. 152–168. See also Sunil Khilnani, "India Ascendant," *Worth*, September 2004, pp. 30–32; Amy Waldman, "In India, Economic Growth and Democracy Do Mix," *New York Times*, May 23, 2004, p. D3, and her "India Takes Economic Spotlight and Critics Are Unkind," *New York Times*, March 17, 2004, p. A3; and Manmohan Singh, "The New India," *Wall Street Journal*, May 19, 2005, p. A14.

96   For a discussion of the country's educational progress, see Scott Baldauf, "In India, Playtime Ends Early for Preschool Hopefuls," *Christian Science Monitor*, March 2, 2004, p. 7; Manjeet Kripalani with Pete Engardio and Leah Nathans Spiro, "Whiz Kids," *BusinessWeek*, December 7, 1998, pp. 116–122; Michael Krey, "Most Important U.S. Tech School? Indian Institutes of Technology," *Investor's Business Daily*, January 13, 2003, p. 7; Thomas L. Friedman, "A Lesson in India," *International Herald Tribune*, May 21, 2004, p. 7; "Imported from India," CBSnews.com, June 22, 2003; David J. Lynch, "India's Tech Push Includes Focus on Entrepreneurship," *USA Today*, April 12, 2004, p. 9B; and Kanika Datta, "2020 vision for the IITs," *Business Standard*, February 12, 2004, p. 7.

97   For the NASSCOM estimates on IT export growth, see "A Survey of Outsourcing," *Economist*, November 13, 2004, p. 8; "The Latest in Remote Control," *Economist*, September 11, 2004, p. 57; and Laura Mandaro, "India Outsourcing Firms Make Global Push in China, America," *Investor's Business Daily*, June 20, 2005, p. A1.

98   The U.S. Bureau of Labor Statistics figures are cited in Kripalani and Engardio, "The Rise of India," p. 68. See also "A Survey of Outsourcing," pp. 1 and 17; and Amy Waldman, "More 'Can I Help You?' Jobs Migrate from U.S. to India," *New York Times*, May 11, 2003, p. 4.

98   Colin Powell's comments on outsourcing may be found in Barbara Slavin, "Powell Prods India on Outsourcing," *USA Today*, March 17, 2004, p. 1A.

98   For more on India's prowess in software, see Leahey and Lau, "Frontier of a New Global Contest," p. 3; William Pesek Jr., "The Indians Century Dawns in Information Technology," *Barron's*, March 13, 2000, pp. MN20–22; Robert D. Hof with Manjeet Kripalani, "India and Silicon Valley: Now the R&D Flows Both Ways," *BusinessWeek Online*, December 8, 2003; Manjeet Kripalani with Joey Puliyenthuruthel, "Let the Deals Begin," *BusinessWeek*, November 22, 2004, pp. 58–60; "Growing Up," *Economist*, May 22, 2004, pp. 58–59; Manjeet Kripalani with Mark L. Clifford, "India Wired," *BusinessWeek*, March 6, 2000, pp. 82–86; Andy Mukherjee, "Software Industry in India Is Booming," *Honolulu Advertiser*, November 28, 2004, p. F5; and Shailaja Neelakantan, "More and More, Made in India," *Far Eastern Economic Review*, November 27, 2003, pp. 40–42.

99   Infosys's Nilekani's quote on globalization is from "The Remote Future," *Economist*, February 21, 2004, p. 14. See also Rebecca Fannin, "India's Outsourcing Boom," *Chief Executive*, May 2004, pp. 28–32; and Kerry A. Dolan and Robyn Meredith, "A Tale of Two Cities," *Forbes*, April 12, 2004, pp. 94–102.

99   Nilekani's "Every company. . ." remarks are from "The Remote Future," p. 14.

99   Diana Farrell's remarks on offshoring are variously reported. See, for example, Marilyn

Alva, "U.S. Firms' Outsourcing to India Reaps Big Savings, Political Heat," *Investor's Business Daily,* February 20, 2004, p. A14.

99   Nilekani's "win-win" quote is from Thomas L. Friedman, "India Helps Itself to a Slice of American Pie," *Honolulu Star-Bulletin,* March 5, 2004, p. A13. See also Friedman "Sending U.S. Jobs Abroad Is Good Geopolitics," *International Herald Tribune,* March 1, 2004, p. 8, and his *The World Is Flat: A Brief History of the Twenty-First Century* (New York: Farrar, Straus & Giroux, 2005).

100   For an estimate of IT engineers in Bangalore, see "A Survey of Outsourcing," p. 12; and Kripalani and Engardio, p. 69.

100   NASSCOM's statistics on the country's IT industry are from "A Survey of Outsourcing," pp. 10–11.

100   Laxmikant Mandal's comments on Bangalore are from Michelle Kessler, "Job Shift Creates India Tech Boom," *USA Today,* February 4, 2004, p. 6A. See also Thomas L. Friedman, "Banglaore: Hot and Hotter," *International Herald Tribune,* June 9, 2005, p. 8.

100   Vijay Anard's interview is in Saritha Rai, "In India, a High-Tech Outpost for U.S. Patents," *New York Times,* December 15, 2003, p. C4.

101   For more on Nehru's vision of Bangalore, see Stremlau, pp. 157–158. See also Simon Winchester, "The Legacy," *Smithsonian,* August 1997, pp. 47–55.

101   For additional information on Vivek Kulkarni, see Saritha Rai, "As India's Economy Rises, So Do Expectations," *New York Times,* January 30, 2004, p. W1.

103   Nags Nagarajan's views are expanded in Thomas L. Friedman, "What Goes Around Comes Around—Even Jobs Outsourced to India," *Honolulu Star-Bulletin,* February 26, 2004, p. A11.

103   For a discussion of Infosys's spectacular growth, see Saritha Rai, "Indian Services Giant Hits $1 Billion Mark," *International Herald Tribune,* April 14, 2004, p. 11, and "Outsourcing Fuels a Sales Surge at Infosys," *International Herald Tribune,* p. 11; J. Bonasia, "Infosys Move Spotlighting 'Insourcing,'" *Investor's Business Daily,* April 12, 2003, p. A4; Khozem Merchant, "The Future on India's Shores," *Financial Times,* April 24, 2004, p. 8, his "Outsource Boom Benefits Infosys," *Financial Times,* April 14, 2004, p. 22, and his "Golden Statues Mark Progress," *Financial Times,* November 19, 2004, p. 5; Eric W. Pfeiffer, "Infosys, the First Indian Company to Trade on NASDAQ," *Forbes* ASAP, August 23, 1999, pp. 21–24; Joanne Slater, "Infosys Adapts to Stay on Top," *Far Eastern Economic Review,* December 25, 2003–January 1, 2004, pp. 62–63; and J. Bonasia, "Indian Firm Takes Outsourcing to Next Level," *Investor's Business Daily,* December 28, 2004, p. A5.

104   Bill Gates's remarks and visit to Infosys are reported in Amy Waldman, "Bill Gates Finds a Seattle in India," *New York Times,* November 14, 2002, p. A10. See also Saritha Rai, "Gates Woos India Software Writers," *International Herald Tribune,* November 11, 2002, p. 14.

104   Infosys's Nilekani's quote on raising the standard of living may be found in David Lynch, "Imported Jobs Building a New, Middle-Class India," *USA Today,* March 22, 2004, p. 6A. See also "India's Shining Hopes," *Economist,* February 21, 2004, p. 15; and Khozem Merchant, "Coming of Age Brings Challenges," *Financial Times,* June 1, 2004, p. 3.

105   Kris Gopalakrishnan's remarks are from "Infosys of India to Establish a U.S. Subsidiary," *International Herald Tribune,* April 9, 2004, p. 13. See also Jay Solomon, "A Race to IT Success," *Far Eastern Economic Review,* October 28, 2004, p. 70.

105   Josh Bornstein's passage to India is from Anne Fisher, "Joining the March of Jobs Overseas," *Fortune,* May 17, 2004, p. 54. See also Anne Fisher, "If All the Jobs Are Going to India, Should I Move to Bangalore?" *Fortune,* January 12, 2004, p. 146; Diane E. Lewis, "U.S. Interns Flood India for Tutelage," *Honolulu Star-Bulletin,* November 10, 2003, p. C2; and Jay Solomon, "India Woos More Western Executives," *Globe and Mail,* February 22, 2005, p. B16.

106 Labji Singh's comments are from "Biotech Should Go on Mission Mode," *BioSpectrum,* January 2004, p. 62.

106 The potential size of India's biotech industry is discussed in Khozem Merchant, "The Birth of a Biotech Cluster," *Financial Times,* August 14, 2003, p.8; Manjeet Kripalani, "India's Next Outsourcing Coup: Drugs," *BusinessWeek,* January 19, 2004, p. 13; Andrew Tanzer, "Pill Factory to the World," *Forbes,* December 10, 2001, pp. 70–72; Trish Saywell, "High Return on Drugs," *Far Eastern Economic Review,* December 4, 2003, pp. 43–45; Saritha Rai, "India Drugmakers Focus on West," *International Herald Tribune,* December 27–28, 2003, p. 9; Naazneen Karmali, "Copycats No More," *Forbes,* April 19, 2004, pp. 66–67; S. Subblakshmi, "Genetically Inclined," www.mid-day.com, February 12, 2004, p. IV; and Clive Cookson, "Eastern Rebirth of Life Sciences," *Financial Times,* June 10, 2005, p. 9.

106 For more on Kiran Mazumdar-Shaw, see Mary Ellen Egan, "Big Shot in Bangalore," *Forbes,* October 18, 2004, pp. 88–89; P. Hari, "The World of Biocon," *Business World,* December 2, 2002, pp. 36–44; Amy Waldman, "From Indian Taboo, Biotech Sector Is Born," *International Herald Tribune,* August 19, 2003; p. 11; Naazneen Karmali, "Biocon Booming," *Business India,* December 8–21, 2003, pp. 62–69; "India's Fermentation Queen," *Economist,* September 1, 2001, p. 58; Sadanand Dunne, "Bangalore's New Buzz," *Far Eastern Economic Review,* July 4, 2002, pp. 28–30; and Andrew Pollack, "Medical Companies Joining Offshore Trend, Too," *New York Times,* February 24, 2005, p. A1.

106 Her training in brewing and family days are found in her *Ale & Arty: The Story of Beer* (New Delhi: Viking by Penguin Books India, 2000).

107 For a discussion of the link between brewing and biotech, see Matt Moore, "Biotech Firms Look to Beer to Make Headway in Europe." *Honolulu Advertiser,* July 11, 2004, p. F4.

107 For more on Mazumdar-Shaw's introduction to Leslie Auchinclaus and the early Biocon days, see Egan, p. 89, and Hari, pp. 39–40.

108 India's role as a drug testing lab is reported in Geoff Dyer, "A Laboratory for Globalization: How India Hopes to Reshape the World Drug Industry," *Financial Times,* August 18, 2004, p. 9; Khozem Merchant, "Scientists in India Develop New Cure for TB," *Financial Times,* September 7, 2004, p. 7; Saritha Rai, "Testing Gives India a Shot in the Arm," *International Herald Tribune,* January 15–16, 2005, p. 11; Manjeet Kripalani, "Copycats No More," *BusinessWeek,* April 18, 2005, p. 51; and Eric Bellman, "India Senses Patent Appeal," *Wall Street Journal,* April 11, 2005, p. A20.

109 Dr. Reddy's comments on Biocon are reported in Karmali, p. 63.

109 Bill Harris's positive comments are from Karmali, p. 63.

110 For a discussion of Biocon's successful IPO, see Egan, p. 89; and Eric Bellman, "Bankers Upbeat on India," *Wall Street Journal,* May 4, 2004, p. C14.

111 For more on "Glenmore," see Hari, "The World of Biocon," pp. 36–44.

111 Shaw's remarks on Biocon's corporate culture are from Hari, p. 40.

111 Nirupa Baeja's quote is from Hari, p. 40.

112 Dr. Suryanarayan's quote is from from Hari, p. 40.

113 Mazumdar-Shaw's criticism of New Delhi is reported in "Is the Government Committed to Biotech?" *BioSpectrum,* January 2004, p. 36.

114 Ms. Ramanathan's return is discussed in Maahavi Swamy, "Cleaning Up City Hall," *Far Eastern Economic Review,* April 3, 2003, p. 40.

114 Hans Taparia's quote is from Manjeet Kripalani, "Calling Bangalore," *BusinessWeek,* November 25, 2002, p. 53. For contrary opinions, see S. Srinivasan, "India's High-Tech Center Built on Shaky Foundation," *International Herald Tribune,* September 3, 2003, p. 13; Josey Puliyenthuruthel, "Bangalore: Tech Eden No More," *BusinessWeek,* November 1, 2001, p. 57; and "The Bangalore Paradox," *Economist,* April 23, 2005, pp. 67–69.

115 The "Brides Wanted" ad appeared in Mumbai's *Asian Age,* February 8, 2004, p. 10.

115 The letter to Dr. Broota may be found in her "Sense and Sensibilities," *Swagat,* February 2004, p. 126.

116 The Sandhu and Mann quotes are from Ramesh Vinayak, "Replica Houses," *India Today,* February 16, 2004, pp. 83 and 86. For more on India's contemporary lifestyle, see Scott Baldauf, "Boom Splits Middle Class," *Christian Science Monitor,* May 13, 2004, p. 1; Uttara Choudhury, "India's Rich Buy into 'Lifestyle,'" *International Herald Tribune,* September 23, 2004, p. 22; Michael Schuman, "Hey, Big Spenders," *TIME,* September 2003, pp. 7–12; Joanna Slater, "For India's Youth, New Money Fuels a Revolution," *Wall Street Journal,* January 27, 2004, p. A1; James Traub, "Keeping Up with the Shidhayes," *New York Times Magazine,* April 15, 2001, pp. 32–37; Saritha Rai, "U.S. Payrolls Change Lives in Bangalore," *New York Times,* February 22, 2004, p. 8; Katherine Boo, "The Best Job In Town," *New Yorker,* July 5, 2004, pp. 55–69; and Gurcharan Das, *India Unbound* (New York: Alfred A. Knopf, 2000).

117 Kipling's quote is cited in "India: Fifty Years of Independence," p. 21.

117 Nehru's "opening of opportunity" is from "India: Fifty Years of Independence," p. 20.

CHAPTER 5. HOME TO THE WORLD

119 The Raffles quote is from Barbara Leitch LePoer (ed.), *Singapore: A Country Study* (Washington, D.C.: Library of Congress, 1996), pp. 12–13.

121 William Gibson's "Disneyland" likeness is reported in Margie Logarta, "Oh Behave, Singapore," *Business Traveler,* March 2004, p. 52. See also Caroline Faris (ed.), *Living in Singapore: A Reference Guide* (Singapore: American Association of Singapore, 2002); and Jennifer Gampell, "Where Having Fun Is Now O.K.," *New York Times,* April 24, 2005, p. TR4.

122 Goh Chok Tong's quotes are from "Critical Focus on Staffing Knowledge-Based Economy," *International Herald Tribune,* October 5, 1998, p. 19. See also Michael Richardson, "Singapore's 'Foreigners,'" *International Herald Tribune,* March 30, 1999, p. 13; and "Relax—A Little," *Far Eastern Economic Review,* December 24, 1998, pp.14–15.

123 Philip Yeo's remarks are from "Singapore: New Hub of the Knowledge Economy," *International Herald Tribune,* July 9, 1999, p. 19. See also Yeo's "Opening Address to the Biomedical Association Partnering Seminar 2003," Singapore, Shangri-la Hotel, October 27, 2003. See also Trish Saywell, "Ambition in a Test Tube," *Far Eastern Economic Review,* January 9, 2003, pp. 36–42; her "Medicine for the Economy," *Far Eastern Economic Review,* November 15, 2001, pp. 40–48; and her "Singapore's Man with a Plan," *Economist,* August 14, 2004, p. 60.

123 Mr. Goh's comments on foreign talent are reported in "Critical Focus . . .," p. 19. See also "Singapore: The Next Lap," Government of Singapore, 1991, pp. 25–27; and Shu Shin Luh, "Singapore Recruits Foreigners Despite Qualms at Home," *Wall Street Journal,* October 9, 2001, p. B7.

123 The country's education reform is described in Karin Robinson, "View from Singapore's Hot Seat," *Weekend BT,* January 31–February 1, 2004, p. 8. See also Trish Saywell and David Plott, "Re-imagining Singapore," *Far Eastern Economic Review,* July 11, 2002, especially pp. 45–46; and Ben Bolven, "Let's All Be Creative," *Far Eastern Economic Review,* December 24, 1998, pp. 10–12

123 The injection of outside athletic advisers is discussed in Trish Saywell, "Singapore Shoots for Sports Success," *Wall Street Journal,* December 10, 2003, p. B7A.

124 The latest Trends study is reported in Miranda Green, "Singapore's Children Top the Class in Math and Science," *Financial Times,* December 15, 2004, p. 4.

124 See Chris Prystay and Elizabeth Bernstein, "Gateway to the Ivy League," *Wall Street Journal,* May 6, 2004, p. B1.

125 See Lee Kuan Yew, *From the Third World to First: The Singapore Story: 1965–2000* (New York: HarperCollins, 2000), p. 7. See also his *The Singapore Story: Memoirs of Lee Kuan Yew* (Singapore: Prentice Hall, 1998).

125 Lee's "trained talent . . ." quote is from his *From the Third . . .*, p. 544.

125 "Many middle-class . . ." is from *From Third . . .*, p. 142. See also pp. 664–668.

126 Lee's comments on the "nanny state" are from *From the Third . . .*, back jacket flap. See also "Politically Incorrect," *Far Eastern Economic Review*, September 24, 1998, pp. 10–12.

126 "Without foreign talent . . ." may be found in *From the Third . . .*, p. 144.

126 PM Lee Hsien Loong's remarks on attracting talent are from Quentin Peel, John Ridding, and John Burton, "Heir Apparent Ready to Re-engineer Economy," *Financial Times*, April 12, 2002, p. II. See also Trish Saywell and David Plott, "Re-Imagining Singapore," *Far Eastern Economic Review*, July 11, 2002, especially, pp. 49–50; and Garry Rodan, "The Coming Challenge of Singapore Inc.," *Far Eastern Economic Review*, December 2004, pp. 51–54.

128 Singapore's push into life sciences is reported in David Tong, "Singapore Builds Hub for Biotech," *Honolulu Star-Bulletin*, April 25, 2004, p. C1; Michael Shari, "A Biotech Hub," *BusinessWeek*, November 27, 2000, p. 144; Wayne Arnold, "Singapore Builds a Better Scientist Trap," *International Herald Tribune*, August 27, 2003, p. 1; Saywell, "Ambition . . .," pp. 36–42, and her "Medicine . . .," pp. 40–48; John Burton, "Bringing in the Talents to Create Dynamic Industries," *Financial Times*, April 12, 2002, p. VI, and his "Singapore Aims to Be a Biotechnology Hub," *Financial Times*, June 10, 2005, p. 9.

129 The Edison Liu story is reported in Trish Saywell, "The New Frontier," *Far Eastern Economic Review*, July 11, 2002; and her "Ambition . . .," pp. 36–42. See also "Singapore. Your World of Possibilities," *Contact Singapore 2003*, unpaged; and Charles Piller, "'Brain Drain' Flowing from U.S. to Asia," *Honolulu Advertiser*, December 12, 2004, p. A30.

130 David Lane's comments are from Chang Ai-Lien, "Cancer Expert Excited to Work in S'pore," *The Straits Times*, August 13, 2004, p. 1.

130 Professor Ito's remarks are from Saywell, "Ambition . . .," p. 37. See also "Singapore. Your World of Possibilities," *Contact Singapore 2003*, unpaged.

130 Alan Coleman's quote may be found in Arnold, p. 8.

130 Dr. Liu's quote is from Saywell, "Medicine . . .," p. 45.

132 James Tan's "If we lose 70 percent . . ." is from Trish Saywell, "Big Spending on a New School," *Far Eastern Economic Review*, November 15, 2001, pp. 46–48.

133 For recent changes to the national service program, see Dominic Nathan, "NS Cut by Six Months," *The Straits Times*, June 16, 2004, p. A1.

134 Edison Liu's quote is from his "The Future of Life and Singapore," *The Straits Times*, February 28, 2003, p. 2. See also "Singapore Biomed Sector to Hit 2005 Target Early," *The Straits Times*, June 23, 2004, p. 1.

134 For more on Ron Frank's decision to go to Singapore and the accompanying quotes, see Anna Teo, "Well Schooled," *Weekend BT*, March 15–16, 2003, p. 3; Sumathi Bala, "The City-State Makes Its Point as a Regional Hub," *Financial Times*, January 26, 2004, p. 11; and "New Heights: Report to Stakeholders 2002–2003," Singapore Management University, 2003, updated 27 August, 2003.

135 Dr. Frank's "what's the difference" remarks are from Teo, "Well Schooled," p. 3.

135 For his assessment on SMU's future, see Teo, "Well Schooled," p. 3.

136 Rosa Daniel is quoted in "Singapore: New Hub of the Knowledge Economy," p. 20. See also Michael Vatikiotis, "A Colombian in 'the Louvre of Asia,'" *International Herald Tribune*, December 23, 2004, p. 9.

136 Lan Shui's quote may be found in "Singapore. Your World of Possibilities," unpaged.

136 Joanne Blakemore is quoted in Ram Kapoor, "Livin' La Vida Local!" *Synergy*, July–September 2003, p. 2. See also Faris, pp. 193–205; and Douglas Wong, "Cosmopolitan City for Work and Play," *Financial Times*, April 12, 2003, p. VI.

137 Ex-PM Lee's remarks are from Ben Bolven, "Artistic Dilemma," *Far Eastern Economic Review*, April 22, 1999, p. 61. See also Logarta, p. 50.

137 Allan Wu's quote is from Yvette Sitten, "Star Search: Singapore's Media Scene Heats Up!," *Synergy,* January–March 2004, pp. 2–3.

137 Sunita Rajan's view is discussed in "Singapore. Your World of Possibilities," unpaged.

140 See Philip Day, "Singapore Leads India Charge," *Wall Street Journal,* April 5, 2004, p. A17.

140 George Yeo's remarks are found in Trish Saywell and Michael Vatikiotis, "A Way to Grow Like China," *Far Eastern Economic Review,* October 31, 2004, pp. 4–6.

140 Flextronics CEO Michael Marks is quoted in Assif Shameen, "You Want It, We'll Make It," *Far Eastern Economic Review,* March 20, 2003, p. 33.

141 Lee Kuan Yew's remarks are from Nayan Chanda, "Protectionism Would Work, Job Migration Unstoppable," *The Straits Times,* February 4, 2004, p. 12.

141 PM Lee Hsien Loong's comments on being small are from Mark Landler, "Some Role Reversal in East Asia," *New York Times,* November 27, 1998 p. C5.

141 The World Economic Forum survey is reported in Frances Williams and John Burton, "Singapore Overtakes U.S. to Lead World in New IT," *Financial Times,* March 10, 2005, p. 6.

141 Mentor Minister Lee Kuan Yew's remarks are from Chuang Peck Ming, "Costs Too High in S'pore: SM Lee," *Weekend BT,* January 31–February 1, 2004, p. 2.

CHAPTER 6. THE CHINA SYNDROME

143 For more on Chairman Mao's pronouncement and the October 1st ceremonies, see John McCook Roots, *Chou: Informal Biography of China's Legendary Chou En-Lai* (New York: Doubleday, 1978), p. 101; and Kai-yu Hsu, *Chou En-Lai: China's Gray Eminence* (New York: Doubleday, 1968), pp. 190–191.

144 Deng's "It doesn't matter. . . " quote is from "Behind the Mask," *Economist,* March 20, 2004, p. 3. See also Clay Chandler, "Inside the New China," *Fortune,* October 4, 2004, pp. 85–98; Ted C. Fishman, "The Chinese Century," *New York Times Magazine,* July 4, 2004, pp. 21–51; "Greater China," *BusinessWeek,* December 9, 2002, pp. 50–58; and Keith Bradsher, "The Two Faces of China," *New York Times,* December 6, 2004, pp. C1–4.

144 Schlesinger's "capitalistic communism" is from my "China on the Move," *Journal of Business Strategy,* May–June 1993, p. 35.

145 Goldman Sachs' prediction is variously reported. See, for example, "Behind the Mask," p. 4; "The Dragon and the Eagle," *Economist,* October 2, 2004, pp. 8–9; Frances Williams, "China 'Set to Join League of Biggest Direct Investors Abroad,'" *Financial Times,* May 5, 2004, p. 5; Daniel Altman, "The China Question: Catch Up or Surpass?" *International Herald Tribune,* October 30–31, 2004, p. 14; and Charles Hutzler, "China May Be on Course to Overtake U.S.," *Wall Street Journal,* January 24, 2005, p. A2.

145 Professor Sachs' "center of gravity" quote is from his "Welcome to the Asian Century," *Fortune,* January 26, 2004, p. 53. See also Jonathan Spence, "Imagining China's Future," *Fortune,* October 4, 2004, pp. 213–222; Christopher Langner, "China Tops U.S. as Favorite Investment Spot," *Wall Street Journal,* October 12, 2004, p. A20; Jane Perlez, "China Races to Replace U.S. as Economic Power in Asia," *New York Times,* June 28, 2002, p. A1; Ted C. Fishman, *China, Inc: How the Rise of the Next Superpower Challenges America and the World* (New York: Scribner, 2005); and Keith Bradsher, "China's Economy Rising at Pace to Rival U. S.," *New York Times,* June 28, 2005, p. A1.

145 For more on Deng's "socialism with Chinese characteristics," see Bruce W. Nelan, "Risky Change in a Dynasty," *TIME,* November 6, 1995, pp. 44–46; Jim Rogers, "The China Play," *Worth,* December/January 1996, pp. 29–37; and David Sheff, *China Dawn* (New York: HarperBusiness, 2002).

146 Michael Moritz's prediction may be found in Bruce Einhorn with Ben Elgin and Linda Hemelstein, "High Tech in China," *BusinessWeek,* October 28, 2002, p. 80. See also "VCs Turn an Eagle Eye on China," *BusinessWeek,* June 14, 2004, p. 42; Gary Rivlin,

"Talk of a Bubble as Venture Capitalists Flock to China," *New York Times,* December 6, 2004, p. C10; and Jeffrey E. Garten, "The High-Tech Threat from China," *BusinessWeek,* January 31, 2005, p. 22.

147   For more on the PRC's multinational threat, see Elaine Kurtenbach, "Chinese Investors Buying Up Companies Around the World," *Honolulu Star-Bulletin,* October 22, 2004, p. C2; Williams, "China Set to Join. . .," p. 5; Bruce Einhorn, "Huawei: More Than a Local Hero," *BusinessWeek,* October 11, 2004, pp. 180–184; Alex Taylor III, "Shanghai Auto Wants to Be the World's Next Great Car Company," *Fortune,* October 4, 2004, pp. 103–110; Dexter Roberts, "China's Power Brands," *BusinessWeek,* November 8, 2004, pp. 77–84; Mark Sappenfield, "A Landmark Move for China Inc.," *Christian Science Monitor,* December 9, 2004, p. 2; Fishman, p. 46; Julie Chao, "Big Chinese Companies Going Global," *Honolulu Star-Bulletin,* August 10, 2003, p. E4; and James MacKintosh, Richard McGregor, and Francesco Guerrera, "Chinese Companies Acquire a Taste for Western Targets," *Financial Times,* October 19, 2004, p. 18.

148   Professor Enriquez-Cabot's quote is from Einhorn et al., "High-Tech . . .," p. 86. See also Russell Flannery, "Hiring Hall," *Forbes,* July 26, 2004, p. 80.

148   For more on "stored brainpower," see Rone Tempest, "China Woos Back Its Silicon Valley Set," *Los Angeles Times,* November 27, 2002, p. 1. See also Lynn Pan (ed.), *The Encyclopedia of the Chinese Overseas* (Singapore: Archipelago Press, 1999).

149   Wu Ying's quote and story are from Janet Ong, "High-Tech Luring Laid-off Expatriates Back to China," *Honolulu Advertiser,* January 2, 2002, p. D3. See also "A Comprehensive Mind," *Beijing Tatler,* June 2004, pp. 169–170; Suh-Kyung Yoon, "Why UTStarcom Is New China's Rising Telecoms Star," *Far Eastern Economic Review,* January 31, 2002, p. 42; and Kaiser Kuo, "UTStarcom/Wu Ying," *TIME,* August 2003, p. A18.

149   Robert Lee's description of "welcoming" is from Tempest, "China Woos. . .," p. 1. See also Andrew Browne, "Chinese Recruit Top Executives Trained Abroad," *Wall Street Journal,* November 30, 2004, p. B1; and Kai-Yin Lo, "Chinese Artists Look Homeward," *International Herald Tribune,* October 8, 2003, p. 22.

149   Dongping Zhu's career and quotes are from Bruce Gilley, "Looking Homeward," *Far Eastern Economic Review,* March 11, 1999, p. 51. See also "Alumnus Mines Data for Dollar in Global Operation," *ECE Connection,* July 25, 2001, pp. 1–3.

150   The returning Chinese estimates are from "Greater China," p. 52; See also John Markoff, "Have Supercomputer, Will Travel," *New York Times,* November 1, 2004, p. C1; Jonathan Kaufman, "After Years in U.S., Mr. Luo Seeks Fortune in China," *Wall Street Journal,* March 6, 2003, p. A6; and Tempest, p. 1.

151   Ping Ko's quote is from Tempest, p. 8. See also David W. Chen, "For Many Chinese, America's Allure Is Fading," *New York Times,* September 7, 2003, p. 4; and Ted Plafker, "Foreign Degrees Lose Cachet in China," *International Herald Tribune,* October 19, 2004, p. 9.

151   Professor Zhang is quoted in Einhorn et al., "High-Tech in China," p. 86. See also James Flanigan, "China's Technological Ambitions Take Flight," *Los Angeles Times,* October 19, 2003, p. C7.

151   Patrick Nolan's comments on legal recruiting are from David J. Lynch, "More of China's Best, Brightest Return Home," *USA Today,* March 3, 2003, p. B2. See also Rena SenGupta, "The Allure of China for Lawyers," *Financial Times,* June 30, 2005, p. 11.

151   Ying Luo's "glass ceiling" quote is from Jonathan Kaufman, "After Years in U.S., Mr. Luo Seeks Fortune in China," *Wall Street Journal,* March 6, 2003, p. A1. See also Kerry A. Dolan, "The Drug Research War," Forbes.com, May 28, 2004, p. 1; and Andrew Browne, "Chinese Recruit Top Executives Trained Abroad," *Wall Street Journal,* November 30, 2004, p. B1.

152   Cynthia Chen's quote is from Lynch, p. B2.

152   Edward Tian's remarks are from David Sheff, "China's Change Merchants," *Chief Executive,* March 2002, pp. 51–52. See also Dexter Roberts, "Bringing It All Back Home," *BusinessWeek,* June 22, 1998, p. 58.

152 Chen's quote is from Lynch, p. B2.

152 Patrick Benzie's quote is found in Kathy Wilhelm, "Why Are Talented Strategic Thinkers in Short Supply?" *Far Eastern Economic Review,* June 14, 2001, p. 39.

153 Hu Ping's quote is from Kaufman, "After Years . . .," p. A6.

153 "They can help. . ." is from Alysha Webb, "Back to the Motherland," *BusinessWeek,* August 29, 2002, p. 60.

153 Professor Hai Wen's remarks are from Roberts, p. 58.

153 For more on Chris Bachran's move to China, see Ben Dolven, "Under New Management," *Far Eastern Economic Review,* April 15, 2004, pp. 28–33; "Jinjiang Int'l to Enter Global Markets," TDCTrade.com, March 18, 2004; "Hotelier Taps Hospitality Skills," ChinaDaily.com, March 28, 2004; Elaine Kurtenbach, "Increase in Travelers Behind Hotel Boom in Chinese Cities," *Honolulu Advertiser,* November 12, 2004, p. C3; and Dan Martin, "Isle Native Runs Chinese Hotel Chain," *Honolulu Star-Bulletin,* June 14, 2005, p. A9.

154 See Dali L. Yang, "China's Looming Labor Shortage," *Far Eastern Economic Review,* January 2005, pp. 19–24; and "China's people problem," *Economist,* April 16, 2005, pp. 53–54.

156 Charles Dyce's quote on the importance of commerce is found in Mayhew, p. 16.

157 The Charles Darwin observation is found in Peter Howarth, "In Search of Shanghai," *Financial Times,* October 16–17, 2004, p. W11.

157 Ralph Shaw's comments are from Mayhew, p. 54.

158 Tan Tingao's quote is from Einhorn et al., "High-Tech . . .," p. 80. See also "Silicon Valley, PRC," *Economist,* June 27, 1998, pp. 64–65; and Tempest, p. 1.

158 The James Gao story and quote may be found in Webb, p. 60.

159 Hao Min's repatriation is reported in Bruce Einhorn and Alysha Webb, "The Chips Are Up," *BusinessWeek,* November 27, 2000, p. 139.

159 China's stake in software is cited in Winter Wright, "New Kid," *Far Eastern Economic Review,* July 11, 2001, p. 38. See also Evan Ramstad, "China's Great Hi-Tech Leap," *Far Eastern Economic Review,* May 13, 2004, pp. 38–39; Justine Lau, "Frontier of a New Global Contest," *Financial Times,* June 1, 2004, p. 3; and J. Bonasia, "China's Software Biz Takes Root," *Investor's Business Daily,* March 2, 2005, p. A4. The IC Insights estimate is from Otis Port, "China Check," *BusinessWeek,* January 31, 2005, p. 12.

160 The Gartner prediction is from Wright, p. 38. See also Michel Vatikiotis and Murray Hiebert, "Dancing Elephants," *Far Eastern Economic Review,* April 29, 2004, p. 12; and Saritha Rai, "Chinese Race to Supplant India in Software," *New York Times,* January 5, 2002, p. B1.

160 Mr. Son's dire assessment is from "Speaking Out: The View from the Top," *Business-Week,* August 25, 2003, p. 113.

160 Ling Hai's return and quote are reported in Wilhelm, p. 39.

161 Bradley Mayhew's quote is from his *Shanghai* (Footscray, Vic., Australia: Lonely Planet Publications, 2004), p. 8.

162 For more on Zhang Xin and her remarks, see John Ridding, "First Out of the Blocks to Modernize," *Financial Times,* March 20–21, 2004, p. W3. See also Kathy Chen, "China's 'It Couple' Builds Sleek Towers and a High Profile," *Wall Street Journal,* July 22, 2004, p. A1; Annie Wang, "Holding up Half the Sky," *Fortune,* October 4, 2004, p. 172; Mark Stevens, "Off the Great Wall," *Departures,* May/June, 2004, p. 168; and R. Scott Macintosh, "A Modern, Aesthetic Chinese Style," *International Herald Tribune,* February 19, 2004, p. 21.

163 Sutter Hill's Barker's description of ZSP is from Sheff, p. 55.

164 For more on Edward Tian and his remarks, see Sheff, p. 55. See also Alejandro Reyes, "Networking for a New China," Asiaweek.com, March 30, 2001; and Joel McCormick, "China.com," *Stanford,* September–October 2004, pp. 36–43.

164 Charles Zhang's remarkable ascent and accompanying remarks are told in Brian Robins, "Zhang on a Mission for Blood Ties with China," *Sydney Morning Herald,* June 25,

2004, p. 25. See also Daniel Roth, "In Search of China's Bill Gates," *Fortune,* October 4, 2004, pp. 162–164; and Kaiser Kuo, "Sohu.com/Charles Zhang," *TIME,* August 2003, p A11.

164   His dealing with government comments are from Andrew Tanzer, "Search Fox," *Forbes,* March 8, 1999, p. 108; and James Kynge, "Global Contagion Spreads Eastwards," *Financial Times,* November 13, 2000, p. VIII.

165   Peggy Yu's quotes are from Bruce Einhorn," The Net's Second Superpower," *BusinessWeek,* March 15, 2004, p. 56; and "Peggy Yu, Co-Founder, Co-President of Dangdang.com," *China Online,* 2002. See also "An e-tailer with a Lot Riding on Bicycles," *BusinessWeek Online,* March 8, 2004; John Pomfret, "A Brain Gain for China," *Washington Post Foreign Service,* October 16, 2000, p. A1; "The Clang of a Virtual Cash Register: Dingdong.com," *Beijing Scene,* February 25–March 2, 2000, p. A1; and "China's Amazon," *Economist,* August 23, 2003, p. 52.

166   Yu's comments on motherhood are from Pomfret, p. A1. See also Clay Chandler, "Little Emperors," *Fortune,* October 4, 2004, pp. 138–150; and Carol Hymowitz, "Chinese Women Bosses Say Long Hours on Job Don't Hurt Their Kids," *Wall Street Journal,* May 17, 2005, p. B1.

166   BGI professor Jian Wang is quoted in David Murphy, "China Uncorks the Gene in a Bottle," *Far Eastern Economic Review,* March 22, 2001, p. 4.

167   Jing Cheng's contributions are discussed in David Stipp, "China's Biotech Is Starting to Bloom," *Fortune,* September 2002, pp. 127–134; his "Can China Overtake the U.S. in Science?" *Fortune,* October 4, 2004, pp. 187–196; and "Biotech's Yin and Yang," *Economist,* December 14, 2002, pp. 71–73.

168   Jing Cheng's long-term prediction of China's success is from Stipp, "China's Biotech…," p. 134.

168   Xia Guangzhi's comments on recruiting Thornton and other foreigners are from James Kynge, "A Revolution Stirs in the Willow Groves," *Financial Times,* March 27, 2003, p. 20. See also his "China Looks Overseas to Add Tech Vigor," *Financial Times,* May 28, 2003, p. 19; Philip Tinari, "China's MIT Upgrades Itself," *Wall Street Journal,* July 28, 2004, p. A11; Lionel Barber and Charles Pretzlik, "A Leader Among Mandarins," *Financial Times,* August 22, 2003, p. 6; and Clay Chandler, "From Marx to Market," *Fortune,* May 16, 2005, pp. 102–112.

168   Hongjiang Zhang's "best Tsinghua students" quote is from Alan Wheatley, "Beijing," *International Herald Tribune,* August 23, 2002, p. 14.

169   His "The biggest challenge" is from Gregory T. Huang, "The World's Hottest Computer Lab," *Technology Review,* June 2004, p. 7.

169   Harry Shum's remarks may be found in Wheatley, p. 14, and are discussed in Chris Buckley, "Research Labs Power China's Next Boom," *International Herald Tribune,* September 13, 2004, p. 10. See also Huang, pp. 1–8.

169   Kai-Fu Lee's comments are from Huang, p. 4. See also John Markoff, "Silicon Valley's Primal Spirit Lives on, in a Part of Beijing," *New York Times,* August 4, 2000, p. A4.

169   Bill Gates's sentiments on China are found in Huang, p. 2. See also Ted C. Fishman, "Betting on China," *USA Today,* February 17, 2005, p. 11A.

170   "It's frightening. . ." is from William J. Broad, "U.S. Is Losing Its Dominance in the Sciences," *New York Times,* May 3, 2004, p. A19.

170   For more on China's educational reforms, see Robert Marquand, "In Modern China, Parents Pushing for Super Tykes," *Christian Science Monitor,* May 10, 2004, p. 1; and Leslie Chang, "Chinese Job-Search Mismatch," *Wall Street Journal,* June 21, 2004, p. A7.

172   See Yilu Zhao, "China's Wealthy Live by a Creed: Hobbes and Darwin, Meet Marx," *New York Times,* February 29, 2004, p. D7.

173   For more on the gap between rich and poor, see Jim Yardley, "An Explosion of Beggars in China," *International Herald Tribune,* April 8, 2004, p. A1, and his "In a Tidal Wave, China's Masses Pour from Farm to City," *New York Times,* September 12, 2004, p. D6;

Keith Bradsher, "China's Strange Hybrid Economy," *New York Times,* September 21, 2003, p. D1; "The Eagle and the Dragon," p. 4; and Charles Hutzler and Kathy Chen, "China Grapples with Social Ills," *Wall Street Journal,* March 2, 2005, p. A14. See "The Silent Majority," *Economist,* April 9, 2005, pp. 32–33; and "Inglorious Riches," *Economist,* March 20, 2004, p. 16.

173 China's upwardly mobile are described in Henry Sender, "China's Consumers Show Desire to Spend," *Wall Street Journal,* August 9, 2004, p. A2; Shashank Bengali, "Racetrack Sign of China's Velocity," *Honolulu Advertiser,* August 8, 2004, p. A8; Keith Bradsher, "The Ultimate Luxury Item Is Now Made in China," *New York Times,* July 13, 2004, p. 10; and Clay Chandler, "China Deluxe," *Fortune,* July 27, 2004, p. 154.

174 Charles Zhang's quote is from "Inglorious Riches," *Economist,* March 20, 2004, p. 16. See also Lifen Zhang, "Getting Rich Is Glorious," *Financial Times,* December 7, 2004, p. 3.

174 See "Inglorious Riches," p. 16.

CHAPTER 7. CROSS-STRAIT COMPETITION

175 The Arthur Clarke quote is from Norman Pearlstine, "The Man and the Magic," *TIME,* 29 December 1997, p. A8.

175 For more on the Chang story, see Andrew Tanzer, "Silicon in, Cash Out," *Forbes,* March 13, 1995, pp. 54–56; and Mark Landler, "From Taiwan, a Fear of China Technology," *New York Times,* October 3, 2001, p. C1.

177 "Taiwan has become . . ." quote is from Erika Brown, "Chang's Law," Forbes.com, September 16, 2003, p. 3. See also "Chipping Away," *Economist,* April 25, 1998, pp. 64–65; and Dean Takahashi and David P. Hamilton, "Taiwan's Foundries Lead Recovery in the Chip Industry," *Wall Street Journal,* June 1, 1999, p. B4.

177 Chintay Shih's remarks are from "EBN's Hot 25," *Electronics Supply & Manufacturing,* July 9, 2004, p. 1.

178 Paul Wang's quote is found in Andrew Tanzer, "Silicon Valley East," *Forbes,* June 1, 1998, p. 127.

178 Ta-Lin Hsu's sentiments appear in Tanzer, "Silicon Valley East," p. 125. See also Shawn W. Crispin, "An Asian Adventure," *Far Eastern Economic Review,* May 22, 2003, p. 54.

179 The Jardine quote is from Vivian Kim, Francis Dora, and Brian Bell (eds.), *Insight Guide Taiwan* (Singapore: Apa Publications, 2003), p. 27.

179 Gideon Nye's sentiments are found in Kim et al., p. 27.

181 President Chen's sentiments are variously reported. See, for example, Rose Brady (ed.), "So Much for China's 'Great Healer,'" *BusinessWeek,* January 24, 2005, p. 55; "Chen Redux," *Economist,* May 22, 2004, p. 37; Jason Dean and Anthony Kuhn, "Test of Sincerity," *Far Eastern Economic Review,* June 3, 2004, p. 35; Richard Halloran, "Taiwan's Role Key in U.S.–China Link," *Honolulu Advertiser,* July 4, 2004, p. B3, and his "Taiwan Leaders Spar Openly over China," *Honolulu Advertiser,* May 15, 2005, p. B3; Michael D. Swaine, "Trouble in Taiwan," *Foreign Affairs,* March/April 2004, pp. 39–49; Kathrin Hille and Richard McGregor, "Taipei Calls Off War Games in Goodwill Gesture," *Financial Times,* September 11, 2004, p. 6; and Bruce Einhorn, "Why Taiwan Matters," *BusinessWeek,* May 16, 2005, pp. 76–81.

182 K. T. Li's remarks are found in "A Eulogy for K. T. Li," *Commercial Times,* June 1, 2001, p. 6. See also Tanzer, "Silicon Valley East," p. 126.

183 Ta-Lin Hsu's quote is from Tanzer, "Silicon Valley East," p. 126.

183 For more on Hsinchu Science Park, see Eunice Hsiao Hui Wang, "Technopolis Development in Taiwan: An Information Technology Capabilities–Enhancing Approach," in Mehroo Jussawala and Richard D. Taylor (eds.), *Information Technology Parks of Asia Pacific* (Armont, N.Y.: M. E. Sharpe, 2003), pp. 193–226; Michael M. K. Lin and Charles V. Trappey, "The Development of Taiwan's Integrated Circuit Industry," *IEEE Transaction,* Part C, October 1997, *20* (4), pp. 235–242; Ben Dolven,

"Power-Pack Park," *Far Eastern Economic Review,* August 6, 1998, p. 15; and Andrew Tanzer, "Made in Taiwan," *Forbes,* April 2, 2001, pp. 64–60.

184　Morris Chang is quoted in Andrew Tanzer, "Brain Drain in Reverse," *Forbes,* April 17, 1989, p. 115.

184　Bobo Wang's story is found in Tanzer, "Brain Drain. . .," p. 115; and in his "Bobo Wang's Mid-life Crisis," *Forbes,* June 24, 1991, pp. 110–111. See also Damon Darlin, "Taiwan, Long Noted for Cheap Imitations, Becomes an Innovator," *Wall Street Journal,* June 1, 1990, p. A1; and "Taiwan: Bobo Wang," *Fortune,* Fall 1990, p. 82.

186　Miin Wu is quoted in Thomas Crampton, "Taiwan's Industrial Ambitions," *International Herald Tribune,* March 18, 1999, p. 15. See also Tanzer, "Silicon Valley East," p. 123.

186　Chi-Chia Hsieh's quote is from Tanzer, "Brain Drain . . .," p. 114.

187　See Alan Brown, "Taipei: The Good with the Bad," *Travel and Leisure,* November 2000, p. 34. See also Roger Mark Selya, *Taipei* (New York: Wiley, 1995); Kathrin Hille, "Taipei Discovers Luxury Living," *Financial Times,* January 22–23, 2005, p. W14; and Andrew Yang, "A Young Taipei Finds Its Groove," *New York Times,* January 23, 2005, p. C7.

191　Taiwan's economic repositioning and Stan Shih's remarks are from Bruce Einhorn, "Minds over Matter," *BusinessWeek,* November 2000, p. 142. See also Jason Dean, "A Hi-Tech High," *Far Eastern Economic Review,* February 19, 2004, p. 46; and Shuhei Yamada, "Taiwan PC Makers Quietly Rule the Roost," *Nikkei Weekly,* December 6, 2004, p. 23.

191　Morris Chang's quote is from Russell Flannery, "And Now, Some Good News," Forbes.com, April 30, 2001, p. 3.

192　"Manufacturing is our safety net" quote is found in Crampton, p. 15.

192　Ho Mei-Yueh's remarks on the shortage of people are from Don Shapiro, "The Need for Alliance," *Topics,* June 2004, p. 23.

193　Emily Hsu's quote is found in Lin Mei-Chun, "Creating a Strong Base in R&D," *Topics,* June 2004, p. 41.

193　C. Y. Chang's admonition is reported in Alexandra Harney, "A Struggle to Stay in Front of Its Neighbour," *Financial Times,* December 18, 2001, p. 13.

193　For more on Morris Chang's change of heart, see Mark Landler, "Reprocessing China," *International Herald Tribune,* October 4, 2001, p. 11; his "From Taiwan . . .," p. C7; Chris Buckley, "Chips Made to Order and a Forecast That Sees a New Order of Business," *New York Times,* October 23, 2004, p. B1; and Terril Yve Jones, "Spying Case Underscores Rivalry of Asian Chip Firms," *Los Angeles Times,* January 3, 2005, p. C1.

193　President Chen's comments are from Harney, p. 13. See also Jason Dean, "Collateral Damage," *Far Eastern Economic Review,* July 29, 2004, p. 32; Keith Bradsher, "Jobs Flow to China, but Taiwan Still Thrives," *International Herald Tribune,* March 19, 2004, p. 17; Bradsher, "After an Exodus of Jobs, a Recovery in Taiwan," *New York Times,* March 19, 2004, p. W1; Bradsher, "Taiwan Watches Its Economy Slip to China," *New York Times,* December 13, 2004, p. C7; and Chang Yun-ping, "President Lauds the Nation's Economic Policies at Events," *Taipei Times,* July 1, 2004, p. 1.

194　His "no sunset" remarks are found in Harney, p. 13.

CHAPTER 8. MIDEAST MIRACLE

198　For a history of Jewish migration, see Joan Comay, *The Diaspora Story* (Tel Aviv: Steimatzky, 1981).

199　For a discussion of Rabin's appeal to immigrants, see "High-Tech Opportunities in Israel," Israel Ministry of Foreign Affairs Report, May 29, 2002, p. 5.

200　See James Bennett, "Sharon's Wars," *New York Times Magazine,* August 15, 2004, p. 32. See also "Israel's Unlikely Dove," *Economist,* October 23, 2004, p. 11; Harvey Morris, "Israel's Pragmatic Warrior," *Financial Times,* December 21, 2003, p. 7; and Benjamin Schwartz, "Will Israel Live to 100?" *Atlantic Monthly,* May 2005, pp. 29–32.

200 Sharon's airport reception is discussed in Greg Myre, "Israelis Roll out Red Carpet for 400 Immigrants," *International Herald Tribune,* July 15, 2004, p. 4.

200 Nefesh B' Nefesh is described in Greg Myre, "New Group Helps U.S. Jews Move to Israel," *New York Times,* July 15, 2004, p. 1. See also Gene Sloan, "More Americans Venturing Back to Israel," *USA Today,* March 5, 2004, p. 1D; and "Agency, Nefesh B' Nefesh Team Up," *Jerusalem Post,* August 17, 2004, p. 4.

201 Sharon's comments about aliyah are found in Myre, "New Group . . .," p. 1.

202 The Sanders and CFI are reported in Jane Lampman, "Mixing Prophecy and Politics," *Christian Science Monitor,* July 7, 2004, pp. 15–16.

202 Hanina Tadir's remarks are from Ken Ellingwood, "Capitalism Comes to the Kibbutz in Israel," *Los Angeles Times,* February 16, 2004, p. 11. See also Karby Leggett, "Pay-as-You-Go Kibbutzim," *Wall Street Journal,* May 26, 2005, p. B1.

203 Ben-Gurion's quote is reported in "Science & Technology," Israel Ministry of Foreign Affairs Report, April 26, 2003, p. 1.

204 King Hussein's comments on Technion are from "Science & Technology," p. 1.

204 The California–Israel comparison is reported in "Something in the Air," *Economist,* February 18, 1999.

204 Michael Moritz's quote is from "First Class Technology Center," Israel Ministry of Industry, *Trade & Labor,* 2003, p. 1. See also C. J. Prince, "Land of Tech and Honey," *Chief Executive,* October 2004, pp. 50–53; John Flanagan, "Israel Offers a High-Tech Development Model for Hawaii," *Honolulu Star-Bulletin,* March 5, 2002, p. A13; Sharon Moshavi, "Desert, Nukes, Spies—and a High-Tech Oasis," *BusinessWeek,* October 13, 1997, p. 14; and Sharmila Dev, "New Interest Is the Key for Israeli High-Tech," *Financial Times,* February 9, 2005, p. 18.

205 For a discussion of the Weizmann Institute, see "Weizmann's Patent Royalties," *Israel High-Tech Investment Report,* September 2004, p. 9.

205 Bill Gates's remarks were made at the World Economic Forum, Davos, Switzerland, January 2000.

205 For a discussion of Israel's national service program, see Jessica Steinberg, "The Military-Technological Complex Is Thriving in Israel," *New York Times,* December 6, 1998, p. D5; William A. Orme Jr., "Israeli Business Flies Like a Dove," *New York Times,* October 18, 1998, p. D3; and Betsy Cummings, "I Got My M.B.A. in the Israeli Army," *New York Times,* March 5, 2005, p. C7.

206 The Yossi Vardi quote is from Bruce Upbin, "Higher Ground," *Forbes,* October 27, 2003, p. 144. See also Del Jones, "A Vanishing Breed: CEOs Seasoned by Military Combat," *USA Today,* January 1, 2005, p. B1.

206 Shabtai Adlersburg's remarks are from Upbin, p. 144. See also Cameron W. Barr, "U.S. Eyes Israeli Software as a Training Tool for Forces in Iraq," *Christian Science Monitor,* September 29, 2003, p. 7.

206 The Landon quotes are from Scott Harris, "Roots in Israel, Head in Silicon Valley," *New York Times,* June 30, 2002, p. D8. See also Upbin, pp. 140–148.

207 Roy Zisapel's remarks are found in Upbin, p. 144.

208 Martha Bennett's quote is from "Israel: Veterans of Technology," *LINES,* September 2000, p. 53.

208 Ms. Maxwell's remarks are from Jessica Steinberg, "New Venturers: Born in Israel, Raised in U.S.," *New York Times,* June 13, 1999, p. D6.

208 For Yoam Millet's quote, see Judy Dempsey, "The Life Sciences Begin to Stir," *Financial Times,* August 7, 1998, p. 22.

209 For more on the Monitor Company report, see "Israeli Biotechnology Strategy Project: Realizing Our Potential," submitted to the Chief Scientist, Ministry of Industry and Trade, and the Ministry of Finance, Tel Aviv, March 2001, especially p. 3.

210 Ofer Carmel's quote may be found in Jay Solomon, "India's New Coup in Outsourcing: Inpatient Care," *Wall Street Journal,* April 26, 2004, p. A1.

212 For more on Jewish migration to America, see Comay, chapter 16. See also Barone, *The New Americans*, pp. 208–248; Jonathan Rosen, "The Citizen Stranger," *New York Times*, September 12, 2004, p. 13; and Elizabeth Armstrong, "350 Years of Jewish History in America," *Christian Science Monitor*, September 15, 2004, p. 11.

213 "We're moving away . . ." is from Bennett, p. 67.

214 For more on TIM, see Avi Machlis, "Grown-up Lessons for Young Companies," *Financial Times*, June 15, 1998, p. 11. See also pard.technion. acil/fastfacts/FastFacts. html.

217 The Poraz quote is from "Banking on Fischer," *Economist*, January 15, 2005, p. 69.

218 Rachel Gold's remarks are from "Aliyah & Klita," Jewish Agency for Israel, October 30, 2003.

220 For more on Israel's diplomatic isolation, see Jay Bushinsky, "When It Comes to Israel. . .," *Jerusalem Post*, August 18, 2004, p. 13; Franklin Foer, "And Nobody Cries Fool," *Wall Street Journal*, August 20, 2004, p.W11; "A Bloody Vacuum," *Economist*, October 2, 2004, p. 23; and Nelson D. Schwartz, "Prosperity Without Peace," *Fortune*, June 13, 2005, pp. 86–94.

220 Gal Fridman's Olympic gold is discussed in "A Windsurfer Nets Israel's First Gold," *International Herald Tribune*, August 26, 2004, p. 18; and Selina Roberts, "Yes, There Really Is an Israel," *New York Times*, August 26, 2004, p. B2.

220 Moshe Arieli's quote is from Josh Mitnick, "For Israel, a First Gold Medal and Affirmation of Statehood," *Christian Science Monitor*, August 26, 2004, p. 2.

221 The Weizman quote may be found in "Ezer Weizman," Jewish Virtual Library, American–Israeli Cooperative Enterprise, 2004, p. 2.

CHAPTER 9. BIENVENIDOS, AMIGOS

223 The Gutierrez story and quotes are from Richard J. Lopez and Rich Connell, "Marines Win Posthumous Citizenship," *Los Angeles Times*, April 3, 2003, pp. B1, B4; Brendan Miniter, "José Antonio Gutierrez," *Wall Street Journal*, April 4, 2003, p. A8; "The Death of Lance Cpl. Gutierrez," CBSNews.com, April 21, 2003; Marjorie Valbrun, "Military Embraces Immigrants," *Wall Street Journal*, April 2, 2003, p. A4; "Immigrant Soldiers," *Wall Street Journal*, April 4, 2003, p. A8; and Gregg Zoroya, "Troops Put Lives on Line to Be Called Americans," *USA Today*, June 30, 2005, p. 7D.

225 The International Office for Migration findings are in "Making the Most of an Exodus," *Economist*, February 23, 2002, p. 41; and "The View from Gringolandia," *Economist*, July 24, 2004, p. 78.

226 See Alan Riding, *Distant Neighbors* (New York: Knopf, 1985), p. xi. See also Jonathan Kandell, "Cross Purposes," *Smithsonian*, June 2005, pp. 90–96.

226 For the interview with Carlos Fuentes, see John Authers and Sara Silver, "A Visionary Approach to Democracy," *Financial Times*, July 31/August 1, 2004, p. W5.

226 See Samuel Huntington, *Who Are We? The Challenges to America's National Identity* (New York: Simon & Schuster, 2004); and Victor Davis Hanson, *Mexifornia: A State of Becoming* (San Francisco: Encounter Books, 2004). Useful commentaries include "Just Like the Rest of Us," *Economist*, April 29, 2004, pp. 11–12; and Deborah Solomon, "Three Cheers for Assimilation," *New York Times Magazine*, May 2, 2004, p. 21.

227 Gregory Rodriguez's sentiments are expressed in "Just Like the Rest of Us," p. 12. See also Mercedes Olivera, "Immigration Wave, Fears Nothing New," *Dallas Morning News*, September 5, 2003, pp. 1–3.

227 See William McGurn, "Land of Hope and Glory," *Wall Street Journal*, May 21, 2004, p. 4W.

227 Primitivo Rodriguez's quote is from Alfredo Corchado, "Returnees Getting Culture Shock from Mexican Politics," *Dallas Morning News*, September 7, 2003, p. 2.

228 Andrés Bermudez's remarks are from Sara Silver and John Authers, "Migrants Make Their Mark in Mexico Poll," *Financial Times*, July 6, 2004, p. 2. See also "Bitten by

Chihuahua and Others," *Economist,* July 10, 2004, p. 32; Ginger Thompson, "Latin Migrants Gain Political Clout in U.S.," *International Herald Tribune,* February 24, 2005, p. 5; and Danna Harman, "Mexicans in U.S. Gain Voting Clout," *Christian Science Monitor,* June 30, 2005, p. 6.

228 The José Lopez story and quotes are from Alfredo Corchado, "Back from U.S., They Offer Jobs—and a Reason to Stay," *Dallas Morning News,* August 31, 2003, pp. 1–3. See also Ginger Thompson, "Mexico's Migrants Profit from Dollars Sent Home," *New York Times,* February 23, 2005, p. A1.

229 Miguel Moctezuma's quote is from Corchado, "Back from U.S., . . .," p. 2.

229 Carlos Gutierrez's sentiments are reported in Corchado, "Returnees . . .," p. 2.

229 Ana Maria Salazar's remarks are from Richardo Chavira, "Drawn to Ancestral Homeland," *Dallas Morning News,* August 4, 2003, p. 1. See also Kathleen T. Rhem, "Hispanic Heritage Aids Official in War Against Drugs," *Defense LINK News,* January 14, 2003, pp. 1–2.

231 For more on U.S. retirees living in Mexico and the accompanying quotes, see Barry Golson, "La Vida Cheapo," *AARP,* March/April 2004, pp. 70–82. See also Seth Sutel, "Americans Head South to Enjoy Their Retirement," *Honolulu Star-Bulletin,* October 24, 2004, p. E6; Janelle Brown, "The Luxury of Home, in Mexico," *New York Times,* January 7, 2005, p. D1; Sally Stich, "U.S. Retirees Look to Mexico for Value and Balmy Climate," *Honolulu Star-Bulletin,* March 27, 2005, p. D6; and Taylor Antrim, "Mexico Dreaming," *Forbes FYI,* April 2005, pp. 65–66.

233 Chad Barton's migration is also reported in Ken Bensinger, "Heading South. Far South," *Wall Street Journal,* September 17, 2003, p. R12.

234 "Mexicans will keep on coming" is from Michael Parfit, "Emerging Mexico," *National Geographic,* August 1996, p. 100. See also Michael Barone, *The New Americans* (Washington: Regnery Publishing, 2001), pp. 115–191.

235 Mario Vargas Llosa's sentiments are discussed in "The View from Gringolandia," *Economist,* July 24, 2004, p. 78. See also Walter Russell Mead, "How a Perfect Dictatorship Collapsed, Right Next Door," *New York Times,* March 26, 2004, p. B37.

236 Professor Grayson's opinion is from John Authers and Sara Silver, "A Flirtation with Power: How Marta Fox Changed Her Husband's Presidency," *Financial Times,* July 17, 2004, p. 13. See also Grayson's "Mexican President Vicente Fox: Bold Leader or Lame Duck," Academic Symposium at the College of William and Mary, Williamsburg, Va., October 15, 2004.

237 The Latinobarómetro poll is cited in "Democracy's Low-Level Equilibrium," *Economist,* August 14, 2004.

237 See John Authers, "Mexico Gets Grace Period via U.S. Link," *Financial Times,* July 19, 2004, p. 24; and Authers, "'A Great Salesman but No Leader': Hope that Vicente Fox Could Change Mexico Is Dashed by Years of Failed Reforms," *Financial Times,* January 13, 2004, p. 11.

237 Mexico's advantage over China is from Juan Forero, "Mexico Manufacturers Lure Business to China," *International Herald Tribune,* September 9, 2003, p. 11. See also Elisabeth Malkin, "Mexico's Industrial Parks Stage a Rebound," *International Herald Tribune,* August 27, 2004, p. 11; and John Authers and Mica Rosenberg, "Mexico Puts Together the Basics of Economic Revival," *Financial Times,* July 20, 2004, p. 14.

238 See Geri Smith and Christina Lindblad, "Mexico: Was NAFTA Worth It?," *BusinessWeek,* December 22, 2003, p. 68. See also "The Triumph of NAFTA," *Wall Street Journal,* January 1, 2003, p. A14.

238 Todd Malan's quote and the foreign investment rankings are from Joel Millman, "Foreign Firms Also Outsource—to the U.S.," *Wall Street Journal,* February 23, 2004, p. A2.

239 Jaime Gomez's remarks are from "Latin America's New Business Elite," *BusinessWeek,* October 15, 1998, p. 2.

239 Alfredo Coutino's quote may be found in Joel Millman, "The World's New Tiger on the Export Scene Isn't Asian: It's Mexico," *Wall Street Journal,* May 5, 2000, p. A4.

239 Economist Garrido's remarks are from Millman, p. A4.

240 Mr. Vallalobos's comments are presented in Mark Stevenson, "China Gains in Export War with Mexico," *Honolulu Star-Bulletin,* November 24, 2003, p. C5.

240 For more on Mexico's proposed "Silicon Border" and the accompanying quotes, see James Detar, "Mexico Seeking Image of Technology Mecca," *Investor's Business Daily,* September 10, 2004, p. A4; and Detar, "'Silicon Border' Aims to Bring Chip Plants to New Mexicali Site," *Investor's Business Daily,* July 12, 2004, p. A6.

241 Professor Molina is quoted in Chris Kraul, "For Researchers in Mexico, Apathy Has Been the Smother of Invention," *Los Angeles Times,* December 4, 2003, p. A5.

242 Miguel de Icaza's remarks are from Ricardo Sandoval, "Mexico Works to Attract Tech Jobs," *Dallas Morning News,* January 2, 2004, p. 3.

242 De Icaza's remarks are from Sandoval, p. 3.

243 The Ross-Merrimer quote is from Golson, p. 75.

245 Ms. Salazar's disappointment is expressed in Chavira, p. 1.

CHAPTER 10. CONFRONTING THE FUTURE

248 Paul Kennedy was cited in my "The Job Wars," *Journal of Business Strategy,* November–December 1994, p. 17.

248 Henry Kissinger's quote is from David Rockefeller, "America's Future: A Question of Strength and Will," *Atlantic Community Quarterly,* Spring 1979, 17 (1), 14–19.

249 Daniel Bell, "The New World Disorder," *Foreign Policy,* Spring 1977.

249 Robert Kaplan is quoted in Neal Peirce, "Keep an Eye on 'Citistates,' Where Economic Action Is," *International Herald Tribune,* January 11, 2000, p. 3. See also John Kay, "Size Isn't All That Matters for Global Economies," *Financial Times,* November 26, 2003, p. 15; and "When Small Is Beautiful," *Economist,* December 20, 2003, p. 108.

249 Lee Kuan Yew's quote is from Nayan Chanda, "Protectionism Won't Work, Job Migration Unstoppable," *The Straits Times,* February 4, 2004, p. 12.

250 Arjuna Mahenchan is cited in Cherian Thomas and Rob Stewart, "India Predicts More Jobs from U.S.," *Honolulu Advertiser,* November 5, 2004, p. C4.

250 Ravi Aron's quote is from Nelson D. Swartz, "Down and Out in White-Collar America," *Fortune,* June 23, 2003, pp. 82 and 86.

251 See "America's Muddled Border War," *Chicago Tribune,* August 5, 2001.

251 The Dilip Soman story is from Christopher Grimes, "U.S. Universities Failed by Visa Process," *Financial Times,* May 12, 2004, p. 6. See also Caroline Alphonso, "Facing U.S. Security Hurdles, Top Students Flock to Canada," *Globe and Mail,* February 22, 2005, p. A1; and Otto Pohl, "Getting a Foreign Education," *International Herald Tribune,* March 25, 2005, p. 1.

252 The Robert Gates quote is from John Griffin, "Foreign Brain Drain Extends Terrorist Attack on America," *Honolulu Advertiser,* May 2, 2004, p. B1. See also Gates, "International Relations 101," *New York Times,* March 31, 2004, p. A23, and his "Land of the Freeze," *Economist,* January 2005, p. 32.

252 See Antonio Regaldo, "Scientists Warn of a Visa 'Crisis,'" *Wall Street Journal,* May 13, 2004, p. B4.

252 Ursula Oaks is quoted in Stacy A. Teicher, "Foreign Enrollment Drops at U.S. Colleges," *Christian Science Monitor,* November 16, 2004, p. 11; and Christopher Grimes, "Academics Call for More U.S. Visa Rule Changes to Attract Brightest Students," *Financial Times,* May 19, 2005, p. 1.

252 Larry Nelson's remarks are from Edwardo Porter, "Foreign Worker Shortage Looming," *Honolulu Star-Bulletin,* April 10, 2004, p. C1. See also Kevin McCoy, "Seasonal Foreign Workers in Short Supply this Year," *USA Today,* March 25, 2005, p.

1B; and Denny Lee, "Few Visas, Fewer Resort Workers," *New York Times,* June 10, 2005, p. D1.

252   Elizabeth Stern is quoted in Edward Alden, "No Entry: Tougher Visa Controls Are Creating Barriers to American Business," *Financial Times,* July 2, 2004, p. 11.

253   The Dumont quote is from Doreen Carvajal, "Reversing the Expat Brain Drain," *International Herald Tribune,* March 10, 2004, p. 11.

253   See Zsofia Vardi, "I Celebrate with Gratitude My Living of the American Dream," *Christian Science Monitor,* September 2, 2004, p. 19.

254   See "A Foreign-Born President," *International Herald Tribune,* October 26, 2004, p. 6.

254   See William McGurn, "Land of Hope and Glory," *Wall Street Journal,* May 21, 2004, p. W4; "Let Arnold Run," *Economist,* December 18, 2004, p. 16; and Martin Kasindorf, "Should the Constitution Be Amended for Arnold?" *USA Today,* December 3–5, 2004, p. 1A.

255   Mohammad Karim is quoted in David Wessel, "Hidden Costs of a Brain Gain," *Wall Street Journal,* March 1, 2001, p. A1.

256   See "USA Hosting Fewer Exchange Students," *USA Today,* November 24, 2004, p. 5D; and "Students Stay Home," *Online NewsHour,* June 24, 2004.

256   See Christopher Caldwell, "The Luxury of Double Loyalty," *Financial Times,* December 4–5, 2004, p. 7; and Maria Puente, "These People Truly Span the Globe," *USA Today,* June 30, 2005, p. 1A.

257   The Fordham report is cited in "Teachers Give Public Schools a Revealing Report Card," *USA Today,* October 5, 2004, p. 22A.

257   See Louis V. Gerstner Jr. "Bad Schools + Shackled Principals = Outsourcing," *Wall Street Journal,* October 7, 2004, p. A18. See also Pamela Mendels, "Fixing America's Future," *CEO Magazine,* April 2005, pp. 23–28.

257   Craig Barrett's quote is from "Intel CEO: Let's End Political Games and Compete," *USA Today,* April 28, 2004, p. 13A. See also Barrett, "Fixing America's Educational System," *Chief Executive,* December 2004, pp. 36–27; and Barrett, "Educational Complacency Will Make U.S. Feel the Pain," *USA Today,* February 24, 2005, p. 13A.

257   See "How to Rescue Education Reform," *New York Times,* October 10, 2004, p. 10. See also Joseph Rosenbloom, "Some Grade No Child Left Behind a Failure," *International Herald Tribune,* February 15, 2005, p. 19.

258   See John Kerry, "Get a Great Education," *Personal Excellence,* September 2004, p. 16. His position is also discussed in Roger Lowenstein, "Help Wanted," *New York Times Magazine,* September 5, 2004, p. 69.

258   See Michael Barone, *Hard America, Soft America* (New York: Crown Forum, 2004), pp. 13–16, 108–121, and 146–162.

258   Jonathan Rauch, "Now, for Tonight's Assignment . . .," *Atlantic Monthly,* November 2004, p. 54.

259   University ranking is from Bowley, "How Harvard Got Ahead," p. W2.

259   Patrick Callan's quote is from Karen Arenson, "National Study Shows Colleges in Need of Help," *New York Times,* September 15, 2004, p. A26. See also William C. Symonds, "Should Public Universities Behave Like Private Colleges?" *BusinessWeek,* November 15, 2004, p. 97.

259   RPI President Jackson's sentiments are from *BusinessWeek,* October 11, 2004, p. 94; and Michael J. Mandel, "This Way to the Future," pp. 94 and 122. See also Elizabeth Armstrong, "Where Are the Future Scientists?" *Christian Science Monitor,* July 29, 2003, p. 13; W. Michael Cox and Richard Alm, "Scientists Are Made, Not Born," *New York Times,* February 28, 2005, p. A17; Sara Rimer, "For Women in Sciences, the Pace of Progress in Academia Is Slow," *New York Times,* April 15, 2005, p. A1; and Laura Vanderkam, "What Math Gender Gap?" *USA Today,* April 12, 2005, p. 13A.

260   Charlene Barshefsky is quoted in John Harwood, "Competitive Edge of U.S. Is at Stake in the R&D Arena," *Wall Street Journal,* March 17, 2004, p. A4.

260 Harvard president Summers' quote is from "Harvard: Tops in . . . Engineering?" *BusinessWeek,* November 8, 2004, p. 11.

260 MIT president Hockfield is quoted in "A Breakthrough for MIT—and Science," *BusinessWeek,* October 4, 2004, p. 100. See also Cornelia Dean, "New Light on MIT Issues, with a (Gasp!) Biologist at the Helm," *New York Times,* May 3, 2005, p. D3.

260 Judith Ramaley quote is from Sharon Begley, "As We Lose Engineers, Who Will Take Us into the Future?" *Wall Street Journal,* June 7, 2002, p. B1.

261 The William Wulf quote is from Kris Axtman, "Where Are NASA's New Ranks?" *Christian Science Monitor,* February 18, 2005, p. 21; and Sharon Begley, "As We Lose Engineers . . .," p. B1. See also David Baltimore, "U.S. Is Losing Its Scientific Edge," *Honolulu Advertiser,* December 5, 2004, p. B3; and Ann Grimes, "Even Tech Execs Can't Get Kids to Be Engineers," *Wall Street Journal,* March 29, 2005, p. B1.

261 Andy Moore's quote is from Sharon Begley, "Angry Engineers Blame Shortage on Low Pay, Layoffs and Age Bias," *Wall Street Journal,* July 5, 2002, p. A9.

261 Thomas Hout is cited in Russell Flannery, "Hiring Hall," *Forbes,* July 26, 2004, p. 82. See also Brian Deagon, "Demand for Engineers Rising Fast in U.S.," *Investor's Business Daily,* January 1, 2004, p. 4.

261 The Palmisano/Clough quote is from "Industry and Academia Weigh In," *Business-Week,* October 11, 2004, p. 228.

262 Bill Gates is quoted in Steve Lohr, "Gates Tries to Inspire Future Techies," *International Herald Tribune,* March 2, 2004, p. 19. See also W. Brian Arthur, "Why Tech Is Still the Future," *Fortune,* November 24, 2003, pp. 119–124.

262 See Robert Pear, "Congress Trims Money for Science Agency," *New York Times,* November 30, 2004, p. A16; Norman R. Augustine and Burton Richter, "Our Ph.D. Deficit," *Wall Street Journal,* May 4, 2005, p. A18; John Markoff, "A Blow to Computer Science Research," *New York Times,* April 2, 2005, p. B1; William R. Brody, "Getting R&D Back on Track," *Chief Executive,* May 2005, p. 24; and Rich Weiss, "Shrinking the Scope of Science," *THE WEEK,* April 22, 2005, p. 12.

263 See Thomas G. Donlan, "The Morals of Science," *Barron's,* August 30, 2004, p. 30.

263 Professor Lodish is quoted in Hollister H. Hovey, "California Funding Draws Scientists," *Wall Street Journal,* November 10, 2004, p. B3A. See also William Safire, "California's Stem Cell Gold Rush," *New York Times,* December 15, 2004, p. A31; and Andrew Pollack, "California Stem Cell Program on Fast Track," *New York Times,* January 11, 2005, p. A15.

263 See "The Rich Ecosystem of Silicon Valley," *BusinessWeek,* August 25, 1997, p. 202.

264 See Phillip Longman, "Multiply and Be Fruitful," *Worth,* September 2004, p. 38, and his interview in "As the World Comes of (Older) Age," *International Herald Tribune,* December 4–5, 2004, pp. 14–15.

265 See David W. DeLong, *Lost Knowledge: Confronting the Threat of an Aging Workforce* (London: Oxford University Press, 2004). See also Pete Engardio et al., "Now, the Geezer Glut," *BusinessWeek,* January 31, 2005, pp. 44–47; Anne Fisher, "How to Battle the Coming Brain Drain," *Fortune,* March 21, 2005, pp. 121–128; and Carol Hymowitz, Joann S. Lubin, and Joe Flint, "'You Retire, You Die,'" *Wall Street Journal,* May 5, 2005, p. B1.

265 The Gallup survey is cited in Marilyn Garner, "The Gradual Goodbye," *Christian Science Monitor,* November 8, 2004, p. 13. See also Kaja Whitehouse, "Keep on Working (Sort of)," *Wall Street Journal,* March 28, 2005, p. R6; and Mindy Fetterman, "Retirees Back at Work with Flexibility," *USA Today,* June 9, 2005. p. 5B.

265 See Mary Quigley and Loretta E. Kaufman, "Hire Calling,"*AARP,* November/December 2004, p. 73. See also Edwardo Porter and Mary Williams Walsh, "With Benefits Wilting, U.S. Retirees Seek Work," *International Herald Tribune,* February 10, 2005, p. 15.

265 Regarding national service, see Kathryn Roth-Douquet, "Military Service Can Open the Eyes of Country's 'Elite,'" *USA Today,* January 18, 2005, p. 13A; and David Brooks, "Ah, Military Service . . . We Love It, We Hate It," *Honolulu Star-Bulletin,* August 3, 2004, p. A11.

265 See George M. Taber, "Capitalism: Is it Working . . .?" *TIME,* April 21, 1980, p. 40.

266 The National Science Board prediction is from Anderson, p. 16. See also *Science and Engineering Indicators 2004,* National Science Board, National Science Foundation, January 2004.

index